Cultivating the Arts in Education and Therapy

Cultivating the Arts in Education and Therapy

Malcolm Ross
University of Exeter, UK

with

Jolanta Gisman-Stoch
University of Silesia, Poland

 Routledge
Taylor & Francis Group

LONDON AND NEW YORK

First edition published 2011
by Routledge
2 Park Square, Milton Park, Abingdon, Oxon, OX14 4RN

Simultaneously published in the USA and Canada
by Routledge
711 Third Avenue, New York, NY 10017

Routledge is an imprint of the Taylor & Francis Group, an informa business

© 2011 Malcolm Ross
With contributions from Jolanta Gisman-Stoch in Chapter 7

The right of Malcolm Ross and Jolanta Gisman-Stoch to be identified as authors of this work has
been asserted by them in accordance with sections 77 and 78 of the Copyright, Designs and
Patents Act 1988.

British Library Cataloguing in Publication Data
A catalogue record for this book is available from the British Library

Library of Congress Cataloging-in-Publication Data
Library of Congress Cataloging-in-Publication Data
Ross, Malcolm, 1932–
Cultivating the arts in education and therapy / by Malcolm Ross. — 1st ed.
    p. cm.
Includes bibliographical references and index.
1. Arts in education. 2. Arts—Therapeutic use. I. Title.
NX280.R67 2011
700.71—dc22
2010051168

ISBN13: 978-0-415-60365-2 (hbk)
ISBN13: 978-0-415-60366-9 (pbk)
ISBN13: 978-0-203-81881-7 (ebk)

Typeset in Gill Sans by
FiSH Books, Enfield

MIX
Paper from
responsible sources
FSC® C004839
www.fsc.org

Printed and bound in Great Britain by
TJ International Ltd, Padstow, Cornwall

For

Kicoula

The Blue Boat

How late the daylight edges
toward the northern night
as though journeying
in a blue boat, gilded in mussel shell

with, slung from its mast, a lantern
like our old idea of the soul

Kathleen Jamie, *The Tree House*

Contents

List of tables and figures   viii

Prologue   I
Introduction   3

Part I
Theoretical   7

  I Towards a participatory practice   8
  2 Five Elements theory   23
  3 The Syncretic Model   37
  4 The Syncretic Model applied   53
  5 The arts and the brain   72
  6 The Tusa interviews   84

Part 2
Practical   109

  7 The irresponsibility of an art teacher   110
     JOLANTA GISMAN-STOCH
  8 A note on creativity   124
  9 Cultivating the arts in education   134
 10 Cultivating the arts in therapy   157
 11 Valediction   177
     Epilogue   192

     Appendix 1: Good habits   195
     Appendix 2: Dangerous play   199
     Bibliography and further reading   203
     Acknowledgements   207
     Index   209

List of tables and figures

Tables

2.1 Tillyard's elements and humours   24
2.2 Chart of correspondences in the Five Elements system   27

Figures

1.1 The Harré matrix   14
2.1 Yin-Yang   25
2.2 Cycle of the seasons   29
2.3 The *Sheng* cycle   30
2.4 The *Ke* cycle   31
2.5 The *Sheng* and *Ke* cycles   32
2.6 The emotional cycle   33
3.1 The Quincunx   39
3.2 The Syncretic Model (original)   41
3.3 The Syncretic Model (revised)   41
11.1 Virginia Woolf's model for *To the Lighthouse*   186

Plates

Tibetan sand mandala and Cycle of the seasons
The *Sheng* cycle and The *Ke* cycle
The *Sheng* and *Ke* cycles and The emotional cycle
The Syncretic Model (original) and The Syncretic Model (revised)

Prologue

'Yes, of course, if it's fine tomorrow,' said Mrs Ramsay. 'But you'll have to be up with the lark,' she added.

To her son these words conveyed an extraordinary joy, as if it were settled the expedition were bound to take place, and the wonder to which he had looked forward, for years and years it seemed, was, after a night's darkness and a day's sail, within touch.

Virginia Woolf, *To the Lighthouse*

I have been asking myself these last weeks, 'What can I do with wonder?' It being summer as I bring this writing to fruition, and my element being Fire, I am filled with wonder just now, which has made it a pressing question for me. What does one do with wonder? But I discover that I have been doing the right thing all along. The writing arises, in its way, as an impulse to praise, or, as the English poet W. H. Auden apparently held, as 'a rite of worship'. Auden believed that a poet feels the impulse to create a work of art when the passive awe provoked by an event is transformed into a desire to express that awe in a 'rite of worship'. To be fit homage, this rite must be beautiful. I doubt that this work of mine is beautiful, but I think it might be 'a rite of worship'.

In his play *The Habit of Art*, Alan Bennett presents Auden towards the end of his life, a literary treasure, but no longer expected to provide much more by way of national enrichment. Here he is, depicted in conversation with his biographer, Humphrey Carpenter.

> Carpenter: Are you writing?
> Auden: Am I dead? I work. I have the habit of art.

A speech or two later, Bennett has Auden elaborate a little:

> Auden: Poetry to me is as much a craft as an art and I have always prided myself on being able to turn my hand to anything – a wedding hymn, a requiem, a loyal toast...No job too small. I would have been happy to have hung up a shingle in the street: 'W. H. Auden. Poet'.

Auden's speech is very much in tune with a passage in Aristotle's *Nichomachean Ethics* in which he insists that the arts are mastered in much the same way as virtue is acquired, namely by cultivating the habit of them. Neither art nor virtue is a gift of nature. The notion of 'the habit of art' is central to this book. I argue that in their twin aspects of *techne* and *poiesis* the arts constitute an order of being – even a holy order – demanding devotion and continual practice. I am aware this is a large claim, and some of my readers will no doubt feel it is a very tall order indeed, where their pupils and patients are concerned. Nevertheless, I am with Aristotle on this.

I shall be trying in what follows to persuade the doubters that the arts must be reclaimed from the 'pastime' curriculum of our schools and from either a merely diagnostic or palliative role in therapy and analysis, to become a way not simply of education and healing, but of life. For, as Iain McGilchrist points out in his book *The Master and His Emissary* (2010), the arts give expression to our deepest yearnings as human beings. 'Through the arts', he writes, 'we reach out to the beyond: to our transcendent, our "immortal" longings'. McGilchrist challenges what he sees as the dominance of the analytical, calculating left hemisphere of the brain in contemporary western culture at the expense of the older, empathic, contemplative right brain. His defence of the right hemisphere chimes precisely with the whole thrust of this book. Having argued that the beautiful inspires a 'disinterested' rather than an erotic or possessive love, he concludes:

> Through the assaults of the left hemisphere on the body, spirituality and art, essentially mocking, discounting or dismantling what it does not understand and cannot use, we are at risk of becoming trapped in the I-It world, with all the exits through which we might re-discover the I-Thou world being progressively blocked off.
>
> (2010: 445)

The Syncretic Model of creativity in the arts presented in this book follows the cycle of change that constitutes the ancient Chinese theory of the Five Elements. It works as a powerful and beautiful metaphor for making a habit of the arts. To be fully human, we must practise the arts through a wide range of disciplined activities of making and receiving, of giving and being given, of conscious articulation and unconscious dreaming, until they form the defining habit of personal being: until they become second nature to us.

Littlehempston, Devon
July 2010

Introduction

To be in the Burren is to be reminded that physical matter is simultaneously inde-
structible and entirely transmutable: that it can swap states drastically, from vegetable
to mineral or from liquid to solid. To attempt to hold these two contradictory ideas,
of permanence and mutability, in the brain at the same time is usefully difficult, for it
makes the individual feel at once vulnerable and superfluous. You become aware of
yourself as constituted of nothing more than endlessly convertible matter – but also
of always being perpetuated in some form. Such knowledge grants us a kind of
comfortless immortality: an understanding that our bodies belong to the limitless
cycle of dispersal and reconstruction.

Robert Macfarlane, *The Wild Places* (2007: 173)

In April 2005, at Cambridge University, a group of educational researchers got
together for a day, under the auspices of the British Educational Research Association,
to explore what they describe as 'three issues vital to education in the twenty-first
century'. The issues were creativity, wisdom, and trusteeship. The keynote speakers
were Anna Craft, Professor of Education at the University of Exeter; Howard Gardner,
Hobbs Professor of Cognition and Education at the Harvard Graduate School of
Education; and Guy Claxton, Professor of Learning Services at the University of Bristol
Graduate School of Education. None of these names needs an introduction to readers of a book such as this. They are authorities in their fields, contributing to
knowledge and understanding spanning learning, healing, culture and human development. Over many years they have each made significant contributions to the literature
of creativity. The seminar was followed by a debate among a number of the
participants, and the outcomes are gathered in a book entitled, *Creativity, Wisdom and
Trusteeship: Exploring the Role of Education*.

Anna Craft and her colleagues are disturbed by various trends in contemporary
education: the almost exclusively economic interpretation of creativity as wealth
creation (now widely advocated across the education world) with little regard for
cultural and ethical considerations; the advance of an almost cynical pragmatism
among students that values education only for its cost-effectiveness in the job market;
the absence from schooling of long-term investment in developing human empathy

and compassion; and the loss of the notions of societal trusteeship and respect for tradition in the scramble for economic success worldwide. The book shines a steady and revealing light on each of these complex and critical issues – and it makes me feel at home, as will become clear when, in the main body of this book, I explore in more detail what Craft and her colleagues have to say.

I find myself in broad agreement with them, and where I differ, it is rather a matter of emphasis than substance. But, more to the point, they seem to have obligingly left room for me – if that is not too presumptuous. They don't see the arts as part of their brief in assessing the problems they identify or as part of the solution they alight upon. I shall be claiming, to the contrary, that the arts are core to the redress we are all seeking. My book proposes another, I think powerful and appropriate, avenue of opportunity for the reconfiguration of our educational, but also of our cultural and therapeutic endeavours. The Syncretic Model, presented in the opening chapters, provides a new (though very old) framework for thinking about creativity (wisdom and trusteeship too) – for thinking about *cultivating the habit of art*. I am delighted to acknowledge what I believe to be a strong kinship with the contributors to *Creativity, Wisdom and Trusteeship*, and am grateful to them for providing exactly the professional context that my own book needs to bring it down to earth and into the real world where what one thinks might make a difference.

You don't have to be a believer to read my book, but you might become one. The person who introduced me to traditional Chinese Five Elements theory, the philosophy behind traditional Chinese acupuncture, is, of course, a believer. When Donna Ashton, my acupuncturist, embarked upon a programme of treatment to heal my broken ankle, she believed (a) that she would be successful, and (b) that her success would come as the direct result of her rebalancing the life-force circulating through the organs of my body, by reconnecting my bodily energy system (my ch'i) to the natural energies, rhythms and influences operating in the cosmos at large, i.e. in nature. Donna believed that my ankle's stubborn refusal to heal, six months on from the accident, was due to blocks and imbalances in the meridians that channelled the life-force around my body. She was confident that her competence was sufficient to identify the source of the trouble and correct the problem I was having.

Donna understood that in looking to repair my body she would need to take into consideration my general mental and spiritual wellbeing. In fact, she made clear from the start, having given me a thorough examination, that where I was concerned, she would begin by treating my spirit. I was, she sensed, at a low ebb, depressed by the accident itself and by what was beginning to feel like a permanent incapacity. After six weeks of treatment, already feeling so much better in myself, an x-ray at the hospital confirmed to my consultant that the break had begun to heal. He was surprised; I was grateful. Everything had been set for surgery. Six months into the treatment with Donna, another x-ray showed the healing to be complete; no trace of the break remained. What is more, speaking now particularly of my mind and spirit, I knew that

Donna had turned my life around. Writing this book could not have happened without her.

During the course of the treatment I had become fascinated by the ideas and principles behind it. Donna agreed to talk to me about Five Elements theory. She lent me books and suggested others I might look at. I almost immediately saw a marked convergence between the Chinese Five Elements model and my own model of the creative process in art – developed in my work in arts education and therapy over the course of many years. This book describes the conversation we had about the two systems and how we came to devise what we have called a Syncretic Model, drawing together over 2,000 years of Chinese thought on the one hand and contemporary Western social psychology on the other. To me, the Chinese model offered another way of thinking about the creative process of art-making, with practical implications for the arts curriculum in schools, for the application of the arts in therapeutic practice and for the training of arts teachers, arts therapists and cultural animators working in the community.

The Syncretic Model serves to extend, even transform, the model I have long been working with. Five Elements theory works for me, not just as a beautiful story but as a potent and endlessly illuminating source of understanding and spur to a regenerative practice. I don't know if it tells us how the world actually is. For Donna it describes a living reality, a system of dynamic energies operating with and through us and creating the force field that is our living, ever-changing environment. Five Elements theory, also called the Five Phases of Change, is for Donna a potent prescription for affecting changes in the patient's body, mind and spirit. As such it forms the basis of her practice as a healer – and it works. For me it has become a new way of understanding how creativity is a force present in the world – and, in particular, present in the world of the artist. I have learned in the course of writing this book to respect powerful, 'hidden' influences at work within and beyond me, helping bring it to fruition. I shall have more to say about this. Meanwhile, I am content that the Syncretic Model attempts a fresh way of understanding how cultivating the habit of art can make a difference, individually and collectively. I should like to think that this book opens, for arts teachers and arts therapists, the prospect of a different story of creativity.

Part 1
Theoretical

1 Towards a participatory practice

This chapter provides the research context for the introduction in Chapter 2 of the Syncretic Model of creativity in the arts. In particular, it sets out the difficulties teachers of the arts have traditionally had in finding a constructive, participatory role when promoting their students' creativity. The chapter covers my own research and teaching since the late 1960s in the quest for a new pedagogy. Key figures in that search include Robert Witkin, D. W. Winnicott, Hans-Georg Gadamer, R. G. Collingwood and Rom Harré, whose cyclical model of the Identity Project is subsequently adapted to create the Syncretic Model itself.

> To Constantine Levin the country was the background of life – that is to say, the place where one rejoiced, suffered and laboured; but to Koznyshev the country meant, on the one hand rest from work, on the other, a valuable antidote to the corrupt influences of the town.
>
> Leo Tolstoy, *Anna Karenina*

A strong tradition suggests that artistic talent is in the gift of the gods, and that, for the lucky few, progress towards success and the continuing command of talent is a matter to be settled between the artist and his or her muse (to use the old parlance). In other words, there's not really much for the teacher of art to do apart from opening the students' eyes to the canon of works constituting the best that has been done in the past, and instructing them in the most popular, practical techniques having contemporary currency. But where their distinctive talents are concerned, in the development of the young artists' defining styles or voices, and in regard to their individual and unique creative energies and imaginations, the teacher must stand back and allow nature to take its course, offering critical and sympathetic encouragement in equal measures, judged appropriate to the circumstances. Teaching the arts, on this reckoning, would amount to little more than servicing a given talent; it would seem that there is little or nothing to be done 'from within the student's expressive act', as

Witkin expresses it in *The Intelligence of Feeling*, since, the act being finally private, there is *no means of an outsider's gaining access to it*.

It is the purpose of this book, as it was of Witkin's, to examine this tradition and to counter it by proposing *a fully participatory practice*, whereby the teacher becomes the intimate companion of the student as a developing artist as she/he works the expressive impulse into a satisfying feeling-form, or moves from merely passive reception of a work of art to a full, imaginative engagement with it. To this end, a model of the creative process in the arts will be presented that provides the teacher with a clear strategy of intervention, a model that is also, at the same time, a set of guidelines for creative self-help.

The different arts therapies have their own professional traditions of intervention, ranging all the way from 'hands-off', reflective dialogue to 'hands-on', free play with the client. Here again, the model proposed in the following chapters will offer clear guidance for a participatory strategy, but only where *the healing potential of real artistic experience* forms the basis of the therapist's convictions concerning their work. Arts therapists who tend to see the arts simply as diagnostic tools or as activities preliminary to treatments of a different sort (e.g. verbally mediated psychoanalysis), may well find my suggestions problematic. Nevertheless, I ask them to read on – not least because I shall try to engage with these concerns. Since the model, to be called the Syncretic Model, for reasons that will shortly become apparent, provides a way of thinking about artistic creativity, it will also suggest a participatory practice to cultural animators and artists working in community settings, providing opportunities for arts experience outside the formal settings of arts therapy, education and training.

The British economist Amartya Sen has proposed a neat formula for what he calls personal 'capability' – the development of which, in its citizens, would seem to be the just aspiration of any civilized society:

TALENT + OPPORTUNITY = CAPABILITY

Sen assumes that everyone has talents if given the opportunity to discover and express them. We can judge no-one's 'capability' without understanding the nature and extent of the opportunity they have had to develop and hone their gifts. In so far as everyone has the inclination to and wherewithal for personal expression, they have a talent for the arts. In some of us that talent will be remarkable both in its specificity and its force. Nonetheless, everyone carries the impulse of self-expression and a propensity for reading the 'signs' of art, and whether their talent is exceptional or run-of-the-mill, 'opportunity' will determine the extent of their artistic capability, both in terms of personal fulfilment and their contribution to the wider community. Opportunity in the arts takes many forms. It might mean having a sympathetic parent or relative (e.g. Van Gogh's brother, Theo); finding a spiritual home (e.g. Joseph Conrad, England); finding a creative partner (e.g. for Benjamin Britten, Peter Pears); finding a sensitive and inspiring mentor (Antony Caro and Henry Moore); making artistic friends (Paula Rego and Vic Willing at the Slade). Opportunity clearly embraces the spheres of education – both formal and informal – and of therapy. My hope in writing this book is that it might offer its readers a way of rethinking the character and quality of the opportunities they represent for their students and clients. If their practice were, as a result of reading this book, to become more fully participatory, I would claim a higher rating for the opportunities they were offering to a 'talent' in the process of its conversion to 'capability'.

The notion of teaching – or healing for that matter – 'from within the expressive act' became the principal pedagogical message to emerge from the research project on the arts in secondary schools in the UK that Robert Witkin and I undertook for the Schools Council in the early 1970s (the 'Arts and the Adolescent' project – Director Peter Cox, Principal of Dartington College of Arts). Doing our research, we found arts teachers largely devoid of a pedagogy where their students' creative work was concerned – pupil creativity then beginning to become a popular idea in schools, particularly where arts and English teachers were concerned. Inspired by Herbert Read's and the Modernist movement's enthusiasm for child (and so-called 'primitive' or naïve) art, famously expressed in Read's dictum 'every child an artist', teachers of the arts were beginning to reach out beyond conventional methods of instruction, but were hesitant about intervening in the mysterious and apparently private processes of creativity, which, to be fair, were little understood at the time. In his book *The Intelligence of Feeling* (1974), Witkin set out the project's conceptual framework for teaching creativity in the arts. Teachers were invited to understand the creative process as a reflexive exchange between feeling and medium, with the making experience culminating in a feeling-form or art work that satisfied the child's expressive desire.

We called this formative process *subject-reflexive action*, in that it was action in a medium determined reflexively by a subjective feeling for the formal outcome that was desired. It was the child's 'intelligence of feeling' in action. Expressive work proper was judged to be directed by feeling impulse rather than procedural rules, by having a good ear, a good eye, a touch, a sense of timing, of rhythm, a feel for how formal decisions are made, the ability to think in terms of contrasts and harmonies, balance and tension, suspension and climax, grace and surprise. All of which meant that a pedagogy centred on teacher rule-direction had to be replaced by one centred on the child's expressive impulse and feeling for forms that were significant, that signified, for them.

If it was now the teacher's task to work with the child's feeling impulse, i.e. with their subjectivity, how was she/he to evoke and recognize it? The project distinguished between reflexive and reactive feelings. 'Reactive' feelings – usually strongly experienced – demanded instant release in action, their, often violent, outcomes being an emotional reaction to a situation, a cathartic discharge triggered by a threat to or disturbance of the subject's homeostatic state. 'There's a snake on the path there;

watch out!' – followed by a squeal as the threat is seen and appropriate evasive action taken. The 'expressive' squeal has no part in 'subject-knowing'. It is intelligent in the sense of its being a practically effective response to danger (a signal to others among other things), but it does not belong to the realm of reflexivity, whereby new understandings of the subjective life are accomplished. No consideration of 'significant forming' occurs in the generation of the squeal. It is about rapid responses and is, generally speaking, soon over and done with. Some 'reactive' responses, like crying in grief, for instance, resolve themselves more slowly and have a longer-term impact upon the restoration of psychological balance and the recovery of feelings of wellbeing.

On the other hand, 'reflexive' feeling, the project argued, works towards new forms of apprehending experience: the spur to action is lacking and instead we are aware of the need to stay with the experience and allow for the gradual shift in apprehension that characterizes deeper, often unconscious, processes of assimilation and accommodation to take their course. We are in the realm of 'knowing'. We might feel the need to take time out, to be alone for a while, to 'sleep on it'. We deploy reflexive feeling when we deliberate on matters of taste, when we make aesthetic judgements, when we brood quietly and expressively upon emotional experience and its deeper meaning, when we wait for feelings to become intelligible to us. The impulse of reflexivity is towards holding on to experience and being enriched and enlarged by it; reactivity, on the other hand, seeks to void, or distance the self from, what is simply too painful – because too disruptive – to bear. In the creative experience of art-making, reflexive feelings guide the formative process by allowing the artist to make the series of adjustments that will bring the work closer to the heart's desire. Reflexivity, the continuous to and fro in attention to a feeling of 'rightness', will, if all goes well, finally issue in a form that is good enough to capture, hold and deliver the artist's knowing.

Teachers involved in the Arts and the Adolescent project needed a new pedagogy that would help attune them to their students' subjectivity, and support authentic self-expression as intelligent feeling at work: in other words, to work from 'within the child's experience'. I was later to discover a similar emphasis in the writings of English philosopher R. G. Collingwood, notably in his book, *The Principles of Art*, in which he argues that the arts 'properly so called' militate against 'the corruption of consciousness'. Collingwood makes a sharp distinction between art that has its roots in human 'expressive' activity and what he calls 'pseudo' art, which makes use of artistic technique (and mystique) to pursue the imperatives of political propaganda, commercial advertising and the marketplace.

With the child at the centre of the arts curriculum, we offered the project's teachers a set of steps by which to proceed, a procedure intended to make the student's expressive act the centrepiece of the creative arts curriculum, and was intended to help the teacher remain in touch with the student's subjective project as it progressed. Underpinning the whole project was Witkin's theory of 'subject-knowing', essentially making the connection between expressive action and self-actualization, a theme that was concurrently also being developed elsewhere by Abrahm Maslow (1968) and, somewhat later, to be proposed by Rom Harré (1983). Our project of the 1970s saw the role of the arts teacher to be the fostering of the student's confidence in their feelings and of their resourcefulness in expressing them 'reflexively'. The creative arts were to counterbalance a curriculum that we felt put too much emphasis on purely vocational or academic goals. As Witkin puts it in his book:

> If the price of finding oneself in the world is that of losing the world in oneself, then the price is more than anyone can afford.

> (1974: 1)

Our message for arts teachers was that it would not do simply to induct the child into the world of the arts and neglect the world of art in the child.

In the event, although the project created serious interest amongst arts teachers at the time, and doubtless helped to promote the child's own creativity to centre stage in the developing debate about the arts in the curriculum, I'm not sure that the pedagogic model itself was to prove all that useful in helping the teacher to a more interactive engagement with the pupil. The initial step of 'setting the sensate problem' proved for many teachers less successful than allowing the children to find the problem for themselves and tune in to it, problem-finding being at least as important an aspect of creativity as problem-solving. It began to look like a rather contradictory move, made to ensure the teacher's status as the one setting the agenda in the classroom. The second step, 'making a holding form' (capturing the basic impulse for the work in a rough outline or sketch), remains a powerful practical idea for helping to set boundaries, for maintaining focus for the individual creative project, and for allowing both teachers and developing artists systematically to track work in progress. The final step, 'the movement through successive approximations to a resolution', made assumptions about art-making as a kind of systematic, whittling-down exercise that were not always borne out by experience. In effect, certain aspects of the recommended routine still seemed to imply a rather too controlling role for the teacher.

In terms of the interaction between teacher and student, I later found a more telling approach in Winnicott's model of the client–therapist relationship. Winnicott insists that no therapeutic progress can be made unless the therapist and the client are capable of playing together. Winnicott was basing his practice as a healer on his observations of mothers playing with their children. Quite apart from the diagnostic and monitoring information provided for the therapist by playful interaction with the client (he worked mostly, though not exclusively, with children), Winnicott was actively supporting the child in their playing, making the playing serve the healing. We shall be returning to Winnicott's notion of play in the therapeutic context later. What reading Winnicott did for me as an arts teacher was to suggest a model for a more directly interactive relationship with the student's work, a relationship in which I might well actually play with/for the student as well as share in a playful and intimate conversation about the ongoing work.

The idea of a playful conversation came to the fore in the research on assessment in the arts for which I was responsible in the 1990s. My partners then were Hilary Radnor, Sally Mitchell and Kathy Bierton (*Assessing Achievement in the Arts*, 1993). Exploring the ways teachers approached assessment in the arts, we became aware that, at least where their students' creative work was concerned, there was a great deal of uncertainty and dissatisfaction. Beyond praising those who were trying hard, few teachers had any other strategies of appraisal with which they felt comfortable. Again, as with the earlier Arts and the Adolescent project, there seemed to be no adequate pedagogy available to teachers of creativity that would provide a proper basis for assessment. Many had strong misgivings over the subjectivity of their own responses even when 'moderated' by formal collective decision-making and adjudication. It was at this time that I first encountered Rom Harré's 'expressivist' model and what he calls the 'Identity Project'. This rather more dynamic way of looking at expressive creativity seemed preferable to the step-by-step approach Witkin and I had envisaged earlier, and, together with my new team, I developed Harré's ideas as the basis for modelling the arts curriculum, and hence for assessing pupils' aesthetic achievement.

Combining Winnicott's influence with Donald Schön's work on the reflective practitioner, we created a procedure for a negotiated form of assessment that we called the reflective conversation. The reflective conversation brought the student and the teacher into a playful, exploratory relationship with the teacher tactfully inviting the student to reflect on the making process and assess their own achievement together with the teacher. The teacher brought their professional responses and reflections to the conversation and a joint statement based on the conversation was agreed. Whilst persuaded of the principle, the teachers found it difficult to put into practice simply because it was so alien to their experience. Something of a sea change in the student–teacher relationship, let alone in the teacher's professional repertoire of skills, would be required to make it happen effectively. And in management terms, the argument was that it would require far too much time to implement, given the pressures on the timetable etc. A nice idea, then, but of limited success.

Harré's model of cultural development has been powerfully influential in my own teaching and research ever since. His thesis was that we build individual identity through participation in a cycle of expressive activities, based on a pair of constructs: private-public, individual-collective. The private-public construct represents what he calls expressive 'display', whereas the individual-collective construct represents expressive 'realization'. He makes these pairs serve as two dimensions of a cyclical matrix, thereby generating four quadrants (or domains) of activity. Harré takes the child's language development as a case in point in explaining his model.

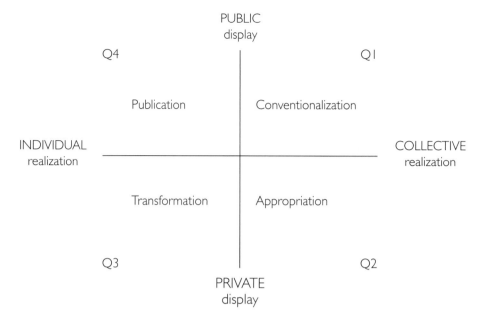

Figure 1.1 The Harré matrix

Q1: Conventionalization. Infants are born into the public–collective real world of cultural artefacts and conventions. They are born with the aptitude to learn. They do so largely on the 'immersion' principle: surrounded by language users, they gradually become users themselves, through imitation, instruction, interrogation and repetition.

Q2: Appropriation. From the public–collective, infants adopt and adapt the language to their own private needs, initially familiarizing themselves with it by playing – usually with the mother. They gradually become independent members of this particular language-using club themselves.

Q3: Transformation. Infants discover that they can engage with a private–collective language in novel ways, ways of their own, to explore and charge the world with private–individual meanings of their own. Language becomes a medium for their own creative problem-finding and problem-solving.

Q4: Publication. They respond to the pull to express their individual ideas in forms of public discourse, so that they can be shared with others, validated and authorized. They become members of the wedding.

The cyclical movement continues as the cultural gatekeepers authorize their use of the language and secure their individual expressive work for the common wealth (return to Q1), thereby renewing the cultural stock. The Identity Project is continuous through life and the developing expressive use of language characterised by each of the successive phases plays a crucial part.

Harré's model struck us as having immediate application to the (public–private, individual– collective) trajectory of the expressive arts curriculum, which we went on to formulate, indicating as we did so the specific role attaching to the teacher's interventions, stage by stage.

Q1: Conventionalization. The student learns about the world of the arts, its conventions, institutions, history and techniques, through 'immersion'. The student becomes an arts user and practitioner by imitation, instruction, interrogation and repetition. Teachers will reinforce these spontaneous activities by ensuring the student's exposure to the traditions and conventions governing participation in the arts world, past and present.

Q2: Appropriation. The student adopts and adapts the languages of the arts to their own purposes and begins to use them expressively – initially as exploratory play. The student develops their own voice, style, tastes and repertoire of skills and preferences among the works of the heritage. Teachers will be on the lookout for, and nourish, the student's emerging artistic preferences and personality, encouraging and resourcing their playful experiments.

Q3: Transformation. The student discovers their own artistic creativity as the capacity to convert materials into the media of symbol use, to produce signifiers of their own. Teachers empathize with the student's particular expressive project, closely monitoring the connection they make between feeling and form (their subject-reflexive activity), watching for signs of loss of connection or authenticity, technical stress, lack of appropriate cultural references, signs of emotional dissonance etc.

Q4: Publication. When the student is ready, the teacher provides encouragement for a sharing of the work with others and participation in a shared, reflective evaluation of it. The developing artist is sensitively helped to let the work go, submit to public examination and move on.

Although the model presents these expressive 'episodes' as a sequence, they ought perhaps to be seen as continuous threads in a flowing tapestry of interconnected activities. The student's overall trajectory may be sequential, but progress from moment to moment is both forward and back, retracing steps and renewing connections across the matrix where fresh material from a different stage is necessary to boost or adjust the direction of the project in hand. This flexible to-ing and fro-ing is represented in the project's published material by arrows crossing back and forth across the phase boundaries. The model is spelt out in terms of the student's personal art-making; it is very easily adapted to their creative use of artworks by other artists – their encounters with the collective arts repertoire. Devising the model was a matter of recognizing our own experience as artists and arts teachers. It served to help us think about that experience systematically. It did not embody its reality; it systematized it conceptually. It helped to answer the questions: What do arts teachers do next? How do their different interventions add up to a coherent experience for the student, a comprehensive pedagogy, experienced as companionship? Before leaving the Assessement Project I shall quote, by way of illustration, from one of the reflective conversations.

I am in conversation with Louise, a 15-year-old secondary-school student. We are in the presence of a life-size, unglazed head, modelled by Louse as part of her art GCSE coursework. The excerpt picks up the conversation about a third of the way in. We have established that the head is female and that she has emerged from a process of improvization, i.e. was not pre-planned. I suggested that the head, with her eyes closed, looked rather like a death mask. The commentary is by Sally Mitchell.

Louise does more than appropriate the idea of the death mask from Malcolm, she begins to transform it through her own sensate ordering. This process continues as she goes on looking, her responses always finding justification in the physicality of the piece, in the form which is the trace of her forming.

At the end of the extract, Louise registers her sense that she is being asked here to address her work in an unfamiliar way. She feels herself on slightly shaky ground, not sure perhaps of how legitimate her responses are or how to provide them. For a time, the actual exploration is suspended, while the conversation partners reflect on what they have been doing.

L   [pause] I haven't really looked at her and said what I think. You know, I don't really know.
M   But you're doing it now?
L   Yes.
M   How does it feel to be doing it?
L   That's…
M   I mean, does it feel wrong to be doing it?
L   No, no, no! It's stimulating my imagination, which is good.
M   I mean, you made her… very much with your hands and your eyes without reflecting too much.
L   Yes.
M   Almost, I suspect, that sort of… even unconsciously. You've gone on making her and said, 'This is right now, and…'
L   Yes.
M   '…that's not quite balanced. I like that colour, I'll have a bit more like that. Now we've got her.' So it was like that?
L   Yeah.
M   We're trying to say, 'What have we got? What have we found?' It's like you've been…

L   Been to a psychiatrist!

M   Well, I don't know! I'm just saying, What have we found? You've gone fishing, you've gone deep-sea diving, you've gone into a wreck – I'm now using a kind of metaphor for your making process. You've gone down there, glided, groped around, you've made it, you've come up, you've brought her up, and here she is. Now, who, what have we got here? And what does she mean? Because, she…I mean, *does* she mean something for you? I don't know, does…I mean does she have any value for you? [gesturing towards the head]

Louise recognizes, by her joking mention of the psychiatrist, the particular tenor of the conversation, but at the same time she does not see it as intrusive. Malcolm offers an extended metaphor, which locates the present activity as a natural continuation of the making processes that have gone before. The diving metaphor encapsulates the movement through appropriation, transformation and publication. The three are crucially linked: you can't surface without having dived; surfacing 'completes' the dive.

Louise clearly accepts this description and promptly answers Malcolm's question as to value with a striking perception, which she is herself surprised by and which initiates an intense period of imaginative discovery.

L   I think she's quite regal.

M   [excitedly] Ah yes! [sits back, folds arms] I mean *I* do. I wanted you to say, and I didn't want to put words into your mouth [leans to look at head, and then up at L], but I have a tremendous sense of her dignity. Because I think she has a…

L   I've just found that!

M   Have you?

L   Yes! Something to do [puts hand to her own face] with the shape of her here [touches the head and her own face in the same place, sits back and looks] – the shadows and her jaw [indicates her own jaw, M sits on edge of seat] – very stiff [M anticipates this description, making a long-face gesture with hands and face, L watching him], very…Queen…Victoria or…I don't know.

M   Yep. [nods]

L   Stiff, sitting quietly by her husband…

The conversation continues. It still has 20 minutes to run. Louise summarizes the effect of the conversation on her by saying, 'She means a lot more to me now than she did before…I want to get her home and have her sitting in the corner of my bedroom.' She gestures, smiling broadly, out towards camera.

The Harré model not only had parallels with the Arts and the Adolescent project schema but with the ideas of another writer beginning to influence my work, Hans-Georg Gadamer, in particular with his book *The Relevance of the Beautiful and other*

Essays. Gadamer offers his own three-part scheme for the elements of creativity in the arts: Play, Symbol and Festival. To illustrate his notion of play, he offers the image of sunlight playing on the sea, or of the swarming dance of gnats on a summer evening. He is talking about a loosening up of attention, a readiness to dream, to be mesmerized, to take in the whole effect (*gestalt*) rather than focusing on the detail. Attention is diffuse but intense, playing with the possibilities of form and allowing possibilities to emerge of themselves. This idea seems to approximate to Ehrenzweig's notion of 'dedifferentiation' (1967).

To illustrate his idea of the symbol in art, Gadamer reminds us of the story of the *tessera hospitalis.* This is the ancient custom of marking the departure of a guest with the breaking of a plate. The host retains half and the departing guest takes the other half with them, the idea being that should the guest ever return, recognition would be immediate on the production of the matching half of the plate. Gadamer is interested in the idea that the artist 'recognizes' the artwork in the course of making it, rather than dictating the outcome through some preconceived plan or prior knowledge. The work discloses (un-conceals) itself to the artist who then 'knows' it, in a moment of recognition, of 'epiphany'.

Gadamer's final idea is festival: he wants to insist on the public destiny of art as belonging to the exceptional, celebratory, 'special' social impulse that distinguishes the holy day from the working week. All normal conventions governing the civil society are temporarily suspended, the rules of authority are inverted and everyone is given permission to act the fool. The Feast of Fools, the carnival, the *jour de fête* are universal traditions with a long history and still going strong. Art, says Gadamer, belongs to this consensual tradition of inverted norms, of religious frenzy and wild, collective high spirits. For Harré's Appropriation, I read Gadamer's Play (*Arts & the Adolescent: Personal Development*); for Harré's Transformation, I read Gadamer's Symbol (*A&A: Control of the Medium*); for Harré's Publication, I read Gadamer's Festival (*A&A: Self-expression*). These were approximations rather than exact matches in what seemed to me at the time to be an underlying inclination towards concordance.

In this chapter I have been sketching a personal story: the way certain ideas evolved within my practice as an arts teacher and researcher. I have never worked as an arts therapist, though my personal friendships and professional connections with the arts therapies extend over many years. My publications are read by therapists in training, and my personal presentations to therapy groups have been surprisingly (to me) well received. The Syncretic Model, however, which is explained in Chapter 3, was devised from the outset with therapists as well as teachers and cultural animators in mind. Its first public exposure was at the September 2009 biennial conference of the European Consortium for Arts Therapies Education (ECArTE) in London. Margot Sunderland, Principal of the Institute for the Arts in Therapy and Education, London, many years before had pointed out the similarity of the Harré model to models familiar to therapists, such as, for example, Clarkson's (1989) Gestalt Cycle.

The position taken in this book with respect to the arts therapies is very simple (perhaps even a little naïve): deploying the arts properly to make a difference in the treatment of emotional illness means, for me, supporting the client's Identity Project, which is understood to be in difficulty due to some weakness or imbalance in their personal creative/expressive process. The therapist makes an assessment of the problem and seeks to restore expressive flow by treating the particular difficulty within a holistic framework. In the analysis above, the role of the teacher is specifically identified. The role of the therapist may be inferred from that of the teacher. In saying that, I am not equating the two. They are marked by many radical distinctions. Most obviously, the teacher, by and large, is engaged in facilitating and trouble-shooting a functioning creative/expressive system such as Harré describes; the therapist, on the other hand, is expert in handling instances of process or systems breakdown in various degrees of complexity and urgency. Therapist and teacher will need different sets of skills and will usually work in different settings. But the aim, as I shall be suggesting again and again in this book, is always the same. As the poet Robert Frost might have said, 'the aim is song'. And for many people it is enough to get them singing again – whatever else might seem beyond their powers of redress. It was another poet, W. B. Yeats, who asked, in his poem 'Among School Children', 'How can we know the dancer from the dance?' I have written this book in the belief that the arts can make all the difference between a life so-called and a proper life. For the teacher and the therapist, it is about knowing the dancer *in* the dance.

Knowing someone from the inside is a task for human empathy. Daniel Stern (1985) developed the notion of 'attunement' to describe the basis of inter-subjective, affective communication between mother and infant. In his studies of early, pre-verbal mother–infant communication, Stern discovered that mothers and their children communicate intensely with each other as a basic, reciprocal form of expression, with the purpose of exploring and coming to know each other's inner emotional worlds. Such communication is conveyed through the mother's handling of her baby, through facial expression and, particularly, through the 'musical' exchange of pre-verbal vocalizations.

> Affective attunement…is a special form of behaviour in response to the communicative affective behaviour of another. Just as imitation is a faithful rendering of the other's overt actions, affective attunement is a faithful rendering of what the other must have felt like when he or she expressed him- or herself with those actions…It is a way of imitating, from the inside, what an experience feels like…
>
> (2004: 241)

Such knowledge is vital to the development of intimacy and the forging of the central relationship of the infant's life. Finding a way to be with the beloved other, according to Stern, comes before the impulse to separation and individual identity. The identity

project, he would say, is forged within a co-created relationship in which two subjectivities learn to interact intentionally together. We are two before we are one: establishing
coherence-in-mutuality is the impulse behind such exploration. This idea seems to offer
us further help in conceptualizing a participatory practice, in developing a way of working with the student or client in the arts from *within* their expressive experience. Stern
goes on to develop his notion of affective attunement in his more recent publication
(2010), and in association with his colleagues in the Boston Change Process Study
Group (2010) – to all of which we shall be returning for closer scrutiny later.

In concluding this chapter, I turn to my friend and colleague Jolanta Gisman-Stoch,
lecturer in cultural animation in Cieszyn, Poland, at the University of Silesia (at
Katowice). Jola also contributes Chapter 7. In 2004 she published a paper in Poland
in which she explored the connection between the structure of the Mesopotamian
epic of Gilgamesh and the Rom Harré matrix. She writes:

> The Mesopotamian epic 'Gilgamesh', dating from the second millennium BC, has
> two principal themes: the relationship between culture and nature, and man's
> unceasing quest for the meaning of life, i.e. to understand the principles of grow-
> ing up. Reading Thorkild Jacobsen's *The Treasures of Darkness*, I was struck by the
> connection between my thinking on the subject of creativity and the structure of
> the Gilgamesh story. In particular, I felt there was a strong link with Rom Harré's
> framework for 'the Identity Project'.
>
> Gilgamesh, the hero of the story, was two parts divine and one part human. He
> was the mythical king of the Sumarian city of Uruk. Immensely strong and fear-
> some he tyrannized his people. They prayed to their gods for help and their
> prayers were answered in the form of Enkidu, a 'natural' man endowed with
> strength and energy equal to Gilgamesh. As the two became friends, Gilgamesh
> moderated his rule. The pair deployed their combined resources outside the city,
> challenging monsters and even the gods themselves. They overcame the monster
> Huwawa of the Cedar Woods; they killed the Bull of Heaven. But the gods were
> offended at their excesses and in punishment caused Enkidu to fall sick and die.
> Bereft, Gilgamesh leaves Uruk on a quest to discover eternal life. He meets
> Utnapishtim, who was made immortal by the gods following the Great Flood, and
> is given two chances of finding immortality. Unfortunately he fails in both of them
> because he can't stay awake and loses his concentration – as humans do. He is
> finally reconciled to his human fate and returns to the city. Approaching Uruk he
> discovers, for the first time, how beautiful it is.
>
> Harré's Conventionalization phase (Q1) I associate with the walled city of Uruk.
> It is the sacred granary or storehouse of the people, guarded by the goddess Ishtar.
> In the city the citizens find protection and healing after their hardships and exertions
> beyond the city walls. The city is everyone's home. This is the phase in which the
> culture is understood as collective wisdom, a shared value system, a storehouse of

ideas, understandings, images, beliefs and cultural accomplishments. In Q1 the main impulse is conservation: the need and the wish to preserve and protect what has been won and what defines the collective. But city life can be debilitating: Gilgamesh, listless within the city's walls, becomes a tyrant given to all manner of excess; Enkidu his friend becomes lazy and bored.

The adventures of Gilgamesh and Enkidu begin with Harré's second phase, Appropriation (Q2). Gilgamesh 'appropriates' the strength of the elders by calling for their blessing, and also for that of his mother, the goddess Ninsun. She says a mother's prayer for him. 'Lord, of heaven, you have granted my son beauty and strength and courage – why have you burdened him with a restless heart? Since he is resolved to go, protect him. O Lord, protect my son, in your great mercy lead him to the Forest, then bring him safely back home.' Q2 allows for individual interpretations of the collective wisdom. Here is the hero's impulse to find his own voice, his own style, to establish his own name in the world. Here lie the 'restless' roots of individuation, the impulse towards 'origination' as the need to authorize one's own being. Gilgamesh, in asking the reluctant city elders for their blessing, says, 'I must travel now to the Cedar Forest, where the fierce monster Huwawa lives. I will conquer him in the Forest. I will kill Huwawa and the whole world will know how mighty I am. I will make a lasting name for myself…Give me your blessing before I leave.

Harré's Transformation phase (Q3), lying between what is private (personal and closed) and what is individual (independent and not collective) is the area of innovation, of creativity. It is a space directed by the impulse to reject, change and break with what has been established. It is the dark space of 'nowhere', the world of inner dialogue and inner struggle, of construction-destruction, of hidden drives and flashes of inspiration. It takes courage, is even a kind of madness. No man surely would dare to enter the darkness and depth of the Cedar Forest: no man has ever found a way to cross the pathless ocean. Accompanied by his faithful friend Enkidu, Gilgamesh dares and does. He kills the Monster. He slays the Bull of Heaven. He puts himself to the test: to conquer or perish – and conquers.

Harré terms the final phase of his cycle Publication (Q4). It lies between the individual and the external, public world. What we experience becomes 'an experience' through the twin processes of communication and celebration. This phase answers to the need we have to share our experience with others, to show, exhibit, publish and be acknolwedged. On his return to Uruk with Enkidu Gilgamesh tells of his adventures and participates in spectacular celebrations. The goddess Ishtar, guardian of the sacred granary, falls in love with him but in his pride he rejects her. This costs him dear. At the height of his fame and fortune his beloved friend sickens and dies. Gilgamesh once more 'goes out from Uruk into the wilderness with matted hair, in a lion skin, in despair'. He faces his final quest for immortality alone.

It seems to me, that what is most important happens beyond the city and its walls. The most interesting moments somehow are the opening and closing of the gates. It is important that the city (Q1) has gates that open both to Q2 and to Q4. The story suggests that what is critical for the survival of any culture is its readiness to pass on its treasures and, at the same time, to open its gates to receive what is new – i.e. new symbolic forms. Similarly there must be a free-flowing exchange between the individual and the collective so that the citizen may build their own house in the city. There is also a question for me. If the final quest for selfhood is deeply personal and individual, what place is there in the student's creative journey for the teacher?'

Jola's question has been the focus of the present chapter and runs right through this book.

2　Five Elements theory

Before going on to tell the story of the conception and generation of the Syncretic Model I shall share with the reader some of the key principles of Five Elements theory, picked up from some basic reading in Chinese Medicine. Grasping these principles, even in outline, will be helpful in interpreting the Syncretic Model itself in due course.

His blood, which disperseth itself by branches of veins through all the body, may be resembled to those waters which are carried by brooks and rivers all over the earth, his breath to the air, his natural heat to the inclosed warmth which the earth hath in itself.

Sir Walter Raleigh, *A History of the World*

Introduction

Jung warns us that the Western mind will always struggle to grasp the ideas underlying Eastern thought, and we do well to heed him as we attempt, in this chapter, to explain and explore the principles on which Five Elements Chinese medicine is based. My approach will be to sketch the theoretical structure lightly rather than attempt a more thorough-going or comprehensive account – which, in any case, would be beyond me. Readers interested in going more deeply into these matters will be referred to several useful texts on the subject. Our purpose here is to explore the metaphorical rather than the healing or therapeutic power of the Five Elements system, to use it to explore the notion of creativity, particularly in the arts – their practice, the teaching of the arts, and their therapeutic application.

Correspondences

An understanding, even a rudimentary understanding, of Five Elements medicine, dating from approximately the fourth century BC, requires that we grasp the principle of *correspondences*, by means of which the unseen world – be it the world of the psyche, the interior world of the human body or the sacred world of the soul and of the divine spirits – is explained, described and integrated into a holistic paradigm. Thinking in correspondences means thinking associatively: in terms of the health of the person it means a way of thinking that corresponds to the way the natural world is ordered, and, to a somewhat lesser degree, to the structures of power relations in the human, social world. Human affairs seem to mirror cyclical patterns of nature; our fortunes wax and wane like the moon, rise and fall like the tides, follow the same patterns of decay and renewal to be observed in the annual cycle of the seasons. Similarity and difference generate whole strings of correspondences, with the notion of oppositional forces achieving moments of equilibrium and harmony within an overarching experience of change. We come to understand that there is no point either in waiting for a final point of resolution, or in looking back to a supposed golden age when all was beautifully ordered and balanced and fixed. If we achieve order and balance within, or between ourselves and the environment, it is only to lose them again and resume the task of trying to re-establish them. Paul U. Unschuld, in his extended survey of medicine in China, writes of the ancients' understanding of the principle of correspondence, thus:

> The cyclical patterns evident in the movement of the tides, and in the alternation of day and night, may have led these thinkers to a world view marked by a characteristic dynamic underlying apparent stability and continuity. Natural events were explained by a model of the ceaseless rise and fall of opposite yet complementary forces.

(1985: 55)

Thinking in correspondences seems a very old and universal way of thinking. Later in this book I shall tie it to symbol use and metaphor and will be suggesting it is an essentially poetic way of picturing the world. It lies at the root of medieval Western thought with its hierarchical Great Chain of Being and its complementary theory of the humours and the elements (Tillyard, 1942: 69):

Table 2.1 Tillyard's elements and humours

Element	Humour	Common quality
Earth	Melancholy	Cold and dry
Water	Phlegm	Cold and moist
Air	Blood	Hot and moist
Fire	Choler	Hot and dry

Tillyard (ibid.: 91) offers the following quotation from Raleigh's *History of the World* as illustration of traditional Elizabethan thinking in correspondences. Raleigh is explaining the functioning of the human body by analogy with the Earth:

> His blood, which disperseth itself by branches of veins through all the body, may be resembled to those waters which are carried by brooks and rivers over all the earth, his breath to the air, his natural heat to the inclosed warmth which the earth hath in itself... the hair of man's body, which adorns or overshadows it, to the grass which covereth the upper face and skin of the earth... Our determinations to the light wandering and unstable clouds, carried everywhere with uncertain winds, our eyes to the light of the sun and the moon, and the beauty of our youth to the flowers of the spring which in a very short time or with the sun's heat dry up and wither away, or the fierce puffs of wind blow them from the stalks.

Thinking in correspondences comes close to thinking in feeling and seems to be about helping us to *feel emotionally at home* in a dangerous and unstable world.

Yin-Yang

Unschuld (1985: 55) now introduces one of the central organizing principles of this strand of Chinese thinking, the yin and the yang:

> These opposing forces were designated by the symbols yin and yang, which originally meant 'shady side of a hill' (yin) and 'sunny side of a hill' (yang). The Shi-Ching, a collection of ancient folk songs from the first millennium BC, contains what are possibly the first beginnings of the yin-yang lines of association. Yin is associated with 'cold', 'cloudy', 'femininity', 'inside', and 'darkness', while yang symbolizes a line of correspondence associated with 'sunshine', 'heat', 'spring', 'summer', and 'masculinity'. In the yin-yang doctrine, the terms yin and yang no longer retain any specific meaning themselves; they function merely as categorizing symbols used to characterize the two lines of correspondence.

Figure 2.1 Yin-Yang

When we come to explore these contrary and complementary principles in connection with creative work in the arts, we shall be noting the reciprocal relations between moments of creativity and moments of reflection, between adaptation and accommodation (Piaget), between expression and impression (Witkin).

The Five Elements

The traditional Chinese conception of the elements differs rather radically from our more familiar Greek-derived Western conception. Whereas in the West we have tended towards a purely material, physical idea of the basic constituents of the phenomenal world, for the Chinese the elements were understood either non-materially or only partially so. They are given dramatic realization. In moving from one system to the other, we are exchanging the notion of 'constitution' for the notion of 'influence'. Modern Western physical theory works with the idea of the elements as represented in the periodic table. For the Chinese acupuncturist, each element is a particular force-field of energy – each element contributes its own characteristic influence to the way the life-force (the ch'i) flows around the body of the patient.

The flow of ch'i in the body is understood in Chinese medicine as being influenced by the behaviour and condition of the five elements operating via a number of channels (or 'meridians') running through the body. Rothfeld and Levart (2002: 20) elaborate:

> These meridians flow along the surface of the body and through the internal organs, just as underground rivers nourish and support the earth. Located along the meridians are a series of passageways through which you can access and strengthen qi, break blockages, and redirect energy. These acupuncture points can be likened to gates that skilled practitioners can open or shut to influence the direction and flow of energy in the body.

Each meridian is named after the organ(s) with which it is associated. There are 12 meridians in all.

Each element has its own yin organ, yang organ, season, climate, nourishing focus, emotion, colour, flavour, odour, sound. Rothfeld and Levert (2002: 27) offer a very helpful chart (see Table 2.2 below).

For the acupuncturist, of the utmost importance is the connection (or correspondence) between the flow of ch'i within the body, and the quality of the ch'i flowing in the universe at large, determined, among other things, by the weather and the seasons of the year. Acupuncture treats blocks and imbalances around the body to restore the creative flow of cosmic energy – and the patient to health. We shall be testing the corresponding role of the arts teacher or art therapist in treating the blocks and imbalances of the natural flow of creative energy to the artist and art receiver.

Table 2.2 Chart of correspondences in the Five Elements system

	Wood	Fire	Earth	Metal	Water
Yin Organ	Liver	Heart/ Pericardium	Spleen	Lungs	Kidneys
Yang Organ	Gallbladder	Small intestine/ Tripple heater	Stomach	Large intestine	Bladder
Season	Spring	Summer	Late summer	Autumn	Winter
Climate	Wind	Heat	Dampness	Dryness	Cold
Nourishes	Tendons Ligaments	Blood vessels	Flesh Muscles	Skin Hair	Bones
Emotion	Anger	Joy	Sympathy	Grief	Fear
Colour	Green	Red	Yellow	White	Blue
Flavour	Sour	Bitter	Sweet	Pungent	Salty
Odour	Rancid	Scorched	Fragrant	Rotten	Putrid
Sound	Shout	Laugh	Sing	Weep	Groan

The *Sheng* and the *Ke*

Unschuld introduces two additional, essential features of the Five Elements system. We have spoken of the flow of ch'i around the body. The body is understood as a dynamic field in which contrary and complementary forces continuously interact. These forces (the Five Elements), in a healthy person, are thought of as being in continual flow: when all is well the individual feels balanced, relaxed, energized and in good shape – mentally, physically and spiritually. For all that these forces are conceived as physical, their influence is felt through every aspect of the person, and to be in good shape means having mind, body and spirit working well together as aspects of the authentic, autonomous self. It follows that a block, weakness or over-activity in any area of this complex system undermines the harmonious functioning of the system as a whole. A little local difficulty on the slip road into Reading will eventually, and probably sooner rather than later, tie up the entire M4 and have knock-on effects far beyond. I know; I have been there.

The distinctive forces associated with each of the five elements interact with each other in two basic ways: they nurture each other and they 'control' each other. Unschuld explains:

> Tsou (c350–220) did not use abstract terms as central symbols but rather chose five tangible natural phenomena: metal, wood, water, fire, and soil. They constitute an easily understandable foundation for the five lines of correspondence, convey-

ing at the same time a number of mutual relationships among various lines. The best known of the total of sixteen are relationships of mutual destruction and of mutual generation. They can be expressed, symbolically, in the following manner: water overcomes fire; fire melts metal; metal – in the form of a knife, for instance – overcomes wood; wood – as a spade – overcomes soil; soil – as in a dyke – subdues water. Water/watering produces plants and trees, that is wood; wood brings forth fire; fire produces ashes, that is, soil; soil brings forth metal; when heated, metal produces steam, that is, water.

(1985: 59)

The 'nurturing' influence is called the *Sheng*; the 'controlling' influence is called the *Ke* (pronounced *Ko*). Unschuld makes the point early in his book that no-one has ever attempted to stabilize the Five Elements system (or its many variants) to establish a consistent, unified or authorized version. Each generation of philosophers and practitioners tweaks the system in their own way and in the light of contemporary thought. There is no absolute or definitive account of the *Sheng* and *Ke* cycles – they amount to a range of somewhat loosely nuanced understandings of positive (+) and negative (–) influences. Most starkly understood, they evoke the contrary forces of construction and destruction. As such they suggest that living in this world, for most of us, means coming to terms with the condition of instability and conflict. Such is the hand that we have been dealt by fate. If it were any comfort, and perhaps it is, faced with the unrelenting pressure of entropy towards our own personal death, we can align ourselves determinedly (and tragically, if that's the way you see it) with the life-force of creativity. We shall be casting art into such a wide-eyed role, aligning ourselves with artists and philosophers who see the gesture of the artist as essentially one of resistance.

To return to the role of Five Elements theory in Chinese medicine, the 'gesture' of the wise and good person is a moral one: i.e. so to order their lives on the basis of virtue as well as prudence as to work with the life-force to achieve a long, healthy and, upon reflection, worthy and satisfying life. Five Elements theory is not a fatalistic or a deterministic account of life; it says, here is what we are made of, these are the forces that help shape our lives; understand them and work with them, and become expert in the continuous management of change, since that is your destiny. Unschuld again:

Unlike the proponents of demonic medicine, the followers of a medicine of influences, grounded in systematic correspondence, were convinced that it was worthwhile to subject oneself to rules of conduct in order to remain in good health. This was the basis of the re-introduction of morality into the understanding of well-being and illness. Climatic influences emanating from the points of the compass, from the stars, from food and drink, from heaven and earth, from rain and wind, from heat and cold, and from numerous other phenomena were no longer inherently evil. Survival in this field of influences was possible if man adapted himself – by means of a lifestyle based on well defined norms – to the system of influences and emanations and did not contravene it.

(ibid.: 73)

We shall, in due course, be asking ourselves about 'the rules of good conduct' that might keep our expressive creativity in good shape. By exploring the dynamics of the Five Elements system in terms of the arts, we shall be able to set out the actions appropriate for artists, for arts students (developing artists) and their teachers, clients and their therapists, at different phases of the creative process. Creativity in the arts is a matter of the proper conduct and handling of the powerful natural forces available to us; of being at one with the influences and emanations that constitute the creative environment – body, mind and spirit in dynamic interaction with materials and the environment. Facing a large student audience and expected to inform and inspire them, I remember feeling entirely unequal to the task. Until, that is, I reminded myself that this was my Sun moment, my Fire time, and that if I tapped that energy in myself (I was feeling all Moon and Water at the time) and in my audience, it would work. The audience would respond, would catch my fire. They did.

A dynamic system

Modern Chinese medical practitioners have consistently adopted a particular set of diagrams to illustrate the relationships between the five different elements. Behind these relationships lies the eternal pattern of the revolving seasons:

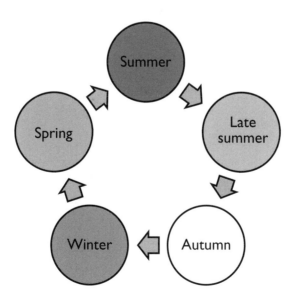

Figure 2.2 Cycle of the seasons

The five elements are superimposed upon this pattern. The *Sheng*, as 'nurturing' cycle, looks like this:

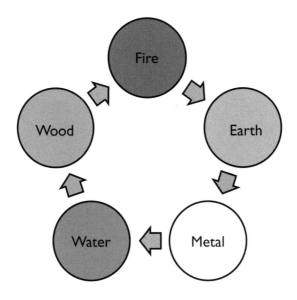

Figure 2.3 The *Sheng* cycle

The ordering of the elements around the cycle never varies, as Unschuld explained above:

Water nourishes **Wood**
Wood feeds **Fire**
Fire nourishes **Earth**
Earth produces **Metal**
Metal produces (by condensation) **Water**

Nourishing, as life-giving and life-sustaining, is one of the two defining principles governing the Five Phases of Change – the creative cycle of being.

The complementary principle, the *Ke*, is, as we have seen, variously identified as destructive or controlling. We shall be looking at two other important principles describing the operation of the cycle: 'too much' and 'too little'. The five influences, in their complementary functions of sustaining and controlling, may veer towards alternative extremes, being, for some reason, either too strong or two weak. A 'destructive' account of the *Ke* cycle might suggest an extreme application of the principle of control. No doubt there are times that call for severity – but that said, it is now usual to see the *Ke* cycle less dramatically: as resisting, guiding, structuring, constraining, guarding, controlling (even cherishing) the operation of individual elements.

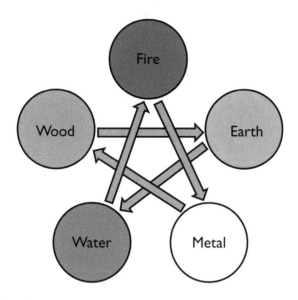

Figure 2.4 The *Ke* cycle

The controlling pairings are a constant series:

Water controls **Fire**
Fire melts **Metal**
Metal subdues **Wood**
Wood controls **Earth** (as root systems stabilize soil)
Earth channels or contains **Water**

When we move on to explore the creative arts process in the context of teaching and therapy, these two organizing principles – nurturing and controlling – will be seen as the determining features of an adequate and effective practice. It now seems sensible to present a contemporary illustration of Five Elements theory showing the double influence of the *Sheng* and the *Ke*.

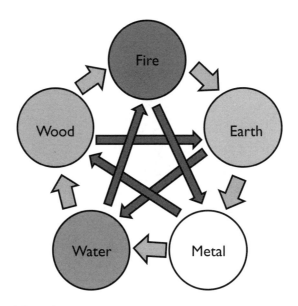

Figure 2.5 Sheng and *Ke* cycles

We have already touched on the twin principles of yin and yang. While each element has its yin aspect and its yang aspect, the elements of Wood and Fire are seen as predominantly yang in their influence, whereas the elements of Metal and Water are dominated by the yin principle. Earth comes closest to a settled balance between them. Where health is the issue, then the energy flow or balanced dynamic between these complementary principles is of the essence: the tide rising and falling, the light dying and dawning. The Incy-Wincy Spider syndrome: down comes the rain, but then out comes the sun. Rothfeld and Levert (2002: 22) make a telling connection between yin-yang and aspects of Western physiology:

> Remarkably, Western physiology is filled with examples of this yin-yang equilibrium. The sympathetic nervous system, which prepares us for fight or flight, can be thought of as a yang system, and its partner, the parasympathetic nervous system, governs the yin activities of rest and digestion. The systolic pumping of the heart is yang; the diastolic relaxation is yin. Even our hormonal systems are known to have a diurnal (day-night) variation. The yang hormones (such as cortisol and the sex hormones) are active in the day time, and the yin hormones that help the body to rest and regenerate (such as melatonin) are active during the night.

Each element is associated with a characteristic emotion.

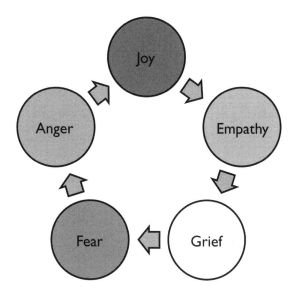

Figure 2.6 The emotional cycle

Let's now take a look at the character of each element in turn.

Metal
Season: autumn
Colour: white
Property: dryness
Emotion: grief
Organs: lungs (yin), large intestine (yang)

The gathering and sorting of the harvest, separating the chaff from the grain, the seed from the fruit, is all part of the total creative economy of change and survival. The yang organ of metal is the large intestine, central to the processes of digestion and elimination. The yin organ is the lungs, governing the breathing process. The Metal phase is about values, conscience, judgement, searching for where one's treasure lies and protecting its purity: virtue, incorruptibility and good authority. It is also about seeking inspiration and the love of untainted innocence. To its inspirational character we should add the aspirational. Metal marks both the beginning and the end of the creative and the educational journey. Metal is home to the seer, the wise ones, the guardians. The danger for Metal lies in its incipient rigidity, its reactionary tendencies, its conservatism, its sedentary security, its refusal to let go, its closedness, its 'dryness', its tendency towards a fortress attitude. A deep inclination to sorrow marks this transitional phase.

The sense of loss, the melancholy aspect of autumn, nostalgia, looking back, the poignancy of fading beauty, can be profound. Where autumn is referred to as the fall, I see an implicit weight of grief – I even pick up echoes of the book of *Genesis* and the story of the human fall from grace. Metal's intimations of nothingness, together (as we shall see) with Water's anxiety constitute the default construct of human existence suggested by Martin Heidegger (1929). But Metal is also where our reassurance lies.

Water

Season: winter
Colour: blue
Property: cold
Emotion: fear
Organs: kidneys (yin), bladder (yang)

Winter is the time of hibernation, of conservation, of nursing the embryo or the seed of creativity, of keeping the candle flame alive at the heart of darkness, drawing deep on the store of reserves gathered in the autumn. Here it is spiritual rather than purely physical energy that is at work – keeping one's hopes up through the long dark days of doubt, danger and embattled idleness. The workings of frost and ice are necessary to the fertilization of many seeds and must be endured. But the future is fraught with risk, and fear can freeze us solid or, alternatively, flood and overwhelm us. But the Water element also compensates fear with courage and wisdom. Water is the essence of life; all that grows depends upon it, and all living things are constituted of it. The Water phase is about power and potential (sexual, mental and spiritual). Its great strength is its adaptability – and its desire, its hunger for maintaining the creative 'flow'. The poet Gerard Manley Hopkins, fearful of his poetic sterility, calls upon God: 'O thou Lord of life, send my roots rain.'

Wood

Season: spring
Colour: green
Property: wind
Emotion: rage
Organs: liver (yin), gallbladder (yang)

The element of Wood has all the features of spring about it. Wood is responsible for the creative moment, the sudden, we might say, 'furious' impulse to break through the restraints imposed by Winter, and risk asserting the primacy of the new overturning the old. Wood is aggressive in its own interests, will not be denied or gainsaid, has all the nerve it needs to take on a moribund world and carry it forward to new life. It is as if it had no choice: it has the bit between its teeth and no hurdle, no barrier is too high for it. But

Wood is also known for its free-and-easy ways, its happy-go-lucky ability to relax and 'go with the flow'. It can be sure of itself because it is inherently both flexible and well organized. For summer sunshine to have something to ripen, and for the harvests of late summer and autumn to be worth celebrating and gathering in, spring (Wood) must ride roughshod. Wood must 'have the gall' to dare. Wood is the bearer of hope.

Fire
Season: summer
Colour: red
Property: heat
Emotion: joy + love
Organs: heart/pericardium (yin), small intestine/triple heater (yang)

The element of Fire rightly suggests heat, warm-heartedness, enthusiasm, passion and pleasure, especially interpersonal pleasure, the sunny disposition. Summer is for high days and holidays. Joy and laughter are in the air; life is to be celebrated and shared. Fire, too, can rage. The creative impulse discharged by Wood, swells with confidence and finally bears fruit and becomes the focus of praise and admiration. Fire is also protective and high-minded, and this means maintaining a measure of vigilance. Chinese medicine proposes this function for the 'pericardium' and the 'triple heater', which, if weakened, leave one's deepest feelings, one's loving and being beloved, dangerously over-exposed. When dejection strikes, the Fire may quickly go out. Courage (*le coeur*) is the essence of Fire: cheerful, heartfelt yet always potentially dangerous. Fire is the realm of 'spirit' (the *Shen*).

Earth
Season: late summer
Colour: yellow
Property: dampness
Emotion: empathy
Organs: spleen (yin), stomach (yang)

Mother Earth – the nourishing root and fertile ground of creative being. Earth Mother love, the essence of empathetic, compassionate feeling, the dual capacity to identify with the other positively and unstintingly and yielding up one's own inner strength and abundant resources. The living foundation of life itself – confident, authentic, generous, pragmatic (down to earth), driven by a commitment (a stomach) to take life on, full on, for energizing and protecting the entire living system. Late summer, more temperate than high summer, sees the ripening of the fruit and the beginnings of harvest. For the husbandman, it is a time to savour the quality of one's produce and prepare for the rigorous demands of gathering, threshing, sorting, marketing and storing. Virgil called Earth 'the first of the gods': the ground of divine being.

Chinese medicine based on Five Elements theory (The Five Phases of Change) makes the assumption that although we are all subject to the different influences of each of the five elements affecting the flow of ch'i (the life-force) through the body, we are also particularly susceptible to the energy of one element (occasionally two). So we may be inclined especially towards the character of Fire (as I am) or of Water, or Wood, or Earth or Metal. This predisposition, while not finally determining our overall health, lifestyle or behaviour, will be markedly influential on our mental, physical and spiritual lives and must be taken into account when coming to understand and relate to the person, and during diagnosis and treatment. Character, including creative character, would seem to arise for each individual as the combined effect of predisposition or elemental endowment (inclination), modified by opportunity or experience. Before treatment can begin, the acupuncturist is at great pains to reckon up the respective impact of both inclination and experience in shaping a particular patient's condition at any given time and suggesting a line of treatment for the ailment complained of.

3 The Syncretic Model

This chapter brings together Harré's matrix of the Identity Project and the Chinese theory of the Five Elements to make the Syncretic Model of Creativity in the Arts. The story of the model's development is told and basic concepts connected with Chinese medical theory re-introduced, with particular emphasis upon 'thinking in correspondences'. Each of the five elements is separately explored for its medicinal and creative significance, and the Syncretic Model is explained as a guide to teaching and therapy in the arts. The chapter closes with a brief look at the Tao of Art.

> A great motif in religion and art, any great symbol, becomes all things to all men; age after age it yields to men such treasure as they find in their own hearts.
>
> Ananda K. Coomaraswami, *The Dance of Shiva* (2009: 84)

Introduction

'A model,' according to particle theory scientist Lewis Dartnell, 'is a representation of a complex system that has been simplified in different ways to help to understand its behaviour'. The Syncretic Model, as its title suggests, attempts to bring different models of the complex activity of human creativity together: in particular, to reconcile a modern Western with an ancient Eastern conception, a psychological with a 'natural' or biological model. Rom Harré's, as we have seen, is a personal, psycho-social paradigm; Chinese Five Elements theory is a holistic vision of the world and its multilayered, dynamic existence. Harré presents the drama of modern existence at the level of individual identity; Chinese Five Elements theory sees this drama played out on a cosmic stage. I shall attempt to show how the one fits within the other.

Model making

Having outlined Five Elements theory, we may now proceed with a consideration of the Syncretic Model itself. In my continuing discussions with Donna during and immediately following my successful treatment, I began to speculate that there might be a significant level of correspondence between Five Elements theory or, as I discovered it also to be called, the Five Phases of Change, and my old friend the Rom Harré matrix, which I had adapted to serve as a model for the arts curriculum in schools, in my work with Sally Mitchell *et al.* (*Assessing Achievement in the Arts*). It seemed to me that the two models shared a common focus: human creativity. Furthermore, the diagrams used to describe acupuncture theory and practice, some of which we have cited already, appeared to invite comparison with Harré, and so began my own quest in the spirit of syncretism. Donna allowed herself to become more and more involved to the point where we agreed to explore these ideas together. So as to make the arrangement manageable we looked for a deadline or cut-off point, and this we found, courtesy of ECArTE, who welcomed a paper from us, delivered jointly on 16 September 2009 at their conference at the Central School of Speech and Drama in London. Having successfully delivered on our promise to ourselves, we continued to meet on our original terms, as acupuncturist and patient. This book, however, is evidence that, for me, the original impulse was far from exhausted. It goes without saying that, but for Donna's support, I simply could not have written it.

My first attempt to bring the two traditions together was set out in a note I wrote to Donna on 8 March 2009. I proposed the following correspondences:

Q1: Conventionalization = Metal/Earth
Q2: Appropriation = Water
Q3: Transformation = Wood
Q4: Publication = Fire

Donna's response was encouraging but she insisted that we could not merely elide the elements of Metal and Earth. Their separate identities had to be respected, she said, and any model built on the principle of correspondence had to show them as independent influences within an integrated system. Metal, in my diagram, seemed to be in the right position – but Earth definitely was not. She also pointed out that my proposed identification yang/public and yin/private, would need further thought, and probably adjustment. In answer to my subsequent question, 'Where can Earth go?' Donna had no hesitation: 'In the middle,' she said. This was a crucial moment – everything followed from that insight of hers. She was able to show me that the modern acupuncture diagrams I was familiar with, though conveniently devised for contemporary purposes, were in fact adaptations of much earlier models that showed Earth at the centre of a simple, squared matrix. In the course of the following weeks, Donna came up with several ancient Chinese examples, mostly connected with Taoist philosophy, including the key models of He Tu and Luo Shu.

We subsequently found other such cosmological models, very similar visually. There is, for instance, the well-known model of the *axis mundi*, there is the sand mandala of Tibet, which has the holy mountain Kailish at its centre (the mountain is a traditional symbol for Earth, being grounded in this world and pointing to heaven). The Wheel of Fortune, depicted in the medieval manuscript of the *Carmina Burana* (1230), a miscellany of bawdy songs and parodies, shows the wheel as a circle within a cruci-form framework. The earliest models of the world were simply indicative of the four directions: north/south, east/west. Interestingly, this is the symbol of Earth in Norse mythology. In the Cattedrale di S. Martino, in Lucca, is a carved figure of a maze with the same configuration, only, in this instance, circular rather than square.

Since those early researches I have come across a popular Western five-segment model, the quincunx. Sir Thomas Browne in his book *The Garden of Cyrus*, makes much use of this figure in analysing basic structures in nature. He points, for example, to its presence on the skin of the pineapple. Macfarlane and Seamus Heaney have both written about the quincunx recently.

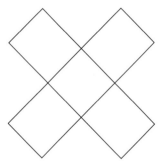

Figure 3.1 The Quincunx

One of the strangest treatments of the quincunx figure that I have come across was made by the surrealist artist René Magritte in 1928. It shows a cluster of amoebic white blobs on a black ground: four, disposed in the conventional pattern, around a smaller blob floating in the middle. Like us, Magritte was also drawn to label his quad-rants, in his case: Q1: *horizon*, Q2: *cris d'oiseaux*, Q3: *armoire*, Q4: *personnage éclatant de rire*. He called the work, *The Living Mirror*. He left his central blob nameless.

Having authorized our intuition of placing Earth at the centre, we needed to modify Harré's four-part matrix in order to accommodate it. Doing so gave us the essential configuration of the new 'synthetic model', as I was then rather awkwardly styling it.

It is worth pointing out that arranging the elements in this way meant abandoning the convention of having the four points of the compass as the principal structuring device. Losing the compass points, however, frees the model up for universal application. Our Syncretic Model, based on the correspondences we saw between the creative process that was Harré's Identity Project, and the Chinese Five Phases of Change, worked for me as significantly enriching and enlivening my understanding of the creative process in the arts. I felt I understood Harré's four phases so much better, and so much more concretely, seeing them in terms of the naturally recurring cycle of the seasons. Placing Earth/authenticity/empathy at the centre gave the new model the traditional configuration of the quincunx: four segments distributed about a pivotal fifth.

There was, at the time, as I have already said, an important distinction between the way Donna thought of the model and how I thought of it. For her it was another way of describing a living, healing reality, and served to guide healing treatment to restore the balanced flow of cosmic energy through a patient's body. It was a practical model for guiding treatment. For me it was a beautiful metaphor – a suggestive device for refreshing and expanding reflection and theory-building as the basis of, or counterpart to, creative practice in the arts and education. However, as time has passed, I have become increasingly conscious of the creative process within myself as a naturally recurring interplay of forces, with their own patterns and rhythms, and am ready to grant that those forces are not insulated from or unconnected with influences coming from beyond me – the kinds of influence cited by Unschuld earlier: e.g. time of year, food, weather, relationships, unconscious mental processes etc. In short, even as a creative individual, I may not be an island. 'Inspiration' – what lies beyond our conscious control – still counts for an awful lot in artistic creativity for instance. If this should prove to be the case, then there is a lot more to being creative, to being a creative artist or writer, than having a specific talent or a snappy set of techniques for doing creative business in spite of, or ignorance of, one's surroundings and one's inner 'treasures of darkness'. The model might be more like an account of reality than a beautiful metphor. There might be more to creativity than is dreamed of in our – Western – philosophy. I am more than half persuaded. Here, then, is the full Syncretic Model, as Donna and I presented it that afternoon in September 2009 to the ECArTE conference, and as I have continued to present it to other audiences since.

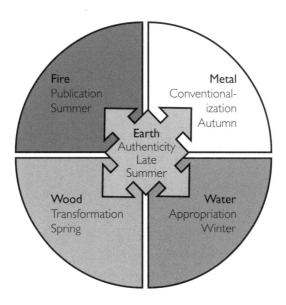

Figure 3.2 The Syncretic Model (original)

Since that original presentation, I have tried other diagrammatic representations, the most recent of which was a Venn version, which is appealing in its way, but not one I am wholly confident about yet. I have adopted a somewhat simplified version of the original as my principal reference point for the discussion of the Syncretic Model in this book.

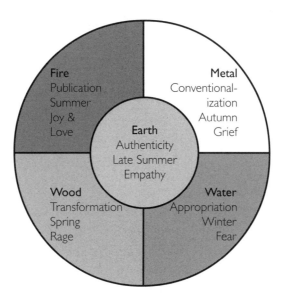

Figure 3.3 The Syncretic Model (revised)

The creativity story has no beginning and no end – just as the cycle of the seasons is continuous. Winter is as significant to the scheme of life as is summer; spring is of equal importance to autumn. Linking each season is the song of the Earth – the principle of empathy. It is the same whether we consider the creative life of the individual or of the collective, the creative life of the professional artist or of the child in school. Let's now look at the elemental phases of the cycle more closely, considering them as descriptions of the different stages in the creative process of the arts.

Metal: autumn

With the arrival of Michaelmas daisies in our gardens we know the year is beginning to draw to a close. The fields are shorn and the tawny stubble awaits the plough – farmers' thoughts are already jumping ahead to next year's spring crop and the early lambs, even as the last of the harvest is gathered in with an eye cocked to the coming equinoctial storm. In the railed gardens of city squares, the trees are turning gold. Metal – autumn introduces its own distinctive note to the harmonious chord sequence that is the music of creativity. Where late summer was generous and reflective, Autumn is necessarily more critical, more judgemental. The seed merchant enters the scene, cups the new grain in his hand and reckons its 'nose'. Landowners cast an appraising eye over their tenants and the returns their labours will have made. It is a time for appraisal, for the laying of fresh plans, for the prudent setting aside of seeds and supplies for the future, for the proper management of resources, for making qualitative judgements, for separating sheep from goats, the chaff from the wheat. Metal marks the dying of the creative year, the end of this particular creative project. The altars of city churches are decked for harvest festival. It is the time of the saints, of all souls, of Hallowe'en. If successful, we shall be cherishing its beauty, our joy tinged with sadness, for beauty is always touched with poignancy. Little wonder if the season has a touch of sadness about it, a strong sense not so much of what has been achieved (that came earlier in the cycle) but of the fragility of our achievement and the joys of making and sharing now only a memory, even the sense of nostalgia suggestive of the waning of the influence of home, the fading of beauty, diminishment of power, reduction of the life-force, loss and separation. Hence Metal's complex and necessary emotion: grief.

'Letting go' of a project, of a creative effort that has cost so much and with which, perhaps, one has become too closely identified, is not easy. More difficult still is to submit oneself to the detached judgement of others, of the critics, the connoisseurs, the sponsors, the collectors, their agents and commissioners. We are to be known and to be judged by the only significant and most demanding evidence: our fruits. There can be no special pleading, because what is now at stake is not simply the individual artist's future, but the future of the cultural tradition itself. The quality of the collective conversation. The guardians will decide: that is what the guardians are for.

And under that kind of scrutiny we must be careful to stay grounded, to retain our faith in the essential authenticity of the work – even in the face of disappointment and a lack of understanding. But we need that wider, public perspective that autumn brings, that sense of proportion that allows us to see a particular experience, one charged with subjective emotion, in a more objective, purer, clearer light. Others can help us here. We need the assurance that authority can provide. Our little craft must prove itself seaworthy. Meanwhile, the flame of creativity must be preserved, the seed, the inspiration for the next project, buried deep and secure for the approaching time of incubation. And so the cycle closes on an inspiring note of purity and innocence, and with the clear aspiration of regeneration. For central to Metal is the idea of the search, the quest for meaning and for ultimate values. All the great stories of the heroic journey or search (Gilgamesh, the Grail, Odysseus) take their inspiration from Metal. Within the walls of Uruk, the guardians preserve the truth of the quest. We arrive at the beginning, born into a culture that exists and persists despite us, as T. S. Eliot says, only to recognize it for the first time. Annie Dillard captures something of the defining mood of Metal in describing Toby's death in her novel *The Maytrees*:

> Nights he rose to take companionable leaks with Jupiter. Comically, when he took his last outdoor shower a week ago, he did not know it would be his last. Nothing marked or would mark his last piece of pie, swim, tune – as presently he would see his last everything, kid, dawn, spoon, and familiar face – if he had not already. When he knew he would die, he found it first impossible, then sad, to near the fall's lip, to yield to the ripping loss of the coloured world and himself in it.
>
> (2007: 180)

Metal's *Sheng* (nourishing) element is Earth. Where would the critics be without the fruits of the artist's labours? Without the artist's abundance, fertility and commitment. Without their own authenticity. Judgement should be infused with empathy. Metal's *Ke* element is Fire. There should be something heart-warming, affectionate and geared to lift the spirit, in the necessarily disciplined and disinterested verdict of the gatekeepers. Something close to mercy. A difficult circle to square perhaps, but necessary if the incentive, the inspiration to further creative work, is not to be snuffed out. Metal holds and guards the treasures of the Earth.

Water: winter

With winter we understand that it is a time for consolidation, for nurturing the creative seed, allowing for its incubation, keeping it warm and safe. The produce of autumn is stored and used in the struggle for survival – and the potent seeds to be sown in the spring lie dormant, waiting. The Chinese element for winter is Water, its defining task is the maintenance of the flow of creativity from generation to generation, and this makes it a time of faith, of preserving the creative spirit through its necessary period of dormancy, of gestation, of incubation, of gathering strength. A profound thoughtfulness presides over this quiet and complex time. We are not speaking here so much of particular projects as of a more generalized life-instinct, the desire to live, to make one's mark, to take one's chance, the find or realize oneself. Will is involved here and especially 'caring' – self-belief and courage. Creative particularity comes with the spring surge. Water is fed by Metal: winter life is sustained from the storehouse of the fruits of autumn.

For the artist, this phase of the creative process is also associated with keeping the creative, the expressive faith and drawing strength from work already completed, by oneself and by others, from ideas already in circulation and from the repertoire that time has preserved and continues to honour at the heart of the cultural heritage. Here we see the nourishing *Sheng* cycle at work. From the *Ke* cycle comes the structuring or handling (I want to say cherishing) influence of Earth: the impulse of authenticity. We know that the characteristic emotion of Water/winter is fear, and it is not difficult to recognize this emotion colouring the vision of the artist as he/she confronts the blank canvas, the empty space, the unmarked sheet of paper, poised to express their own particular and distictive expressive voice. To the rescue ride Metal, with its venerable and precious treasures gathered from the past, and, as a steadying influence, Earth, with its endlessly optimistic song of the future, and its boundless gift of empathy. 'Have faith, be confident, be gentle with yourself, hold on. Wait. You will be ready when the time is right.' This is wisdom speaking.

Wood: spring

Winter is followed by spring. Spring takes over the creative seed, gives it an injection of energy and a clear sense of direction. Wood particularizes the project, transforming latency into actuality. The green Wood, the traditional haven of lovers and setting for the pastoral paradise, bursts into life in a riot of new growth. The parks and avenues are bursting with greenery. Among the animals and the birds the same surge of energy is seen: nest-building, courtship, mating, procreation abound. It is as if all that energy conserved and accumulated during the long sleep of winter now breaks out in a furious determination to have its way. A strengthening sun gleams from the towers of glass. The force is irresistible – concrete cracks to let the pale shoot find its way into the light and upward to the sun, itself freshly returned to the world with renewed strength – and a plan. Never was there better organization, sensibly matched by flexibility. The laws of growth transform seed into plant and organism. Lines of supply are established and development proceeds apace. Pollination is effected, courtesy of the insect world, and the new season's fruit is set in gardens, orchards and allotments far and wide.

For the artist, too, there is a sudden unstoppable surge of energy. The dormant idea springs to life and the first expressive gesture establishes the direction of the new creative project, as materials are transformed into symbols. Already the work carries the author's unmistakable signature for, as at every succeeding phase of the process, it has to pass the critical test of authenticity: this is my own, honest work, and even now, in its rough and tentative beginnings, it speaks in my language and answers to my desire. Its fierce optimism and assertiveness is fuelled by the deep faith and commitment of Water – winter. Its tendency to simply burn itself out is restrained by the steadying hand of Metal that will eventually cut out and prune back what is redundant and irrelevant, to allow the full maturation of what is healthiest and most necessary. Spring's fury or rage will later be countered by autumn's sober and more reflective manner, the artist's wilful prodigality tempered by an awareness of the timeless values embedded in the heritage; by the perspective that history and judgement give.

Fire: summer

As I look out from my table at the window onto a snowy garden this January morning it is difficult to imagine how it was, back in the summer or how it will be in five months' time. The windows will have been thrown open, the lawn already perhaps showing signs of drying out, the first flush of the roses and other flowers will be over, the sharp shadow of the house cast upon the little patio as the sun arcs high across the southern sky. Summer is the season when passion runs high, when friends are invited round for supper at a table on the grass, and the dappled shadows of the beech tree play over us as another scorching day draws to its cool close. The pavement café tables are busy under their awnings, the great sporting occasions thronged with ecstatic fans. Up and down the land the festival season reverberates to the stamp and throb of revellers. Summer grows fat and strong on the back of spring's heroic efforts, and, given spring's direction and impetus, now brings the creative project to fruition.

   For the artist, it is a time of final realization, of the full flowering of one's efforts, and for turning to one's friends, to the rest of the creative team, in a gesture of rejoicing and sharing, for the conversations and celebrations that will see the work to completion. So there is a readiness to take advice, to reconsider, to edit and revise; above all, to finish, publish and, if necessary, be damned. There is an impulse of praise in the air: one long day succeeds another with barely a pause for breath. However isolating the earlier phases might have felt, summer lifts the spirits, brings conviviality and gladness, particularly when the project seems to have been blessed beyond our hopes for it. The temperature peaks; so too do the spirits. Beware! Moments of conflict are soon sparked into conflagrations. With a production threatened by administrative nit-picking, I once laid about me with a flame-thrower. And yet we are just as soon ready to lurch into debauch and calculated indulgence. The ever-present influence of Earth, seeking the sense of an authentic work achieved, bestows restraint and restores composure to a moment that has to have been liberally fuelled by an abundant supply of creativity, of Wood. And lest we get too carried away by the heady spirit of festival, Water – winter is there to cool the fever with its reminder of the risks attaching to every creative project, and the trials still to be faced. Water, with its quiet and compelling wisdom, its patient mission of fertility.

Earth: late summer

The shift to late summer is often barely perceptible, and yet, for the careful observer it is distinct enough. In some respects it offers the best of all worlds. The days are warm still – even hot at times. Conviviality persists – in late beach parties and walks along the riverside. Shade is plentiful, though the signs among the trees of the coming fall are there already, green yielding to subtle shades of yellow, russet and gold. In the countryside, the harvest, begun under the aegis of Fire, is now in full swing; the hay is in and the early corn cut. The journey home on the train is refreshed at the open window, an evening saunter to the pub or the pool, still a happy prospect. Fruit is ripening and it is time to gather the first of the nuts and berries. The mood is one of gentle reflection, of sincerity and fellow-feeling, of relishing the fruits of our labours and cherishing life in ourselves and in others. The pervasive sense of 'reception', of being blessed and being valued, is all part of Earth's motherly spirit of generosity, reciprocity and empathy. This is the time of libations. Back from our holidays, feet on the ground, given decent weather we walk abroad delightedly upon the Earth that is our most precious gift, and our home.

For the artist it is a time for taking stock of one's achievement, for making contact with our roots, for testing our authenticity. The Earth is forever there for us, forever renewed, unstinting in its gift of life and in supplying the essentials for creative living. It is whence we came and whither we are bound. Not for nothing do we cherish the identification of the Earth with mother. Earth is nourished by Fire: the quality of the work is underwritten by the helpful encouragement and praise of others and our own insistence on making final adjustments and seeing it through. Earth is stabilized by Wood: the work, now being released into a life of its own, is rendered robust and durable by the creative energy which initiated and continues to sustain it.

Jola offers this comment:

> Asking his mother in the granary for blessing Gilgamesh needs the blessing of Earth.
>
> He says 'no' to Ishtar because Ishtar incarnates everything a woman can be except a mother. Ishtar for him means, maybe, Metal – anyway she is the Goddess of war. Gilgamesh doesn't want to be conventionalized. He is afraid of both being 'understood' (in the terms Lévinas uses it, i.e. being killed), of not being loved any longer, being labelled and put, out of reach, on the granary shelf.

The final move on, or return, to Metal/autumn sees the individual in their role as a member of the wedding, as the inheritor of and contributor to a particular cultural legacy.

Harré calls this phase Conventionalization. Here the individual is embedded within a tradition and investing in it. Metal yields its influence to Water, autumn to winter – and winter looks both ways, backwards towards a tired but abundant past and forwards towards the New Year in waiting and with everything to play for. In terms of the Harré matrix, winter/Water approximates to Appropriation – to the phase in which the tradition is personalized as a private aspiration of the emerging individual identity. Moving on to spring/Wood, Harré's Transformation phase receives the impulse for lift-off, and powers itself into orbit – into a particular orbit, private and specific to this particular artist at this particular moment. Summer/Fire is Harré's time of Publication, of the full flowering, the coming to fruition of the project as a public, shared but distinctively individual action in the world. This is its inclination now, towards letting go and feeding back, in the spirit of the joyful gift.

Harré's model has four rather than five phases: Harré's matrix lacks our fifth and central element/season, Earth/late summer. In the Syncretic Model, we place Earth in the centre, following the older Chinese tradition, seeing its influence as pervasive throughout the cycle, as the recurring impulse towards authenticity – put another way, towards the intuitive and proper authority of the author. Empathy, in that context, translates as the maker's compassionate feeling for the making and for what he/she has made. When, in the course of the creative cycle, the artist comes down to Earth, the work faces its most rigorous trial: the celebrations over, in the privacy of their own heart, the artist must judge the work as good enough – which is to say, as answering to the original impulse (preserved and nurtured by Water/winter), and as the fruit of an authentic endeavour deserving not only of survival but to be treasured (Metal/autumn).

Later in this book, Earth will be identified with the intelligence of feeling, informing and funding the artist's creative making in her quest for significant form. Empathy will take on an imaginative, intelligent and formative character. Since Earth is influential at every phase of the cycle of creativity we must expect to find the intelligence of feeling a pervasive and determining presence. Earth's authentic quality is variously nuanced around the cycle. At Metal, authenticity occurs as the search for the genuine, the principal; at Water it means good faith; at Wood, invention; at Fire, (ap)plausibility. Authenticity at the centre of the model is truth, sooth, troth.

The artist is a soothsayer: a truth-sayer, with the accent on the saying and the pledging of one's troth. The project of art is to *tell* the heart's truth, and its mission begins and ends in such a telling. Art celebrates the extraordinary human gift for telling one's heart's truth and sharing another's. Its 'magic' lies in the mystery of this gift or power, latent in inert materials and common speech, of evoking the heart's deepest longings and understandings. No one has ever plumbed the secret that defines poetry or music, painting or dancing. None the less, art is a practice of animation, and the way to perfect it and venerate it lies in making a habit of it.

We have established sufficiently close a correspondence to allow us to equate the principal moments of the Harré cycle with those of the theory of the Five Elements – accommodating the fifth Chinese element, Earth, as a new feature of the matrix. Both cycles describe a process of waxing and waning, of growth, decay and renewal. Whether we consider ourselves as part of a larger system of influences, subject to the rhythms of the cosmos, or whether we understand the creative process as an inner cycle of linked, essentially mental processes, we are, none the less, responding to the natural scheme of things. Human creativity has its rhythms and its idea of order, and to ignore either is to trivialize the notion itself and to risk its violation. Such is the burden of this book. To cultivate the habit of art is to comprehend and align oneself to creative rhythms at play in the world and 'rituals of worship' wired into our brains. Their understanding and mastery require the dedication and sustained application we would associate with any human commitment to excellence, to a discipline that is bigger than we are, in the service of which we find some of our deepest satisfactions. The psychological character of Harré's cultural model finds correspondence with the biological and spiritual character of the Chinese. Both in their different ways speak to the creative process in art, theorized elsewhere in this book and documented in the witness of artists themselves. This is the Way, the Tao, of art.

The Tao of art

Thirty spokes unite at the wheel's hub:
It is the centre hole that makes it useful.

(Lao Tzu, *Tao Te Ching*, XI)

Taoism is best thought of as a spiritual philosophy. It is not, in the Western sense, a religion, which is to say a set of ritual practices and beliefs based on the worship of a supernatural being or beings; rather it is a way of life that draws its spiritual power from an understanding of the hidden structure of the world, in which the essence or force of life is to be found in all things, linking the material with the immaterial, the human spirit, mind and body, with the energy vitalizing the entire cosmos. Taoism was firmly established in China by the fourth century BC, its principles spelt out in a small book, thought to have been written by Lao Tzu and published about 250 BC, called the *Tao Te Ching* (The Book of the Way and its Virtue). Perhaps its defining spiritual activities are meditation and the martial art the *Tai Chi Chuan*, but given the identification in the Tao of creativity with the generative and regenerative life forces in nature and in man, the Tao has always been closely related to Chinese art. Among the many other expressions of Taoism was the discovery and healing practice of acupuncture – and Five Elements theory or the Five Phases of Change, to be fully understood, must be placed within the wider context of the spiritual philosophy, the Tao.

Taoist art is a celebration of the artist's capacity to penetrate the veil of the material world to reveal and connect to the essence or spirit – the sacred energy – within. Perfecting their art was for the Taoist artist (and here we include the performing as well as the forming arts) a life-long discipline in the habit of spontaneous, intuitive expression. It was about cultivating the art of un-concealing (showing) the hidden soul or character of the natural world. Art-making and receiving were understood as forms of meditation – thereby belonging, it would seem, to Aristotle's domain of 'contemplative action'. For the Taoist artist this meant attuning one's own soul to the soul of the world – it meant making oneself transparent, empty, a medium, a channel. The cult of celebrity and personality is anathema to the spirit of Taoism. Nor was the art of the Tao about interpersonal communication or, in the narrow sense, about personal or self expression, though it required the mediation of the gifted and dedicated individual for its realization. I am reminded here of a passage in Hannah Arendt's introduction to Walter Benjamin's *Illuminations* (1992: 52):

> What mattered to him above all was to avoid anything that might be reminiscent of empathy, as though a given subject of investigation had a message in readiness which easily communicated itself, or could be communicated, to the reader or spectator: 'No poem is intended for the reader, no picture for the beholder, no symphony for the listener.'
>
> ('The Task of the Translator')

The Taoist artist cultivates the habit of art as a spiritual discipline that serves the living flow of cosmic energy, uniting the creative resources of mind, body and spirit with their corresponding vital forms in the cosmos at large. The final end of such a transmission is the rebalancing of the person's creative energies and their re-attunement to the grand patterns of the natural world, to the flow of the cosmic dance. Illumination, disclosure or enlightenment (Walter Benjamin's term is 'un-concealment') was the artist's spiritual reward. It is in this sense that art is held to be regenerative, that art belongs to the cosmic dance of continuous renewal.

Here is Ben Willis writing about the Tao of dance:

> Tao is, like the martial arts and other athletics, the art of movement. The dancer works from a base of self-discipline, concentrates energy in the body's spiritual centres, and moves in a spontaneous, intuitive response to a purely intuitive medium, music. The dancer identifies with, becomes one with the music in much the same way as does the musician, and so swims in the pure river of ch'i, of spirit…Like the musician and the athlete, the dancer's practice consists of

constant training to ready the physical instrument for the maximum intuitive/spiritual response.

(2000: 123)

Just such an understanding seems to inform Gabrielle Roth's Five Rhythms dance workshops. Technique, in the Taoist scheme of artistic creativity, is not the conscious application of skills and conventions, still less a self-conscious display of invention. Rather, it is the intuitive co-response (correspondence) of the trained body to the imminent moment – to the movement of spirit. It is as unconscious, spontaneous and perfect as the instinctive move of the trained athlete when the heat is on. In the creative world of the Tao artist, 'things are liberated from the drudgery of usefulness', to quote Walter Benjamin.

Conclusion

At the top of this chapter, I cited Lewis Dartnell's definition of a model. Modelling or representing simplified accounts of complex systems as a way of understanding them has a long tradition going back to the earliest human representations of the physical world, the heavens, the spiritual world, and to cultural activities such as hunting. The modelling impulse has inspired myth-making, storytelling, dramatic rituals, dancing, painting – all the arts, in fact, since their obscure beginnings. Nowadays, modelling (often involving scientists and artists working together) is largely done by means of fast computers. I recently googled some astonishing models of bird-flocking and galaxy formation. In this book we supply and explore one of the earliest models of complex human behaviour: the ancient Chinese model of the Five Elements. And yet, as we shall see, it is still more than capable of yielding wide-ranging and useful insights into contemporary human creativity in general and into what we are calling 'the habit of art' in particular. As Unschuld informs us, there are 16 relationships implicit in the original Chinese model, of which we have abstracted only two, the *Sheng* and the *Ke*. Although it is perfectly correct to see the different phases of the model as an ordered sequence or set of interrelated cycles, following the broad temporal pattern of sunrise, noon, sunset, midnight, the seasonal waxing and waning of the year, and the life-cycle itself, none the less there is much more going on within this complex system of continuously interactive energies.

For the system of human creativity is about the continuous interaction of our physical, mental and spiritual intelligences and these operate not simply as chains or strings but as networks and circuits. In its way, the Chinese model maps the brain itself as it processes and integrates into one life-sustaining system the workings of body, mind and spirit. I take the position in this book that creativity is the brain behaving at optimal level as a complex system of interactive intelligences functioning to sustain and perpetuate the life of the individual and the species. Minds proceed from moments of equilibrium to moments of disequilibrium: creativity is the autonomic response of the brain in achieving a new point of balance through adaptation or change, and thereby re-establishing the creative flow of consciousness. Each crisis takes us, if we are lucky, to a different level of articulation. The Syncretic Model offers a plausible representation of the basic functions of the brain and proposes a set of activities and interactions around and across those functions that govern artistic creative activity and contribute to human wellbeing.

But we are not simply creatures tied to events; we can and do deliberately precipitate crises of disequilibrium for their adaptive potential. All play is of such an order. Art as a form of play is of such an order. Art involves the deliberate triggering of disequilibrium, and the work it then takes to remake the self and discover a new point of balance or harmony. Think of bird flocking – as I was when I followed the Google link. The amazing and beautifully synchronized manoeuvres of flocks of birds (swarms of gnats, shoals of fish) arise, I am reliably informed, from the amazing vision of the individuals within the group. Each one is finely attuned to respond to the movements of its immediate neighbours and this allows for instant changes of direction and height, resulting in the thrilling wave formations for which there is neither a master plan nor a charismatic leader. The spirals, flanges, vortices, clouds and skeins that constitute this spontaneous, improvised dance are the result of wave mechanisms resulting from a vast number of synchronized individual responses. This image probably tells us more about how human creativity works in the brain than any other I can immediately think of.

But this dance can be easily impaired and the whole system crash should one element fail the whole. And there is the notion of optimum performance, which seems to be characterized by the flexibility, immediacy and adaptability 'wired into' the dance that so mesmerizes and enchants us. Again it is all about eyesight – in particular, about range. The 'flocking' modellers show that blind birds simply collide, make no progress and have no fun, whereas those with too wide a visual range produce a kind of monstrous uniformity and compliance more suggestive of the totalitarian mastermind than the collective dance of convivial individuals. (Are there hints here of right- and left-brain functions?) All of which suggests that our handling of the Syncretic Model must allow not simply for the underlying rhythms of the great primeval cosmic forces influencing behaviour generally (and I include the influence of the mother upon her child as a cosmic force) but the moment-by-moment functioning of the infinitely elaborate networks and circuits which carry and process information in the brain and order conscious and unconscious responses in constant flow. So whereas the Harré model gave rise to a numbered sequence of phases (Q1, Q2, Q3, Q4), in the Syncretic Model we have followed the Chinese in resisting such a numbering, thereby establishing the openness of the system and hinting at a bewildering level of complexity and range of interactive possibilities beyond the scope of this book's compass. Human creativity occurs as the adaptive co-ordination of somatic, intellectual and affective intelligences in the ceaseless interplay of the five elements or phases of being:

conservation (Metal), reproduction (Water), exploration (Wood), illumination (Fire) and integration (Earth). This complex structure, by means of which we keep our heads and find our balance as human beings, also constitutes the habit of art: greatly simplified, we offer it as our Syncretic Model of artistic creativity and explore its application in the training and practice of the arts teacher, arts therapist and cultural animator.

On page 1 of the Colour Plates we illustrate one of the most beautiful, contemporary versions of our matrix: the Tibetan sand mandala.

4 The Syncretic Model applied

The theme of the participant practitioner is further pursued in this chapter: first of all, through Donald Schön's account of the professional whose skill is 'reflection-*in*-action', and then through Daniel Stern's notion of 'affective attunement' and its implications for the interaction between professional and client. Partnering the creative process in art is explored in terms of the cyclical activities of the Syncretic Model – as are the complementary activities of partnering art reception and art criticism as different aspects of the habit of art.

> Through certain kinds of exchange with others, you become more yourself.
>
> Boston Change Process Study Group

> Free-will cannot be debated but only experienced, like a colour or the taste of potatoes.
>
> William Golding, *Free Fall*

Introduction

In this chapter I shall be suggesting the Syncretic Model's practical possibilities in outline, before going into more detail in connection with arts education and therapy. I shall be writing inclusively for the arts teacher, the arts therapist and the cultural animator. I shall be drawing not only on the Syncretic Model itself but upon Daniel Stern's notion of 'attunement' and Donald Schön's principle of the 'reflective practitioner', both of which I see as helpfully complementary. The question I shall address here is this: What help can the Syncretic Model offer the arts practitioner who wishes to reflect, following Schön's distinction, both *on* and *in* their practice?

Schön's reflective framework

Schön's (1983) thesis is that all true professionals improvise: this is the skill that defines them and sets them apart from the 'servicing' sector. They don't simply follow the book or stick to a routine; they commit themselves with an open mind to the ongoing presence of their client and feel their way, more by intuition than design, into a 'creative' relationship out of which an effective assessment and strategy can be allowed to emerge. The medical practitioner, for instance, who simply ticks off the presented symptoms and reaches for the prescription pad is, in Schön's terms, not responding professionally. A teacher who slavishly works through the prescribed pages of the National Curriculum and 'delivers' the pre-ordained lesson is not a professional in Schön's sense. He makes a key distinction between what he calls reflecting-*on*-action and reflecting-*in*-action. Reflecting-*on*-action takes place at a distance from the field of action itself and occurs as retrospective evaluation with the benefit of hindsight on the one hand, and as forward-planning on the other. Reflecting-*in*-action, on the other, hand is what professionals do when they are participating fully in an ongoing encounter with a client or group of clients, not simply following a prepared plan or reacting routinely but improvising creatively within an evolving situation. Elsewhere in this book I call such responsiveness 'reflexive'. In the analysis that follows I shall be assuming that arts teachers, therapists and cultural animators (collectively 'arts practitioners') operate using both systems of reflection (often together), that they are reflectors-*on*-practice and also reflectors-*in*-practice. To deliver a 'participatory practice' you must be able do both, and know which is the more appropriate in any given situation.

Schön provides a framework for reflecting-*on*-action: he invites the professional to plan their work and assess their performance retrospectively under four heads: (1) Repertoire of Skills; (2) Values; (3) Overarching Theory; (4) Role Relations. This same framework, incidentally, can be used to write a departmental Statement of Intent, laying down what the department considers itself to be about. For example:

> (1) Using our personal empathic intelligence, and professional skills as artists and arts practitioners (teachers, therapists, cultural animators), we shall cover, nourish and challenge our clients' 'habit of art'.
>
> (2) We shall encourage our clients to connect artistic experience with personal meaning by helping them to become autonomous, effective art-makers and art-receivers on their own account.
>
> (3) We are guided in our work by an expressive theory of art that makes everyone an artist. Our mentors include Winnicott, Witkin, Gadamer, Harré, Schön and Stern.
>
> (4) We companion our clients as instructors, exemplars, co-creators, monitors, guides, friends, guardians and assessors. We are committed to taking care of every one of them.

Having written extensively about Schön's work elsewhere (Ross *et al.*, 1993) I shall add nothing more here. There is, however, rather more I feel I need to say about Stern's ideas.

Stern and the inter-subjective relationship

Daniel Stern (1985, 2004, 2010), like D. W. Winnicott before him, is a paediatric psychologist whose early focus was on infant development. Despite the particularity of his background I feel arts practitioners generally have a lot to learn from him. His study of the mother-infant relationship and, in particular, his formulation of the idea of 'affective attunement' as the process of forging mother-infant intimacy through non-verbal expressive interaction, laid the foundation of a sustained exploration of how we communicate our feelings to each other *explicitly*, of how we come to know each other empathically, and of the implications of an empathic understanding and interaction for the particular practice of psychotherapy.

In 1994 he co-founded the Boston Change Process Study Group (BCPSG) with a number of fellow analysts. Their purpose seems to have been two-fold: to understand the process of change within the therapeutic context (how does/might intended change within the patient happen in therapy?) and to encourage the growing shift from a predominantly verbal reflecting-*on*, with the patient's inner world as the focus of an 'analysis', to one that placed greater emphasis on the therapeutic impact of the inter-active, moment-to-moment, therapist–patient relationship, i.e. reflecting-*in*. (Incidentally, Stern and his colleagues have no difficulty with the term 'patient'. In this general chapter I shall continue to use the collective word 'client' generically.) This shift or change of approach in psychotherapy they consider now to be pervasive in general therapeutic practice: they call it 'the pendulum swing from a one- to a two-person psychology'. Whereas a one-person psychology sees the roots of the patient's 'complaint' within the hidden inner world of the patient alone, a two-person psychology focuses on the patient's relationships with others. Doing so is seen as fundamentally shifting the balance of power within the relationship from one essentially governed and regulated by the investigating and managing therapist, to one in which therapist and patient co-create the agenda and co-manage the healing.

Stern and his colleagues describe the relational process they are interested in as dialogical: affective understanding is built in feeling in response to what they call 'affective cues' (body language, facial expression, non-verbal vocalization, expressive speech) rather than exclusively through transactional verbal discourse. Stern repeatedly makes the point that although implicit and explicit understanding interweave throughout the therapeutic process, where implicit knowing is concerned there is no need to verbalize and bring to consciousness in that way. There is, he argues (2004: 130), a special dimension of consciousness dedicated to implicit or empathic understanding: what he calls 'inter-subjective consciousness'. Its medium is the infinite variety of expressive signals or cues that the client and therapist use to engage inter-subjectively with each other. He calls these signals 'forms of vitality' or 'affective cues'.

The new therapeutic dialogue aims at creating an experience of inter-subjective understanding where the patient has been experiencing painful incoherence and frustration in her 'real' relationships. At the root of the healing encounter lie what Stern calls the twin impulses of 'directionality' and 'fittedness'. Directionality is the emergence of a shared sense of 'moving on'; this moving on is accompanied by a growing feeling of relatedness (or fittedness), making for the progressive inclusion and exploration of increasingly complex, powerful emotional content. What Stern and his colleagues describe themselves doing here rings bells of recognition for me, not only in the context of arts therapy but also in the area of arts education, particularly with respect to the teacher–student relationship in the creative process of art-making and art-receiving. I also see strong connections to the reflective conversation, illustrated in Chapter 1, and with Jola Gisman-Stoch's Chapter 7 to follow.

A rather different connection also comes to mind. When Stern writes about building intimacy between patient and therapist, he reminds me of the special intimacy that attends the making and receiving of art itself, what I shall be calling in this book *poiesis*. This process is dialogical between the receiver of art and the art work she/he is interacting with; it is also dialogical between maker and materials, in the negotiation between the maker and the work's emerging intention, the work's 'reaching out', the unfolding meaning of the work. Although he regularly compares the creative process of a relational therapy to aspects of artistic experience (in music, dance and drama), Stern does not take the step that seems so obvious to me and identify the arts as quintessentially the site of implicit knowing. He doesn't engage with the arts therapies specifically.

For Stern, therapeutic treatment is about building the interpersonal relationship between therapist and patient as an end in itself, as bringing about the change in the patient that the therapeutic 'alliance' is pursuing. I tend to feel, however, that such change needs psychological 'distance' to make it stick, needs the special symbol system of the arts to embed a new and autonomous sense of emotional cohesion in the consciousness of the patient. The habit of art is about the patient's being able to make their emotional experience intelligible to others; being able to 'inscribe' themselves within their expressive work. Making ourselves intelligible to others (and others to ourselves, including the possibility of revisiting and re-interpreting 'difficult' experience) is what symbolic interaction does for us.

Stern's work is profoundly important for arts therapists – and not only therapists but also arts educators and all those whose work brings them into creative partnership with people making or receiving art. In much the same way as the therapist seeks to establish a proper degree of intimacy with her patient, so too the teacher does with her pupil. Without such a relationship there can be neither creative arts teaching nor creative arts therapy. However, in both the teaching and the therapy, in my view, there is an objective beyond the mediating relationship, even beyond the experience of coherent emotional communion with another that such a relationship may helpfully deliver. What is beyond the talking about the patient's 'complaint' is the reconfiguring of the patient's intelligence of feeling, and that is achieved expressively, through a particular quality of verbal interaction for sure, but more particularly through the habit of art itself: through symbol use.

In the concluding chapter of their book, the BCPS Group (2010: 194) sets out its 'basic premises'. The group names five premises – and I cannot resist a Syncretic Model take on them:

1   *The Dyadic Nature of the Therapeutic Process: The relationship between therapist and patient is seen as 'the central force for change'. The 'alliance' between the partners is responsible for articulating the intentionality and the direction of the search for coher-ence.* For all that the authors wish to play down the special skills and responsibilities of the therapist, I see this relationship as essentially a professional one, and that means taking the therapist's authority, status and 'distance' seriously. This phase has the stamp of Metal about it.

2   *The Engaged Search for Directionality and Fittedness: The contributions of the therapist and patient must demonstrate the time, effort, and importance of finding directional fittedness – that it matters.* The Water phase is all about caring, about what 'matters', is all about the stored energy that will fuel the commitment to the creative surge when the time is right. It is about knowing where one is going and having the courage to risk the making of relationships – the relationship, where the artist is concerned, with materials and the emergent work. I am reminded of Walter Benjamin's claim: 'No poem is intended for the reader'.

3   *The Creative Negotiation of Sloppiness and Indeterminacy: Fitting together of any two subjectivities* (there is a sense in which the artist and the work are 'two subjectivities') *will require much negotiation, disambiguation, feedback in many modalities, and missed opportunities. Indeterminacy is an unavoidable concomitant of the process. This gives rise to an inevitable sloppiness.* Openness is an essential element in the creative process and defines the character of the Wood phase. The quality of the inter-subjective relationship ('attunement') determines the effectiveness of what Winnicott calls 'reflecting back', between maker and work, and maker and mentor.

4   *Increasing Inclusiveness in the Relational Field: The more one's experiences are shared with a responsive other(s), the more one's thoughts and feelings will be experienced as human and 'relationable', that is, able to be included in one's relationships with others and thereby with oneself. Sharing of meanings and experiences converts experiences of shame, guilt, or deviance into expressions of a joint humanity.* We are aware of Fire as the phase of publication, of the reflective conversation, of widening the range of creative relationships and entering upon a shared process of evaluation and authorization.

5   *Vitalization in the Therapeutic Process: These dynamic processes, once in motion, move toward increasing integration, coherence, and fluency in the patient's ability…to be guided by their own feelings and directions in a balanced way in significant exchanges with others.* Earth, as we have seen, is the phase of authenticity and empathy. It is also the seat of the intelligence of feeling – to which, in his own way, Stern devotes his study of *Forms of Vitality* (2010).

The fit may not be completely snug, but I propose that it is close enough to suggest not only that the Group's thinking and our own are mutually sympathetic to a significant degree, but also that this cyclical pattern seems strangely pervasive in the human story of creativity. A case could be made, it seems to me, that the human story of art begins as the 'special' (implicit) inter-subjective expressive attunement of mothers and infants in the establishment of intimacy, which is to say authenticity and empathy, as an intimation of the poetic dimension of being. The language of correspondences begins as the perception of implicit correspondence between mother and infant: as inter-subjectivity. Recovering the language of correspondences, reconnecting with the poetic dimension of being, is to feel emotionally at home in the world. It's the difference between being 'street-wise' and having an A to Z.

Cultivating the habit of art

Staying with the role of the reflector-*on*-action, we can take a look at how we might begin to shape a programme for nurturing inter-subjectivity in the arts. Here we can draw deeply upon the Syncretic Model. Each phase of the model indicates a vital element of the programme both as recurring pattern and improvisational flux, both as theoretically conceptualized and as pragmatically experienced. My purpose here is to use the Syncretic Model to suggest a systematic way of understanding and exploring the habit of art. This book does not, however, attempt either to detail the contents or set out the methods of teaching and learning or of the therapeutic encounter in the arts. What I do claim for it, however, is that those working in these applied fields, using their skills and understandings as writers, dancers, painters and musicians to enhance the expressive opportunities of their clients, will have no problem adapting the Syncretic Model to their practice.

   At each phase, as we saw in the preceding chapter, there are many forces at work. Each has its dominant characteristic: it is characteristic of Fire to be fiery, of Water to be watery. But the situation is in every instance complicated by the nurturing drive of the *Sheng* and the controlling drive of the *Ke*. So Fire is nourished by Wood and controlled by Water. And there is the constant pull from Fire on to Earth that keeps the creative process flowing. Underlying the quality of Fire is its yang tendency, whereas Water is held within the gravitational pull of yin. As we consider each phase of the creative process in the arts we shall have to take account of all these energies in play, in dynamic tension: teachers and therapists, understanding this dynamic will seek to align themselves with it in partnering their client's creativity, assessing the quality of the flow, on the lookout for blocks, weaknesses and imbalances, intervening to nourish here, to resist there, and always with a view to the next step, to being able to meet the demands of the next phase of the cycle.

Metal/autumn/grief/conventionalization

Metal is the art world that every child is born into. Here are its privileged histories, its inspired and inspiring heroes, its appropriated treasures. Here are its approved practices, skills, understandings, codes and conventions. This is the given symbolic domain that every developing artist must get to know and learn to use for themselves. Here too are its unvarying standards and here preside its critical gatekeepers. This is the site of the art professional's authority as an artist, and her inspiration as a professional committed to nurturing the artist in others. Metal is our point of cultural departure. But it is also our destination as makers and receivers of art; both the beginning and the end of a particular creative, expressive episode (Identity Project). The impulse central to Metal is the quest; the search for the good teacher, for enlightenment, for perfection and truth, for making oneself understood through work. This is the phase of judgement, of gathering up, of treasuring, of letting go, of loss, sometimes of disappointment and existential grief. It is the space of final validation, and of the authority in which our confidence as learners resides. It is the space of investiture and formal authorization, from which we begin anew and (given the cyclical character of the model) to which we return again and again, bearing gifts and receiving recognition, slowly and patiently practising the habit of art. It is the space of the beautiful and the good and the wonderful. It is the place of the professional's holding and of the developing artist's being held. Here innocence and purity are discovered and recovered, and membership of the cultural community granted and confirmed. This is the space of conservation, of the cultural heritage, of the word, of the Guardians.

Metal is nourished by **Earth**: artistic judgement is sweetened by empathy.
Metal is controlled by **Fire**: artistic conservatism is softened by the spirit of festival.
Metal feeds **Water**: the authority and resources of the culture feed individual expressive desire.

Water/winter/fear/appropriation

Water is the phase of individuation, of the beginnings of self-hood and independence as an artist and art receiver. The notion of appropriation signals the beginnings of individuation of the artist within the collective; the selection by the individual of her own personal repertoire from the cultural storehouse; the emergence of personal voice, personal taste, personal style – the building of a living, personal history of art. There is a 'private' feeling of hibernation – of waiting – about it that allows for the quiet gathering of strength and the building of the personal drive and desire to be, that are the essential seeds of self-belief and self-assertion as an artist. Its implicit trajectory is forward, is towards the future (Stern's notion of directionality). The fear associated with this phase is the fear of the unknown, of moving on, the fear of exposure, of risk and failure, of being on your own. But in the healthy individual there is an equal and opposite endowment of courage so that the risk can be run and the fear outfaced. Here lie the roots of playing, the consciousness of handling and being handled in a safe place. Here faith is born. This is the site of individual, imperious desire, born of the guardian's love and commitment: the real beginnings of inter-subjectivity. Here we discover commitment and caring.

Water is nourished by **Metal**: the expressive impulse is nurtured by tradition.
Water is controlled by **Earth**: the creative impulse is resisted by the impulse to truth.
Water feeds **Wood**: the creative impulse feeds the creative drive.

Wood/spring/rage/transformation

Wood is the phase of the creative impulse: the focused, well-organized burst of energy in pursuit of expressive achievement and self-realization. If the right work has been done in the earlier phases (Metal and Water), the artist or receiver of art is now fully primed to invest feeling and imagination in a full-on engagement with the materials of expression, in working towards a new understanding, a new symbolic perception, a new possibility of being-in-the-world. The provocation (imbalance) may be either playfully sought or simply suffered fortuitously: in each case the mental machinery of creativity engages with the problem and drives strenuously and ingeniously for a resolution, which is to say, towards achieving the adaptation that will restore balance and renew flow to the system. Rage is the emotion of spring; it unlocks the possibility of new life, the spurt of growth, the irresistible drive to transform inert materials into symbolic forms (materials into media), to identify problems and pull out all the stops to solve them. It will not be denied. This is the place of alchemy, of transformation. The rage to be, to assert control of one's own creative life, carries all before it. Without that quality of impetuosity, it is doubtful if the inertia of the world could be turned around, the fear of failure mastered, the clutter obscuring vision removed that will allow for the moment of creative illumination, disclosure, un-concealment. Desire is given its head and drives its roots deep into the earth to stabilize it. Fury is the hectic in the blood. This is the irresistible call to change: in the words of the English poet George Herbert:

> I struck the board, and cry'd, No more.
> > I will abroad.
> > What? shall I ever sigh and pine?
> My lines and life are free; free as the rode,
> > Loose as the winde, as large as store.

But, as with each of the elements, its characteristic emotion carries a countervailing influence within it. Not for nothing, then, the more relaxed, more leisurely inclinations of the creative artist as Bohemian or flâneur, arrogantly isolated, their own person.

Wood is nourished by **Water**: the creative drive is fed by the creative impulse.
Wood is controlled by **Metal**: the creative drive is controlled by the force of tradition.
Wood feeds **Fire**: creative ability gives rise to the art work.

Fire/summer/joy/love/publication

Fire is the phase of confident realization, of disclosure, of illumination, of the spirit: what had hitherto been a largely private struggle between artist and materials, the individual and their emotions, now moves into the public domain as it approaches clarification. This is the penultimate phase of creative realization and coincides with a readiness to share, to test with friends, to express the joy of a project approaching consummation, in company with others who offer a degree of critical distance but whose positive commitment to us is never in doubt. Summer sees the flowering, the fruits, come to maturity, ripen in the sun. Its best moments are expansive and confident. So joy is its characteristic emotion, and this shared joy makes up for all the earlier anxiety, frustration, isolation, confusion and uncertainty, which if unrelieved could so easily convert to despondency and despair. The successful work is a joy and speaks to our desire. There will be love for the work and for everyone associated with it or touched by it. The artist is untroubled at this point by the chill, judgemental shadow cast by Metal, because the best efforts have been made and the passions spent. Whether sweet or raucous, here is the impulse to celebration (Gadamer in his scheme calls it 'festival'), ready to let go, to turn the world upside down for a dizzy night or two.

Fire is nourished by **Wood**: the artwork reflects the quality of the artist's creative imagination.
Fire is controlled by **Water**: the integrity of the artwork is governed by the creative impulse.
Fire feeds **Earth**: the art work feeds the intelligence of feeling.

Earth/late summer/empathy/authenticity

With the creative work essentially completed, Earth is the moment of truth for the artist or art receiver; the final moment of reckoning with themselves. How does it feel? Is it right? Can I accept it, own it (own up to it), is it truly mine, will it do, has it integrity, did I mean it? The unique aspect of this phase in the model is, of course, its influence throughout the project: authenticity and empathy touch every phase of the creative cycle. I am inclined to situate Witkin's intelligence of feeling within the Earth phase as the active centre of the model. A feeling of compassion animates the whole undertaking: it is the defining emotional relationship between the artist and the work. It defines the relationship between the professional and the client artist. It is a time for absolute honesty, when the artist is alone with her/his soul. Earth is about being grounded, centred, gifted, finding and securing one's roots. It is about the achievement of authentic being and the readiness to move on to a new beginning, bearing one's gifts, making one's contribution, playing one's part in the larger scheme of things. When all is not going well, there can be hostility and the aggression that goes with defensiveness. But piety (L *pius* = pity) is our preference here: having the confidence and the humility (L 'humus' = earth) to face the Guardians and the judgement of the world. This is the seal of the soul's integrity.

Earth is nourished by **Fire**: the intelligence of feeling is fed by the art work.
Earth is controlled by **Wood**: the artist's authenticity is defined by the creative imagination.
Earth feeds **Metal**: the tradition is sustained by accommodating new works.

Given a nurturing programme based on the Syncretic Model, it is for the professional (and her colleagues) to map specific content on to the framework: content that is appropriate for her particular art subject and for the developing artist's need and ability within the context of education or therapy. These are not areas I shall be straying into here. It has been my purpose rather to present the nurturing and challenging programme of the habit of art as the interplay of powerful emotional, psychological and imaginative forces prompting the artist, the student, or the client to actualize themselves through a life-enhancing series of expressive, practical creative projects of art-making and art-receiving. Learning and healing in the arts are doing and being done to: they are effected through the cultivation of good habits, and what Richard Sennett (2008: 288) calls the 'craft of experience'.

Partnering the developing artist's creativity

The model suggests three specific roles for the arts teacher, therapist or cultural animator: empathic companion, nourisher and controller. The empathic companion joins the student in her/his work at each phase of the model, planning the instructional or treatment programme, understanding the pressures and opportunities associated with each particular phase and deciding upon appropriate kinds of intervention. These decisions will give rise to professional activities that largely take the form of nourishing or strengthening the student's or client's work, or of deciding to challenge or resist it in some way.

I was recently invited to work with a group of completing PhD students whom I judged to be hovering variously between Earth and Metal. They were at the end of their three-year course. We spent an hour or so sharing, mostly the pain, and what little joy there had been – strangely, there had been no previous opportunity on their university course for them to do so – and then we danced for an hour, slow-motion Butoh, to Basquiat Strings and Olöf Arnalds. Finally, sitting on the floor in a circle, there were smiles. It had become clear that their PhD experience had been totally exhausting and not always either constructive or liberating. But even in such a brief, one-off session we seemed to have recovered some authentic ground together. They asked me if they could have a paragraph in this book.

Nourishing is the *Sheng* principle, and challenging the *Ke* principle.

The nourishing process (*Sheng*) will be guided by the notion that each phase is fed by the preceding phase: so we nourish Water with Metal, Wood with Water, Fire with Wood, etc. This interprets as trouble-shooting Wood's creative difficulties by referring back to Water and the initial seeds of self-expression. In the case of negotiating Earth's authenticity, the work will be nourished by Fire's spirit of joyful and loving celebration and fulfilment. Of course, it would be quite wrong to operate this system mechanically. Here the lessons concerning inter-subjectivity learned from Stern and his colleagues are of the utmost importance – as also Schön's notion of reflection-*in*-action. The Syncretic Model is a system in which all the phases are in play and accessible throughout the creative process, and fresh resources may be drawn upon from any quarter at any time, as necessary. But it might be a rule of professional diagnosis (in education as well as therapy), having re-enforced the element in question, to look back to the preceding phase(s) for support in tackling possible blocks and weaknesses that might be affecting what the client is now wanting to do (and might not yet be quite ready for, technically, imaginatively or emotionally).

The challenging principle (*Ke*) I think of as a kind of asking. I like the idea of rogation as a feature of creative teaching. In some ways it harks back to the dialectical method of Plato, except that I'm not really sure just how interested Plato was in answers other than his own, beyond using them as props and scaffolding for his argument. Asking is not simply to be understood literally as the asking of questions; it includes questioning, of course, but means much more than that. Rather it has the connotation of testing, of making demands to test the strength, flexibility and depth of the client's resources, the quality and discernment of their choices, much as attacking forwards in a football match might be said to 'ask questions' of the opposition's defence, or the emerging composition ask questions of its composer. Asking is a form of 'handling', where nourishing is more closely associated with 'holding' (Winnicott). When I suggested to my Polish student, Ania, that she might improvise a dance performance for her fellow trainee cultural animators, this was a challenge she hadn't expected and yet which proved to be one she was, in fact, well able to handle and benefit from. It suddenly occurred to me within the dynamic of the session, and was a good intuition on my part. There will be many reasons why a professional might choose to resist or challenge the client. The effect of a good challenge is positive as well as threatening, making one feel noticed and worthy of real attention at the same time as it throws up unexpected resources in the heat of the moment. Winnicott, in one of his case studies, challenged his client by allowing her accusations of his not caring about her to pass without comment and apparently unheeded, letting her simply play aimlessly in his passive presence until she finally 'arrived' and made herself authentically available to him. The *Ke* rule pairs each phase with an 'opposite number', to brace or challenge (cherish) it:

For a problem with **Water** (desire) – challenge from **Earth** (integration)
With **Wood** (innovation) – from **Metal** (conservation)
With **Fire** (celebration) – from **Water** (desire)
With **Earth** (integration) – from **Wood** (innovation)
With **Metal** (conservation) – from **Fire** (celebration)

Again, this is not a hard-and-fast rule – if it were it would negate the principle of flux that is the essence of the model. Could one even call it a wise 'sloppiness'?

Using empathic intuition ('inter-subjectivity'), the professional who partners the client's artistic creativity reflects-*in*-action, continually monitoring progression through the different phases, identifying blocks and imbalances, and intervening either to nourish and enrich or to challenge and test choices and resilience – in short, to keep learning, or the treatment 'moving along' (Stern, 2008: 149), each phase feeding into the next. The professional's nurturing and challenging needs to be attuned to these processes and possibilities within the client. This way, the professional will be implementing a fully participatory practice.

Assessing and recording progress

In our book *Assessing Achievement in the Arts*, my colleagues and I presented a model of negotiated *summative* appraisal based on what we called the 'reflective conversation'. As we saw in Chapter 1, this is an open discussion between art teacher and art student in the presence of the work and with other relevant material to hand, covering all four aspects of the Harré model. The outcomes of the discussion are then written up, a grade or mark agreed (with an accompanying note explaining any disagreement), and the report submitted to the usual processes of monitoring before the results are confirmed. Teacher and student handle *formative* assessment separately as ongoing personal logs and diaries that track the creative work – edited and made available to the final assessment conversation. I have nothing to add to this idea here except to say that whereas in the original project we took the Harré matrix for our guide, I would now wish to see all five phases of the full Syncretic Model guiding the process. Transcriptions of several such conversations, together with explanatory commentaries, are to be found in the book (Ross *et al.*, 1993).

Where the teacher's professional development is concerned, I firmly believe every arts teacher should have an independent supervisor/professional mentor available for regular consultation – on the model used in the psychiatric and therapeutic professions.

The art receiver

In this book we are largely concerned with creativity in the productive sense: we have been concentrating on the process of *making* art. In Chapter 6, the Tusa interviews, we interrogate the making process of a sample of professional artists, using the Syncretic Model as an analytical instrument. I now wish briefly to touch on the Syncretic Model as a framework to describe receiving or responding to art. Reader Reception Theory (Wolfgang Iser, Roman Ingarden) proposes that the reader of a work of literature (we shall extend the idea to the art receiver more generally) becomes a 'constructive' partner in the art experience by bringing their own life history, as well as their life with literature to the imaginative business of reconstruction and fleshing out the artist's work in their own mind. Every reader 'inscribes' themselves into the text they are reading. Our case is that this process of creative reproduction and reconstruction directly corresponds to the trajectory of attention that constituted the artist's original creative process, and that the Syncretic Model can help us to a fuller understanding of the act of artistic reception or appreciation.

The Metal (conventionalization) phase of the cycle supplies the art receiver with the tradition at its purest, the cultural heritage, with its authoritative conventions of expression, its understanding of the role and nature of art in a particular culture, its technical and participatory traditions, its repertoire of treasured works and its institutions of conservation, exposure, celebration and critical discourse. Every new work, no matter how radical, draws its confidence from the Metal phase (as endorsement or challenge) and can only be fully appreciated by reference to it. The art receiver enters Metal as a seeker after beauty and truth.

The Water (appropriation) phase registers the artist's own distinctive voice, her style, her characteristic point of view, and empowers the particular impulse toward a form of expression that makes her work instantly recognizable to others. The art receiver makes her own company: this is my Van Gogh, this is my Mozart, this is my

Virginia Woolf. Somehow, art today, to keep art in step with life, seems to require this strong sense of the artist's authorizing presence, compounded of fear and courage, despite theories proposing 'the death of the author'. The art receiver is at great pains to furnish her own distinctive storehouse, to build her own repertoire and to embrace the challenge, satisfy her hunger for facing new works (including new old works) as winter yields to spring.

The Wood (transformation) phase brings the adventuring receiver to her hope for a particular new work to be received and appraised. For the maker, this phase marks the transformation of materials into media, the sudden dramatic encounter with inarticulate materials in the quest for sign, for signification, for meaning. Where the artist might, as we have seen, improvise a rough-and-ready form to 'hold' the expressive impulse and so anchor the making process securely upon a particular feeling impulse, the receiver, too, might engage in an initial scanning process, to get a handle on it, as it were – on its form, its mood, its energy, its generic line, its likely development. First impressions may be of shock, surprise and confusion, or, on the other hand, of dawning recognition, delight and welcome relaxation in familiar territory. Recognition (Gadamer) seems essential at some point and in some sense, if we are to attune ourselves empathically to what is distinctive in the maker's thought and feeling and 'inscribe' ourselves into the reading. At a live concert recently I was introduced to the music of Morton Feldman. Astonishingly, despite its strangeness, I found myself immediately at home and deeply engaged. It was only afterwards I discovered the shadowy presence of Schubert, Chopin and Bach moving just beneath the surface. The artist's creative mental rage and frenzy may be experienced less dramatically by the creative spectator, but it will still be there in the Wood phase of appreciation, as enthusiasm for the new, as vigorous, focused attention and as a thoroughly absorbed engagement. Leaving a book, the theatre, a concert, a gallery, we may be surprised to find our perception of the world radically altered. Leaving Feldman, I felt my acoustic self to be radically altered.

The Fire (publication) phase makes for our considered, sustained and deepest responses: if the earlier phase of identification of the work's central motif has proved successful (Wood) then the Fire phase allows for its deep penetration, unfolding and savouring. It also sees the judgemental element of appraisal make its first appearance, and gives rise quite naturally to the social impulse to share, to check on the responses of others and to join the discussion (e.g. the reading group). We must also expect to walk out on a work, albeit reluctantly: something I find myself doing, where the theatre is concerned, far too often these days. But there will always be the hope of another to claim our heart.

The Earth (authenticity) phase gives us, the receivers, the opportunity of checking not only the maker's authenticity but also our own. We not only ask, and are right to ask, for the author's truth but must also be true to ourselves as well, given that we are inscribed within it. Our final judgement, to be sound, must also represent our truth, our authenticity. We might speak of reconnecting with our 'good will', our 'good faith' here – the generous as well as the eager impulse that brought us to the work in the first place and made us ready to devote time, feeling, attention, imagination and money to it. Has it met our heart's desire?

The return to Metal, to the storehouse, the repertoire, the great tradition of the arts in our culture is to test our own standards against those of the collective, to nudge the collective perhaps to a subtle readjustment that would accommodate what we have prized. It is also to renew our faith in the habit of art and begin the whole cycle again.

The art critic

In the reflective conversation, illustrated in Chapter 1, we have seen how reflecting *on* a particular work with the artist him/herself, can also be a form of reflecting *in* – a kind of co-creative critical encounter. By way of illustrating the deployment of the Syncretic Model as an instrument of more formal art criticism, of personal reflection *on* a work, I propose to spend a moment looking at a piece of critical art writing. Art criticism, like art reception, is a dimension of the habit of art, and professionals in the applied arts need to understand how their clients might want to respond creatively not just as art makers and art receivers but also as art critics. I think it reasonable to see, in this piece of writing, a good deal of what would go to make up the more formal act of critical appreciation; the coming to terms with a work of art, directly, face-to-face and expressing a view. I have chosen a piece from the *London Review of Books* (25 February 2010: 18) by the magazine's cover designer and art critic, Peter Campbell. Campbell reviews an exhibition of photographic colour prints by the American artist William Eggleston, then on display in London at the Victoria Miro Gallery. I have chosen this piece partly because the colour illustration that accompanied the article disturbed, even rather irritated, me (I was not sure why at the time), and before reading Campbell I had pretty much decided that the exhibition would not be for me. However – and this really is the point – Campbell, in the course of his review, quite succeeded in changing my mind. He helped me to 'see' the print and I found myself coming to like it. The print is called *Untitled (Room with Old TV, Lamps, Wildwood, New Jersey, 2002)* which is pretty much what the picture shows.

The scene, as Campbell later describes it, is nothing if not 'inconsequential'; a more or less incoherent clutter of rather grotesque glass and plastic domestic objects from the 1950s, arranged on a non-descript 'vanity' table, with a pair of sheeny red plastic bucket chairs and, half-hidden beneath the table, five variously coloured plastic hoops. Were it not for the view from the window above the table, we might be looking at the interior of a village jumble sale or at a pile of items in a junk shop. The table seems to back onto a wide picture-window with a roller-blind, looking out onto a row of dreary house fronts with blank windows. The feeling of 'inconsequentiality' is increased by the odd angle at which the photograph has been taken: it is tilted out of the horizontal by a fraction, as if the photographer hadn't bothered or learned how to hold the camera level. Altogether, a bit hit-and-miss, you might say. For his part, however, Campbell wants to say that the casualness and inconsequentiality couldn't be more pitch-perfect.

In terms of the Syncretic Model, Campbell cycles through the phases pretty much as we have set them out. He certainly covers all the bases. He devotes a high proportion of his review to the Metal phase, placing Eggleston in context for us, which is very much what we ask critics to do. With the Feldman piece of music I was able to do this 'implicitly' for myself. With the Eggleston, this felt entirely right as a way of helping me tune in to what otherwise simply proved too 'different' to grasp, too strange and challenging to find a way to like. So he tells us about the way colour works in art and poses a general question: 'Is correct drawing or true colour of the essence?'

By way of an answer he considers Van Gogh's way with colour (Van Gogh also had an exhibition open in London just then) and, in particular, the influence of Indian paintings on his style. Next comes a brief introduction to the history of the art photograph and the traditional dominance of the black-and-white print over colour. For most of the twentieth century, Campbell says, 'Colour was an intrusion, a vulgar distraction'. But, moving on now to the second phase of the model, Campbell points out how Eggleston makes colour the whole point of his photographs, and with his 1976 exhibition at the New York Museum of Modern Art, his distinctive mixture of colour and inconsequence began to be appreciated. 'In 1976 it was colour that set him apart,' writes Campbell. How can such deliberate inconsequentiality come to feel consequential? As we find ourselves drawn to study the illustration more attentively (the Wood phase), Campbell, seemingly anticipating the reader's difficulty, wades in with a strong controlling dose of Metal – historical context, and so forth. In the *Ke* cycle, Metal controls Wood. By the time Campbell has got us looking again at the picture, he has already established Eggleston's personal voice for us (Water phase) – his signature attachment to inconsequentiality of subject (later described as 'sour') and a particular quality of colour (later called 'sweet'). Campbell explains how the 'dye transfer' process is responsible for Eggleston's 'exceptionally saturated, intense colour', and our perception and enjoyment move up a gear.

In his review, Campbell does not focus on any particular works other than the one illustrated. His primary intention is to place Eggleston's work as a whole within the context of modern art as a way of helping us to 'see' it – in effect, to provoke us and prime us for the exhibition itself, so that we shall find the work for ourselves. He has, however, provided us with the illustration, to serve as a sample of what the exhibition has to offer. What he says about the way Eggleston's prints signify as art (Wood phase) can be applied to the picture illustrated. So we can see what he means when he suggests 'that colour is central to the way they work on your imagination'. When we ask what these pictures are about, given their apparent inconsequentiality, Campbell suggests that the answer lies somehow in the unsettling relationship between 'the unexplained strangeness of the ordinary or tacky' and the 'rich, subtle, pretty even' colour effects achieved by the artist.

Again, speaking of the work as a whole, and thereby addressing the concerns of the Wood phase through the identification of Eggleston's signature at the Water phase, Campbell manages to catch the sensate germ or construct ('holding form') at the metaphorical centre of the work's significance. Witkin would speak of 'the sweet–sour dialectic' (Witkin, 1974: 171). The reason these prints 'have enough individuality and bite to work as gallery art' is that they 'so often bring sweet or brilliant colour and sour subject matter together'. They capture an important moment in design history, and the history of art photography.

In a critical review there is perhaps not much scope for the Fire phase, but I feel it to be implicit somehow in the way I gradually warm to Campbell's project, to his voice as he gently implicates me in the work of appreciation, and in my growing sense of commitment to and affection for the work he has befriended.

This was, for me, a very astute observation by Campbell and immediately opened the way to an understanding of what is special about Eggleston's work – we might say, his world picture. I understood what had been going on in my looking and why I had found the picture at first so disturbing. I recognized a typical construct in the realm of modernity. I was bound to say, 'Yes, this too is how the world really is'. Or perhaps I should have said, having been there, '... really was.' We are firmly with empathy and authenticity in the Earth phase here. I look at *Untitled (Room with Old TV, Lamps, Wildwood, New Jersey, 2002)* and, seeing it afresh, find it 'rich' and 'subtle' and 'pretty even'. Suddenly, I am not only intrigued where I was merely puzzled, but fond where I was irritated. With my emotions now fully engaged I could see the 'truth' at the heart of Eggleston's vision.

Campbell comes full circle (back to the Metal phase) in suggesting that these strange prints, defying, as they do, so many of our more comfortable notions of what kind of thing art is supposed to be and do, carry the agenda of modernism in a new and important direction.

This is a serious critique upon serious work, written with real understanding and a strong commitment to the 'life' of the work. However, Campbell keeps his own balance and critical distance, adding a subtle note of reservation to put the achievement of the piece into perspective. 'Some things that are truly grey get lost in colour. Even the weather looks bright.' So here, then, is Eggleston: an artist of singular vision, if not quite our man for all seasons. As for Campbell himself, he has exemplified admirably the role of critic as the art lover's Good Companion.

Elemental profiling

What this present account lacks and what may hopefully be supplied in the future is a procedure for preparing an elemental profile for each client based on an identification of their 'governing', or characteristic, element. As we have already indicated, Five Elements theory holds that we are each distinguished by a dominant element. So I am Fire and Donna is Water. In acupuncture practice, based on this theory, knowing the patient's characteristic element is very important for the practitioner when making a diagnosis and assessing an appropriate course of treatment. I am convinced that such a development is possible in the context of arts education and therapy and would imagine that it could prove of immense help to teachers and therapists anxious to play to their charge's natural strengths and inclinations and to help individuals manage and cope with difficulties to which they are typically predisposed. The work just hasn't been done that would allow this yet, if it were thought to be desirable – which it might not be. The idea that each individual has such propensities and inclinations will not be strange to the experienced practitioner, whether teacher or therapist. Meanwhile, paying due attention to the Water phase (appropriation) would allow such a profile to be sketched, without the more radical – and probably controversial – elemental analysis I am describing here.

Conclusion

I have personally found that the Syncretic Model also works as a way of understanding problems in the broad field of human creativity and personal relations. I have used the model to help students address a range of issues.

Two musicians, for example, working in schools together, were experiencing difficulties establishing a balanced working partnership. We looked at how the Metal element of the more extrovert of the two had the effect of cutting back the creativity (Wood) of the less assertive partner. The answer seemed to be to make a point of planning the sessions jointly around their shared commitment at the Water phase. This seemed to work.

A PhD student was looking for a suitable instrument with which to analyse the writer-reader relationship in a series of didactic books for boys written by a popular Victorian author. By generating questions from each of the five phases of the model, a viable analytical matrix emerged.

Analysing a particularly difficult workshop and its traumatic consequences for me personally, I concluded that the 'frozen' (Water) students I had found myself trying to work with had needed so much of my personal warmth (Fire element) to unlock them that I was left, by the end of the session, a heap of ash. They literally made me sick.

As a purely speculative case study I have chosen my great heroine among modern writers in English, Virginia Woolf, who wrote what is my favourite book of the modern era: the novel *To the Lighthouse*. She finished revising her final book, *Between the Acts*, and passed it to her husband Leonard to read on 25 February 1941 in complete despair, saying she no longer knew how to write. On 28 March, with the war increasingly frightening her, she walked from her garden to the river and drowned herself.

I have asked myself if the Syncretic Model might have anything to say that would throw light on her sad end, and it seems to me that there might be a lesson there. Virginia habitually found herself not only exhausted as she came to the end of a spell of sustained and intense writing (Wood), but with all the signs of another dark episode of her own particular 'madness' (hallucinations) returning. Her personal writings at these times suggest an overwhelming anxiety about the reception her published work would receive at the hands of the critics. Leonard, her husband, who was deeply sympathetic to her work and always her first reader, was invariably enthusiastic about her latest book (Fire). But this didn't help to alleviate her deeper anxiety about reception more widely. It was the final word of the critics that would be decisive for her, and of which she lived in so much dread (Metal).

Two factors, it seems to me, materially contributed to her difficulty – apart from deeply ingrained personal problems dating from her earliest years, together with the tension of the war. In the first place the conflict between Metal and Wood in her psyche as a writer meant that the wear and tear on her emotional and creative resources were almost insupportable. She wanted to please but she also insisted on doing as she pleased – and that meant flying in the face of convention, inventing an entirely new kind of novel, thereby cutting herself off from the more positive, 'holding' influence of the Metal phase. She placed herself beyond the pale, outside the circle of power. Her Wood element could not be cherished by her Metal, only cut to the quick; furthermore an antagonized public was likely to make her pay for having the temerity to go so precariously out on a limb.

The second factor working against her was, I believe, the unsuitable treatment prescribed for her by her doctor and implemented by the family: complete isolation and idleness (no writing materials allowed) and a meat-free diet. Leaving the diet aside – I wouldn't know – one would have thought that the enforced isolation and inertia could have done her no good at all. If we look at the model, she needed to be allowed convivial company; more particularly, the 'special' company of friends with whom to celebrate her having come through. She needed to move on from Wood to Fire, and thence to 'come down to' Earth, gently. Had her creative cycle been allowed fully to express itself, who knows if she might have managed to keep her Metal element under control in the wider scheme of things and been prepared to face it with greater equanimity when it finally came around. As it always did, Metal proved to be her undoing – fatally so in the end. With the war taking its toll, her self-confidence (Earth) exhausted and overwhelmed by fear (Water), Virginia Woolf could not find the courage to go on. Only the courage for the final act.

5 The arts and the brain

Consciousness studies is a fast-developing dimension of neuroscience. This chapter focuses on recent writings in the field that propose a central place for artistic activity in the structures and programmes of the brain. More particularly, the right hemisphere of the brain is deemed to be responsible for handling affective information, for managing the life of the emotions, for our propensity to play and to find illusion important in experience; in short, for our life in art. This brief survey closes with Jaak Panksepp's claim that hope itself might be a programme of the brain.

It is clear that nearly all of whatever brain activity it is that corresponds to aesthetic experience is unconscious, and it is even doubtful that the ideal viewer of a great artwork should be conscious, because one (often claimed) effect of great art is to merge subject and object in an aesthetic epiphany that transcends the individual consciousness.

Joseph A. Goguan

Introduction

In recent years scientists have made remarkable progress in the quest to understand the workings of the physical brain. Technological advances such as brain imaging have allowed them to monitor the brain in action, to identify areas and neuro-circuits active under certain circumstances and when engaged in particular operations. Although never at the forefront of investigations, the arts and associated mental activities, such as 'right-brain thinking', and the work done by feelings and emotions, the discovery of 'mirror neurones', have been the subject of focused studies, and the outcomes, now increasingly available in academic publications, make interesting, even exciting, reading for those of us with a professional stake in the world of the arts, including arts education and therapy. The brief review that follows makes no claim to being exhaustive – time allows here for only a sampling exercise. But I believe this can provide a useful introduction to a rapidly expanding field, and should be sufficient to alert the arts community to a powerful new resource. For artistic responses, it seems, are wired into the human brain, and perhaps into the primate brain more generally. Art is one of the ways we think about and come to know ourselves and the world in which we live. As the pioneer brain scientist J. Z. Young might have said, art, it seems, is a 'programme of the brain'.

The soul in the brain

From the many books on the subject recently published by leading neuroscientists, I have chosen to draw principally upon Michael Trimble's *The Soul in the Brain: The Cerebral Basis of Language, Art and Belief* (2007). Michael Trimble is Professor of Behavioural Neurology at the Institute of Neurology, University of London. In an earlier book, *Biological Psychiatry*, published in 1988, he gives a comprehensive account of the impact of neuro-chemical and neuro-pathological research on the practice of psychiatry, and in particular confronts the criticisms levelled at the new 'biological treatments' of mental illness. It is a dauntingly thorough survey, and while evincing his root interest in and understanding of epilepsy and its associated effects upon the subject's feelings, emotions and personality, gives no obvious clue to the concerns at the centre of *The Soul in the Brain*. In his new book he sets out to map language development, the arts (in particular poetry and music) and religious experience onto what he calls 'their underlying neurological basis'. He sees the 'expressive' function of language as the common thread linking those other cultural achievements. On the basis of his own investigations – initially in the context of his work with epileptics – and drawing on related studies by colleagues across the various branches of neuroscience, as well as philosophers and writers on the arts, Trimble states his position thus:

> These cultural activities, I suggest, are deeply embedded in our nature and could not be so ingrained without corresponding brain structures, which have developed over millenniums of evolution.
>
> (2007: 72)

Developed, that is to say, in the service of species survival; specifically, in the service of reproduction, and family and community building. If we are to accept this claim – and it now seems a position beyond dispute within the neuroscience community – it has consequences for our understanding of the origins and continuing significance of the arts, not least for accounts of artistic experience that promote the role of culture over the role of natural selection. Neuroscience has demonstrated, using MRI observation, that cultural factors, for example artistic education, can materially affect the character of brain activity as between experts and novices, suggesting that where the expert seems to 'see beyond' the physical features of the subject, the novice gets locked into merely trying to 'copy' them. (see Robert L Solso, 'The cognitive neuroscienc of art', in *Journal of Consciousness Studies*, Volume 7, No 8/9, 2000). Either way, what this means is that the conventionalization/Metal phase of our Syncretic Model should now include an understanding of the biological (perhaps including the genetic) forces that help to shape aesthetic and artistic experience. The possibility, even the necessity, of the artistic life is imprinted within our brains.

Left brain, right brain

In answering some of the questions to which his claims give rise, Trimble makes much of the latest understandings of the different functions served by the right and left hemispheres of the brain. He begins by explaining the comparative neglect of human creativity (by which he tends to mean, specifically, creativity in the arts) by neuroscience over the years of its development. He says it reflects science's long tradition of valuing left-brain over right-brain activity. Language was generally seen to be largely the business of the left brain – and language, particularly the discursive and propositional language of science, philosophy and the law, has been the dominating influence in shaping the character of the modern state. More recent studies, however, have challenged the traditional view, not only as defining contemporary culture, but also as an adequate account of language itself. Trimble argues that the affective (expressive) aspects of speech, for instance, and the powerful role played by the emotions in decision-making, not to mention the huge reliance we place upon our intuitions when reason seems to fail us, all derive from the right hemisphere, making language itself impossible to describe or understand if the left hemisphere is privileged.

Things, Trimble observes, are now changing. What he calls 'protolanguage', otherwise 'pre-verbatim communication', among primates, lies at the root of the expressive potential of language (echoes of Stern here?). It has all the characteristics associated with prosody, the special features of language as poetry: physical and auditory 'gestures' involving such features as duration, stress, contour, timbre and grouping. Rhythm plays a central part and arises and functions to express and sustain the emotional intensity of an utterance. The language of feeling is the oldest language we have, and persists in all its force as a defining feature of the right hemisphere of the brain. Trimble cites E. D. Ross (1997) who argues that, whereas the primary emotions are seen to arise in the right brain, the task undertaken by the left brain is to suppress their essentially disruptive impact (see Nussbaum, cited later in this book) and impose more positive, more comfortable secondary emotions upon the subject, thereby protecting social bonds and boundaries. But here is a potential experiential loss, one that could prove a block to full perception, a leaching of existential truth. *Trimble proposes that the arts help to preserve that truth symbolically.* The arts help to maintain our sense of life's personal meaning and significance for us, using 'the oldest language we have', the language of feeling, which is the language of metaphor, of myth: *poiesis*.

The pre-verbatim has been understood to be a richly metaphorical, affect-laden, and textured biographical memory. What cerebral circuitry underlies this preconscious, preverbal potential poetical repository? The contention here is that the right hemisphere must play a major role.

(2007: 186)

Trimble goes on to single out *play* as the natural mode of operation for the right brain. He describes play as 'saturated with metaphor, the creation of other worlds with alternative meanings'. Play he sees as kin to ritual, as linking the arts with religious experience. All of which Trimble draws together under the banner supplied by Nietzsche in his distinctive apologia for the arts:

Nietzsche argues that since God is dead and life made intolerable by pain and suffering, consolation can come only from creativity and art, in particular, music. Hence his famous apothegm, 'The existence of the world is *justified* only as an aesthetic phenomenon' (Ja Sagen). In this context, tragedy for Nietzsche has an aesthetic value. It is not wisdom or catharsis that is achieved but an affirmation of life in the context of death.

(ibid.: 195)

Saying yes; which recalls the point made earlier, that the arts defend and assert the idea at the heart of personal being, that life is not simply to be protected and reproduced but rather must have meaning. That meaning, according to Trimble, is aesthetic in origin. Nietzsche apparently had his own idea about the lateral compartmentalization of the brain, claiming that there were

two chambers of the brain, as it were, one to experience science and the other to experience non-science … The source of power is located in one region; the regulator is the other. Illusions, partialities and passions must provide the heat, while the deleterious and dangerous consequences of overheating must be averted with the aid of scientific knowledge.

It seems to me that in citing Nietzsche's ideas on the arts, Trimble brings his own argument into line with ideas familiar to us in the writings of Adam Phillips and Seamus Heaney. Where Phillips understands the role of art in asserting the sovereignty of the self against existential annihilation, for Heaney poetry offers a means of what he calls 'redress'. Cognition itself, Trimble argues, is profoundly dependent upon the affect-laden operations of right brain. We engage with the world in feeling, and handling, sorting and expressing feeling is an essentially intelligent process – in effect, the province of art. I take this to be a direct vindication of the speculative work Robert Witkin and I were doing in the early 1970s on 'the intelligence of feeling'. Trimble again:

The long-lasting, lingering, limbic links to the right hemisphere firmly bind and bond us to our evolutionary past and, I suggest, dominate our cognition to an extent that has been completely underestimated. For us, language precedes reason, and our language is derived from the heritage of the primitive proto-language of our biological ancestors.

(ibid.: 197)

The sense of wonder, of awe, of the sublime, our experience of the sacred, the holy, the numinous, feelings universally associated with religious experience in its raw rather than in its doctrinal form, all derive from the right hemisphere, as radical intuitions of personal being, personal meaning in the world. Little wonder that so much of human art has been historically associated with religion, and that both art and religion have their common roots in ways of handling the primary emotions. The drive to make, use and cherish the arts derives from our need to explore and manage the primary emotions symbolically in the creative experience of living.

Transcendence

In his book *The Master and his Emissary* (2010), Iain McGilchrist fully endorses Trimble's account of the importance of the balancing role of the right hemisphere of the brain in the economy of mind. He argues powerfully that right-brain activity always has been, and remains, the default modality, the 'master', of the human mind, despite the huge investment made over the course of history in its 'emissary', the left hemisphere. He points out that, despite its inclinations towards the left brain, twentieth-century philosophical discourse has unknowingly corroborated the claims of the right. He lists the following themes as typical of right-brain functioning:

empathy and inter-subjectivity as the ground of consciousness: the importance of an open, patient attention to the world, as opposed to a wilful, grasping attention; the implicit or hidden nature of truth; the emphasis on process rather than stasis, the journey being more important than the arrival; the primacy of perception; the importance of the body in constituting reality; an emphasis on uniqueness; the objectifying nature of vision; the irreducibility of all value to utility; and creativity as an unveiling (no-saying) process rather than a wilfully constructive process.

(2010: 177)

McGilchrist, while acknowledging that in all practical matters the brain operates as a whole, with both hemispheres contributing in their unique ways though not necessarily carrying equal weight, he none the less makes regular reference to the predominance of right-brain influence in the arts. In particular, I am grateful for the light he sheds on art's transcendent trajectory: on the connection between what he calls human 'longing' and the expressive impulse of 'reaching out' to transcendent values, including the realms of the infinite and the spiritual. I would now want to say that it is longing, rather than desire, that is the impulse behind Water's drive. McGilchrist writes: 'Art…in its nature constantly impels us to reach out and onward to something beyond itself and something beyond ourselves' (ibid.: 308). This impulse cannot, he says, be merely dismissed as 'romantic', a convenient but spurious argument deployed by reactionary left-brainers anxious to muzzle this potent intuition for life's bitter-sweetness, to sideline empathic knowing.

Had I but world enough and time, I would make much more extensive reference to this important book, for in almost every respect it is close kin to our project. But I came upon it too late in this writing for that.

Saying yes

We have already cited Nietzsche's positive take on the message or role of the arts. In short, saying yes to life. Trimble makes a great deal of the positive thrust of art and thoroughly endorses Nietzsche's position, as, incidentally, do many of the other scientists whose work we look at below. He considers the ancient paradox of art exemplified in the continuing popularity of dramatic tragedy. As we have already discovered, for Trimble the importance of art lies in its life-affirming character. Tragedy, for all its grim, even terrible, events, comes down firmly on the side of life, not least in demonstrating the extraordinary dynamic that regulates the emotional life. Nietzsche has hinted at it already: power is somehow contained by countervailing power; energy meets energy in thrust and counter-thrust. Nothing is lost. We are part of an unending process of change that balances surge with decline, exhaustion with resurgence. It isn't simply, or at all, that our favourite stories always end like fairy tales, with everyone living happily ever after. Rather, it is that life itself goes on, and that is enough – and additionally, of course, that the impact of the creative activity of the artist is essentially affirmative, that meaning always trumps incoherence, that life holds its own answer to death. Death, indeed, as the poet John Donne proclaims, 'Shall have no dominion' – over the human imagination, over the human spirit.

All this, it seems to me, repeats the message inherent in the Syncretic Model. When Trimble writes of the relations existing between the so-called primary emotions, it is remarkable how close he comes to repeating the dynamic account of the emotional life represented in the ancient Chinese theory. Here is a reminder of the original Chinese system of the primary emotions:

Metal: grief
Water: fear
Wood: rage
Fire: joy and love
Earth: empathy

Trimble writes:

> Of all the human passions, fear, anger, and bereavement stand out as universals. They are deeply entwined in the stories of the great tragedies, but are also *bound to one another* [my emphasis]. Fear generates anger, and both anger and fear are core emotions in bereavement. As outlines, fear and anger are limbic, especially emygdala-driven emotions; as for grief, the neurobiology of bereavement has not been studied. Fear has an evolutionary history far older than human kind. All mammals know fear, and fear and anger relate to social dominance. Grief and mourning, on the other hand, have a cognitive component that over-rides fear and anger, since grieving is about loss; and because it is about loss of a person or persons to whom one is attached, empathy is involved, as is recognition of the future and the potential of others to mourn for oneself. In preliterate societies, the development of empathy and the ability to appreciate that other individuals have minds (the theory of mind) must have been crucial, to the driving of primate and then human evolution.
>
> (2007: 192)

This passage is rich with resonances for the Syncretic Model, not least in mirroring the workings of the complementary engines of the *Sheng* and the *Ke*. It is particularly intriguing to note Trimble's picking up on the role of grief in resisting anger, and of empathy in assuaging fear. His point about the central role of empathy is also well taken.

Apollo and Dionysus

Whilst there would seem to be general agreement among consciousness studies experts that a balance between left- and right-brain influences would appear to be the 'natural' arrangement, and indeed might once, at an earlier point of our biological history, have been the case, our evolution as a species, especially within the culture of the West, seems to have brought them into a degree of competition – certainly to have disturbed the balance between them. This point forms the crux of Iain McGilchrist's book cited above. For Nietzsche, their rivalry is embodied in the struggle between the traditions of Apollo and Dionysus. Trimble quotes the extreme views of the feminist writer Camille Paglia, pitting left brain against right:

> Apollo is the hard cold separatism of Western personality and categorical thought. Dionysus is energy, ecstasy, hysteria, promiscuity, emotionalism – heedless indiscriminateness of idea or practice. Apollo is obsessiveness, voyeurism, idolatry, fascism – frigidity and aggression of the eye, petrification of objects... Words themselves the West makes into objects. Complete harmony is impossible. Our

brains are split, and brain is split from body. The quarrel between Apollo and Dionysus is the quarrel between the higher cortex and the older limbic and reptilian brains.

(2003: 196)

For his part, Trimble is more optimistic, seeing a potential for harmony and balance between the Apollonian challenges and constraints of form, and the headstrong, ecstatic demands of the essentially Dionysian expressive impulse. Without wishing to push the connection too hard, what we might have here is an echo of the role played in the Chinese system by the principles of the yin and the yang.

For arts educators and therapists this discussion raises a particularly intriguing and taxing set of questions: How are we to give Dionysus, the right hemisphere of the brain, his due? After all that has been said about the importance of what Paglia calls the neglected older reptilian brain, how are we to prevent the propositional left brain from dominating our practice? How is the 'talking cure' to avoid becoming merely another 'talking shop'. How is our teaching to avoid becoming talk about art rather than doing art? How is right brain to be accessed in the classroom, the studio, the clinic, as the poetic, the prophetic, the ecstatic mind? When Dionysus joins us, how do we handle him? Or as Adam Phillips puts it, What are we to do with 'the beast in the nursery'? (See his book of that title for some powerful hints.) There are, of course, many well-known examples of artists using extreme means to make this connection, through drugs and alcohol use, for example. Trance states seem a regular feature of much religious ritual – often self-induced through music and dancing. Dionysus is the lord not only of the dance but also of pop music, and probably all other festivals everywhere, including the village fête. He might not be so far away from the classical concert hall either – though he probably stays at home for the last night of the Proms. It seems to me that *play* affords the teacher and the therapist an immediate and potent technique for opening up the lifeline to the god. D. W. Winnicott certainly thought so.

Creativity and madness

In an interesting review of the old question of the possible connection between creativity and madness, N. Barrantes-Vidal, writing in the *Journal of Consciousness Studies* (Vol. 11, Nos. 3/4, 2004), while stating quite categorically that 'states of madness do not lead to creativity', remarks that they, none the less, 'share common causative *traits*'. His account of those traits offers us an interesting picture of the character of the ecstatic or Dionysian right brain. In invoking the presence of the god in the classroom and the clinic, we need perhaps to be clear what we are bargaining for.

Substantial clinical work has shown that both creativity and the temperamental roots of psychoses have common features at a biological (e.g. high levels of dopamine), cognitive (e.g. a brain organization characterized by a weak inhibitory control that enables loosened or more flexible styles of mental activity), and emotional level (e.g. high openness to experience and phases of elation and intense enthusiasm).

(2004: 74)

Trimble comes down unequivocally in favour of a positive reading of creativity in the arts. He sees our built-in attraction to the beautiful as a partly religious, partly aesthetic impulse, and as essential to the cussed and determined 'seeking' instinct (for further discussion see below), insatiably active in every human mind – the Water phase of our model. The instinct that says yes to life, despite the dangers, the pain, the grief. Once again, unaware as I must suppose him to be, Trimble repeats the logic of the Syncretic Model: 'Fear,' he says, 'gave way to the quest for beauty, and finally to the realization of joy' (2007: 209) In terms of the model, we might say, Water gives way to Wood, and Wood yields to Fire in the *Sheng* cycle. We might also go on to say that Fire in yielding to Earth submits itself to the empathic principle of the Gift. Artwork is about giving, again and again – just as the earth doesn't know how to say no.

The evolution of creativity can be seen as a basic neurological force, evolving in *H. Sapiens* to a need to explore other worlds, through a belief in the gods, and then to a need to represent them and to communicate such beliefs.

(ibid.: 210)

The Syncretic Model, perhaps, is not 'simply symbolic': I am coming to believe that it reflects the reality of neurological forces at work within the brain and larger forces at work in the cosmos. On the other hand, Trimble sees our capacity for, and need of, illusion, of make-believe, as another distinctive feature of the brain, of the right brain in particualar – an issue we take up again later in this book. He has made it the purpose of his book to restate the case for Dionysus in our clinics and classrooms, for the balancing role of the right hemisphere of the brain, where our religious impulses, magic, expressive language and poetry, music and dance seem to lie inextricably intertwined. My final quotation from his book makes the application of his thought to our model and, in particular, to Harré's Identity Project, resoundingly clear:

The right hemisphere more than the left is involved with the creation of the sense of self, is dominant for control of emotion and for retrieval of autobiographical memories, and is intimately involved with processing personally bonded features of an individual's world – especially that which is familiar and which is necessary for the creation of poetry and music, and probably other artistic forms as well.

(ibid.: 211)

In his typically measured way, Trimble makes his case for the return of Dionysus to re-enchant the arts.

A compelling biological adaptation

We have already quoted from the *Journal of Consciousness Studies*. In concluding this brief excursion into the labyrinth of neuroscience, I shall concentrate on a collection of papers gathered in one volume of a series of special editions of the journal devoted to the subject, *Art and the Brain* (Vol. 6, June/July 1999). As stated at the head of this paper, it is not my intention to provide a comprehensive overview of this emergent field – that would be well beyond the scope of this project; but I believe sampling can be useful and instructive, even if it makes no claim to be representative, indicating, as it does, major support for many of the most cherished intuitions of arts teachers and therapists. As will become clear from what follows, a number of the issues raised by Trimble in his book reviewed above, are of general concern among the consciousness studies community as a whole.

Trimble, as we have seen, gives a strongly positive account of the role of the creative arts in the life of the brain. His sentiments are endorsed in a paper by Bernard J. Barrs, Professor of Psychology at the Wright Institute. Barrs makes the case that emotional events 'are far more informative than closely matched unemotional events'. Emotions help to keep us on our toes. He continues;

> They present the most fundamental kind of information. Emotions move us; that is, they bring unresolved questions to consciousness, again and again, until we literally move our stance toward life, to experience it in a new and more adaptive way.
> (1999: 60)

On this reading the emotional work of the arts is, as Barrs puts it, 'a compelling biological adaptation'. Another contributor, Jaron Lanier, who works in the Inter-Active Communications Department at New York University, stresses the role of the arts as an agent in the continuous development of the mind. Art, he says, is 'hard' (i.e. difficult) for the brain, both to create and to receive: in some ways the harder the better, like higher math. Our highly evolved brain needs the challenge of complex problem-solving to maintain it at the top of its form and to stretch its potential: one reason why more easily accessible art often disappoints. Professor E. Harth of Syracuse University also sees the arts as affording a special kind of challenge to our thought processes. For Harth, the arts are 'tools to think with'. He makes the interesting point that the communicative or social dimension of art is not their primary function, which is to aid and abet thinking, intelligent behaviour itself, making art for oneself every bit as valuable as art for others.

> I have assumed that language may have begun as *monologue*, just as children, in the early stages of speaking, talk mostly to themselves. The value of *monologue*, even for the adult human, lies in its facilitation of thought processes that exhibit the basic pattern of recursive manipulation of symbols and images. Both artistic expression and language are *thinking tools*, their mode of operation patterned after preexisting internal cognitive processes.
>
> (1999: 114)

In their different ways, the contributors to this special issue of *JCS* are attempting to account for the brain's attachment to art — and their often very different takes on the question, I think, helpfully suggest we should not be too 'essentialist' in our own efforts, being ready, rather, to accept that there are probably a number of complementary and interdependent explanations for the presence and persistence of the arts in human history. Jason Brown, Clinical Professor at New York Medical Centre, supports Trimble's point that the arts explore, express and celebrate 'meaning' and value.

> Meaning is knowledge in the service of value, without which a perception is a neural datum. The valuation in meaning is the subjective in knowledge. It transforms concepts to personal beliefs, to the point where the subjectivity of knowing, the *belongingness* of what is known [see the appropriation/Water phase of the Syncretic Model], has a greater immediacy for the subject than the content the meaning is about.
>
> (1999: 153)

It is not a big leap from this position to an understanding of the 'meaninglessness' for children of much of what is currently taught in schools.

Hope

Ralph D. Ellis teaches consciousness studies at Clark, Atlanta University. He also takes up the connection between artistic expression and the realm of personal values:

> The art work must invite us to really make contact with the emotional meanings to which it speaks, rather than to just thinking about them…We act not just in order to attain the end which our value feeling points as desirable, but also in order more fully to *feel* the value feeling itself and to *affirm* that which we value…Living beings want to maintain and enhance their patterns of life and consciousness…This existential point can also be thematized neurophysiologically by thinking in terms of self-organizing dynamical systems that tend to maintain their pattern at a fairly high degree and complexity.
>
> (1999: 172)

Ellis argues that art not only moves us but also provokes us to move, 'presenting us with tools to use in intensifying, explicating and carrying forward our own emotional lives'. He might be describing the operation of the Syncretic Model, echoing as he does T. S. Eliot's lines in *Four Quartets*, 'We shall not cease from exploration/And the end of all our exploring/Will be to arrive where we started/And know the place for the first time.'

D. F. Watt, of Quincey Hospital, Quincey, MA, makes what, for me, is one of the most striking points on offer in the collection. The paper is a review and a powerful commendation of Jaak Panksepp's book *Affective Neuroscience* (OUP, 1998). Watt singles out as fundamental to the brain's creativity, its emotional programme for hope. Hope, he argues, underpins the individual's basic inclination to adopt a creative, a 'seeking', stance before the world.

> Although initially the relationship of a non-specific VTA-LH seeking system to primary or prototypical affect may seem unclear, this 'seeking system' probably underpins a most basic emotional capacity without which others make little or no sense – the capacity to experience *hope*. We are driven to go out into the world and interact by this VTA – lateral hypothalamic system, searching for food, drink, other rewards and pleasures, as well as searching for harder to find, more abstract treasures [the phase of Metal that both begins and ends the *Sheng* cycle] such as purpose and meaning that are essential to humans with their more advanced cortical evolution, as this system clearly has a huge role in prefrontal system syneptogenesis, myelination and development.
>
> (1999: 195)

This paper holds almost breathtaking promise – despite the tough vocabulary. It concludes by proposing 'that affect is a central organizing process for sentience' – which comes as close as I could wish to endorsing the case for a feeling intelligence.

I believe the arts community as a whole, and arts educators and therapists in particular, may look with confidence to the new fields of consciousness studies and neuroscience more generally (neurobiology, neuropsychology, neuro-aesthetics etc.) for support of its own intuitive and practical understandings of the importance of the arts in the formation of individual and collective identity. That so much of the work reviewed above resonates with aspects of the Syncretic Model is particularly gratifying to me. It seems we are seeing the extraordinary convergence of two systems of thought which, though separated by over 2,500 years of history, none the less seem to share a common understanding of the human body, mind and spirit.

6   The Tusa interviews

In the year 2000, John Tusa, Director of the Barbican Centre in London, recorded a series of radio interviews with a group of British artists on the subject of their creativity. The published texts of some half dozen of these recordings are analyzed in this chapter, using the Syncretic Model as the analytical instrument. Writers, painters, sculptors, poets and musicians all report very similar experiences of the Five Phases of Change, suggesting that the Syncretic Model gives a good account of the cycle of artistic creativity as experienced by practising artists. The interviews enrich and deepen the model's meaning and would appear to endorse its application in fields where art making and reception are fostered.

I got the habit, thank goodness.

Paula Rego

We must therefore survey what we have already said, bringing it to the test of the facts of life, and if it harmonizes with the facts we must accept it, but if it clashes with them we must suppose it to be mere theory.

Aristotle, *The Nicomachean Ethics*, X.8

Introduction

Having presented the Syncretic Model and begun to explore its application in the areas of arts teaching, therapy and cultural animation, I want now to apply it to an analysis of the creative experience of professional artists, as a way of testing its basic credibility for the purposes I have in mind. If the model works as an analytical tool in such a context, then we are surely permitted to extend its application in the way I want to do.

In the year 2000, John Tusa, then Managing Director of London's Barbican Centre, former BBC news presenter and Managing Director of the Corporation's World Service, was invited to do a series of in-depth interviews with major figures in the arts world for BBC Radio 3. In selecting their interviewees, Tusa and his director, Tony Cheevers, were at pains to avoid what Tusa calls 'the "stage army" of the familiar, the over-exposed, the establishment orthodox'. The 14 artists selected for the pro-gramme were 'major figures in the arts whose look back at their life and career was worth hearing in its own terms'. The list included Howard Hodgkin, Anthony Caro, Milos Forman and Muriel Spark. In 2003, Methuen published an edited version of the broadcasts under the title *On Creativity: Interviews Exploring the Process*, for which Tusa wrote two accompanying essays: 'On Creativity', and 'On Interviewing'.

The interviews follow a regular structure. They begin with childhood, parents, home and school, Tusa sensitive to the longer-term effects of these early influences. He then explores the origin of the artist's sense of having a vocation – of wanting to become an artist. An examination of college years, of joining the arts community, then leads on to a more detailed, sustained consideration of the artist's working practices. Final exchanges usually cover aspects of publication: audiences, coping with criticism, how a complex work unfolds and how one project gives rise to the next. Along the way there are often references to other contemporary artists working in the same field, and to the contemporary arts scene as the artist sees it.

The interviews are, by and large, extremely well handled and deeply engaging. Tusa's considerable expertise as an interviewer, together with his sensitive and informed grasp of each artist's work, make for rich and illuminating encounters. Whilst never becoming intrusive or harassing, Tusa invariably finds his way to the heart of the matter, and we, as listeners and readers, find ourselves on intimate terms with minds of the greatest interest. Nor are we ever merely lost in technicalities or baffled by art-speak. Tusa manages to keep his interviewees resolutely grounded and accessible.

The interest of this testimony for me is the opportunity it provides for testing the credibility of the Syncretic Model as an analytical instrument. I want to explore the interviews to see whether the Syncretic Model might be discerned as a shadowy presence standing behind Tusa's questioning and the answers he elicits from his subjects. Simply that. Are the five phases present as a common pattern running through these revealing exchanges? Tusa, in his introductory essay, has something himself to say about 'pattern':

> We had no belief that a group of such widely varied artists could be forced into a conforming set of patterns and we had no interest in trying to create patterns where none existed.

> (2003: 5)

However, he admits that 'as time went by', common themes emerged – and he item-izes them. Unremarkable childhoods – 'often lower middleclass, with aspirant tinge'; having an influential teacher or friend; having the courage to make defining choices at critical moments in their lives; coping with being 'appallingly lonely'; having an unerring instinct for what was 'right' in a work; handling creative blocks; given to 'effort and sweat'; seeing particular works as part of a continuing oeuvre; being true to themselves. In largely concentrating on biographical material Tusa hopes to steer clear of creativity theory – which is, of course, what we are interested in, in this book. He has little patience for it.

He does have a quasi-theoretical agenda, however, which boils down to attacking the way the term 'creativity' has become debased by politicians and others using it 'as political margarine to spread approvingly and inclusively over any activity with a non-material element to it'. He also disapproves of the way the term is used in education, where 'anyone's finger painting, anyone's clay bowl was deemed as praiseworthy as anyone else's'. Tusa would rather the word 'creativity' was applied exclusively to the exceptional, original talent; to distinguished artists such as those selected for his interviews. His, then, is the so-called 'genius' school of thought on the subject of creativity. There is a powerful moral thrust to Tusa's argument as well, as he praises his artists for their bravery, their fortitude, their unremitting commitment to 'effort and sweat', their attachment to 'truth', their avoidance of dilettantism. Tusa likes his creatives on the heroic scale. He insists that 'most of us are not creative in this way'. All of which suggests a divergence between Tusa's project and ours. Be that as it may, it is already clear that common ground exists: his observation that each artist's creative life is 'a seamless, instinctive continuum', with each work giving rise to the next, and his emphasis on the artist's instinct for what is right in the work and steadfast commitment to authorial integrity, all anticipate phases of the Syncretic Model. And our idea of creativity being a continuous, repetitive cycle is not entirely out of kilter with the 'pattern' Tusa unwittingly uncovers.

What I am going to do in this chapter is look closely at half a dozen of these interviews, 'panning' for evidence of the model as an unconscious organizing principle at work in their structuring and within the evidence elicited. I shall begin by looking for evidence, phase by phase, element by element, ranging across my sample: Frank Auerbach, Harrison Birtwistle, Anthony Caro, Tony Harrison, Muriel Spark, Elliott Carter. I shall conclude by considering Paula Rago's interview as a whole, pulling out the dynamic interaction between the different phases or elements of her process as Tusa uncovers it. Hers is a complex and particularly cohesive interview. I hope to be able to demonstrate that, within the limits of the exercise, the Syncretic Model does indeed 'harmonize with the facts', and therefore can at least be considered as a plausible theory of creativity in the arts.

The small size of the sample forbids our making any serious claims to research vindication – and no such claims are made. The results of this analysis, however, will give a useful indication of which way the evidential wind might be blowing. It will certainly suggest whether or not further such case studies, and others going beyond Tusa's remit, might usefully be undertaken. Tusa's omission of the performance artist (actor, musician, dancer) needs to be made good some time, as also his ignoring of the theatre director, choreographer, curator, critic and musical conductor, all of whom he would presumably wish to include within the realm of the creative arts. For my part, I would want to test the model on groups of informal artists, including children in schools. The model proposes creativity in the arts to be a universal experience, of general significance in the lives of everyone. That some of us achieve distinguished status does not in the least diminish the importance either of the creative life or of the habit of art in the lives of the rest of us.

Informed of my purposes in this chapter, John Tusa wrote generously to me to say that he thought it 'a lovely idea – very interesting'. I hope, having read it, he still does.

Metal, autumn, conventionalization, grief

If winter is the time to draw upon the cultural stock and make it one's own, autumn sees the gathering in of the harvest and the sorting of the good from the bad. It is also about making a good start. The issue for Metal is standards. Representing standards in the arts are the great and the good of the cultural tradition who, in their distinctive ways, have come to define the canon, the heritage. It is against their inspiring achievements that artists naturally measure themselves, while at the same time pushing the boundaries so as to make the past serve the present, relentlessly seeking new ways of saying the old things, reinventing old ways for saying new things. It is not for nothing that Five Elements theory is called the Five Phases of Change. Change is what the Syncretic Model seeks to address: change as something we must endlessly accommodate and assimilate; change we actively seek and promote in our instinctive pursuit of the new – particularly what might, for our contemporaries, turn out to be shockingly so. The model says Metal (judgement, tradition) reins in Wood (creativity, the new). But it must not chop it off at the roots. Lest Metal should get above itself and block change, Fire is there to soften its edge, to melt it into ploughshares. Aristotle says, if the supreme end of human life is happiness, then the happiest are those who follow the contemplative life.

The artists interviewed by Tusa all refer to the importance of the heritage. Creativity does not come from nothing. Their authenticity must be one with the authenticity of the greats. Their work, too, will be done 'in response to feeling'. The place of conventionalization has always meant, for me, the heritage, the tradition, the touchstones of taste, the vast cultural storehouse that the guardians open to us as we are inducted into the habits and institutions of art, as we pick out our own particular teachers and masters, as we train and grow up into creative art-makers and art-receivers in our own right. Why grief? Well, there's the difficult business of letting go, perhaps even of having fallen short somehow. As creative makers, we cannot simply release the work and think of England, or anything else for that matter. We cannot simply wash our hands of it emotionally because, in the first place, we are implicated in its success or failure, not least because our own standing as artists depends upon it: more particularly, of course, because our heart was in it. All of which can be sobering stuff, even should it go well. Joy and love have to be strong to control grief, to soften the sense of loss that inevitably attends the end of any journey, of a holiday, of a relationship, of a life. Earth supplies the powerful elixir, empathy, so we shall not suffer alone, nor be allowed to be too hard on ourselves – to buckle under the pressure of exposure to critical or merely curious others.

Auerbach sees his own quest inspired by the ventures of the great masters 'who are in pursuit of a private quest, which has results that become more and more visible'. Caro, referring to the huge influence that his time in Much Hadham with Henry Moore had on him, cites the master's generosity with not only his time but also his books.

> Oh, I learned a lot from him because he was very generous with his books, with talking about art to me. He knew I liked to talk about art, I liked to think about it. He let me borrow a book. Probably I borrowed two or three books and then change them, so I'd take home a book at night on Negro art or on Surrealism. We hadn't seen any Negro art. I was at the Royal Academy Schools; you didn't know about Negro art. It wasn't something that was on our syllabus.
>
> (Tusa, 2003: 71)

The Art Establishment can be as conservative as any other establishment in public life. As an artist one needs one's own authorities to look to for inspiration – and one does need them, even if one goes to find them in the New World, as Caro finally did – 'because I wanted to go to the future'. Ready as he might be to let his work go, 'live its own life, like one's children have to live their own lives', he still wants people to respect, look after and take care of them. And they need to be sufficiently robust to be able to take care of themselves. When a client welds one of his pieces into his front gate, Caro protests.

Like Caro, the poet Tony Harrison immersed himself in the tradition, in his case the seemingly unlikely tradition, given his social background, of classical literature, which he encountered for the first time and instantly loved at grammar school. He says he 'devoured' books and relished learning languages. His entrée into the theatre came on the back of 'the apprenticeship and discipline of learning classical metres, rhyming couplets and quatrains and so on' that he put himself through. He continues: 'You've got to learn you know, the mechanics of theatre, the film, and sound, filming, all the techniques. I like all that, as I did like to learn, originally, all the technicalities of poetry itself.' Elliott Carter lays very similar stress on his connection to the European Modernist tradition in music, seeing that tradition (he cites Stravinsky's *The Rite of Spring*) as the root of his own inspiration and innovations. His absolute determination to go his own musical way is partly fuelled by a very powerful aversion to aspects of contemporary life; for example the invasive and multifarious techniques of the advertising industry. The autumn and winter phases are intimately associated with the issue of learning, of getting to know the canon, the repertoire, the language of your own native art scene – or, these days, whatever worldwide idioms you are drawn to. Winter is a good time for sitting down by the fire with a book, a notebook or a score – or to simply practise. It's about working up an appetite.

In the course of this book we regularly return to the question of values. We shall come to understand the central role of good authentic judgement in the creative process of the individual artist, and to see how judgement is built up by means of experience (Aristotle's principles of repetition and the acquisition of good habits), and through the instruction of exceptional teachers and the influence of the masters. We shall ask ourselves about 'first and last things', and the relation of art to wider moral, political and human values. I don't find our artists with much to say on these issues, but then they weren't really being asked about them. They almost certainly would have responded had they been. George Steiner, the literary critic, debunked the cherished idea among many arts apologists – probably inherited from the great Victorian critic and educator Matthew Arnold, and his contemporaries – that the arts, and literature in particular, exerted a moral, ennobling and civilizing influence upon society. Steiner memorably cited the artistic pretensions and predilections of the Nazis as proof that no such connection could be made. But the positive connection somehow persists, and not as an idle fancy. It surfaces in Suzi Gablik's impassioned plea for the 're-enchantment' of the arts. It is also present, as we have seen, in the enquiries of the neuroscience community's investigations of the arts and the brain. For Aristotle, the greatest happiness comes through the practice of 'contemplation' (in contrast to 'calculation'), and the arts, in our sense rather than Aristotle's, are one of the practices of contemplation. A fully invested habit of art, such as the Syncretic Model describes, has values at its centre – namely, authenticity and empathy. It is possible, of course, to build a body of work or to acquire a personal collection or repertoire with no recourse to such values, but we would argue that to do so would be the miss the point: to mistake Auerbach's 'human quality' for Carter's *bête noire*, advertising, for instance. Muriel Spark says that we have lost the connection with the *numinous* because 'we have lost touch with natural things'. Art, uncoupled from natural things and from human qualities like authenticity and empathy, becomes just another branch of the entertainment and commodity markets.

Water: winter, appropriation, fear

Frank Auerbach, asked about his removal as a seven-year-old from prewar Nazi Germany and settlement in England, sees a connection between 'a sort of slight feeling of alienation' and 'a life in one of the arts'. Never really feeling quite 'at home' and yet at the same time conscious of being over-protected, seems to have sown the seed of rebellion in him early, nourishing and colouring his creative impulse emotionally. The idea of becoming a painter he traces back to being given a cake of watercolour, aged three or four: 'I'm not certain that I wanted to paint but I do think that I wanted to do something that was what's called creative'. So the creative/expressive flame was kindled in him quite early. This slightly rebellious streak is still working itself out, he feels.

Over the years, he has drawn down his own, personal selection from 'the world's great images' to fund his creativity – an ongoing act of appropriation.

> I'm one of those people that has art books open on the floor, not always, but very often when I work. And I love, for instance, Mexican sculpture and Franz Hals…All artists who've been curious about their metier, and I think that is almost every artist, have got a vast store of images in their mind. That is a help in that it sets a standard.
>
> (ibid.: 39)

So, both Metal ('it sets a standard') and Water ('a vast store of images') are at work here, powering the creative flow. He approaches each new project hoping things might come more easily for once. They never do. But the impulse forever driving him forward is always the same: the sense of caring deeply, of absolute commitment.

> One has certain deep feelings which express themselves in a plastic way. But there must be some experience that is your own, and you try and record it in an idiom that is your own, and not give a damn about what anybody says to you.
>
> (ibid.: 49)

Appropriation (the Water phase) means having your own repertoire of authoritative sources to draw on, having a voice of your own with which to express yourself, and the courage to confront and overcome your fears when it comes to expressing your deepest, most urgent feelings.

At the age of 8, Harrison Birtwistle began to write music: 'It seemed to be quite the natural thing to do.' Learning the clarinet defined music for him from the beginning as a 'linear idea', rather than a vertical one. As a student at Manchester College, with Maxwell Davies and Alexander Goehr, who were composers already, Birtwistle was a clarinettist. 'But I always knew that I was going to write music.' Messiaen's early influence was pivotal. 'It gives you courage. What I have been on about. Somebody else is doing it, maybe there is something there.' And courage, it seems, is what you need, because writing music is 'the most terrifying thing to do'. Winter fear, then, but with Metal at his shoulder to lend him courage; also winter preserving and nourishing his vocation as a composer.

For Anthony Caro the impulse to become a sculptor surfaced as the desire to work with clay when he was young:

> I just knew that I liked the reality of clay, the stuff that I used to make with it. I worked during my holidays with Charles Wheeler, in Charles Wheeler's studio, and he was very kind to me and I think I just got the idea that this was the right material for me.
>
> (ibid.: 70)

Although he was eventually to move on to working with metal in his search for a personal voice, it seems that his original love of fashioning in clay provides for Caro the continuing thread of his creative narrative.

Tony Harrison knew very early on that he wanted to become a poet – but a special kind of poet. Coming as he does from a working-class family, Harrison wanted to write poetry 'that did some kind of honour to what I was learning [at grammar school], but also would reach people like my parents, and use what I think of as a common language'. So he drew on the formal characteristics of the classical reper-toire and deployed them in the unique expression of his personal voice. Theatre offered him a natural outlet for that voice and at once provided him with his 'public'. With the benefit of hindsight he sees the force behind his own creative drive as the impulse to express himself. 'The idea of articulation, expression, became for me absolutely vital to existence.' That members of his close family should find themselves, quite literally in some cases, unable to speak, sharpened the edge of his determination. He was determined to find his own voice. This is the clearest possible account of appropriation, but also of unquenchable desire and caring enough.

Muriel Spark, the novelist, remembers herself as a child fascinated by other people's speech. Her mother had a somewhat malicious habit of inventing unkind nicknames for family and friends – a kind of mischievous word play. As for Spark herself, 'I was listening to words, voices, remarks, and the nuance and the various levels of meaning'. She was soon writing stories about her family and making up poems. Later she became totally convinced of her 'poetic turn of mind'. Asked by Tusa if the thought of being creative frightened her, she replied:

> I'm really not sure about that. I was just a little worried, tentative. Would it be right? Would it not be right? Can I write a novel about that? Would it be foolish? Wouldn't it be? And somehow with my religion – whether one has anything to do with the other, I don't know, but it does seem so – I just gained confidence, and I don't care if it's foolish or anything, I just write.

> (ibid.: 234)

The creative impulse is finally a moral imperative; a moral virtue even.

For Elliott Carter, too, the impulse to write music is also a matter of profound personal conviction:

> I feel that in the end the music that I have always liked, and the music that I admire and the music that I write considers the public as a secondary matter. The reason we write is because we love to write and we think music is a very beautiful thing and we hope that we can do something nice.

> (ibid.: 89)

He continues to compose because he likes to write music – as simple as that. Creativity begins with enjoying being creative, with finding happiness in bringing something into being. With wanting to be a maker, in Carter's case, of music.

I imagine that every one of the artists interviewed, thinking of their own art form, would readily say 'Amen' to that; and those of us concerned to nourish and cherish the creativity of others, in whatever context, will want to be able to make just such a claim on behalf of those we work with. This is the flame we look for, protect at all costs, and try to rekindle if necessary. Carter's revelatory moment came with his first hearing Stravinsky's *Rite of Spring*. It seemed to speak to him directly. It confirmed him in his wish to become a composer and proposed a language (modernist) that seemed immediate and personal. Even with commissioned pieces, he says he has to feel free to write what he wants to write. Finding his own voice, developing his own distinctive musical vocabulary, became the key to his composing freely and honestly.

Looking back over this examination of the Water phase of the creative process of these artists is to find a powerful convergence, across a range of widely different experiences, towards the sense of a strongly defined and enduring artistic identity, devoted to the habit of art as an irrepressible urge to expression, an appetite for self-realization. This is the creative seed or impulse, often planted early in life, now sustaining the making of art as the vocation of a lifetime. Exceptionally well defined in these particular lives, the expressive impulse is given to each of us, as the drive behind our personal identity project. We shall probably not all be called to give our lives to art: we are all, however, primed to live expressive lives, according to the rhythm of the Five Phases of Change and the discoveries of neuroscience. That seed sleeps deep within the element of Water, which bears it safely forward, nourishing and cherishing it to the moment of awakening.

Wood: spring, transformation, fury

Having discovered strong evidence of Water influence, we shall be equally successful with Wood – and given Tusa's focus on the creative process, this will not be surprising. But what characterizes this explosion of creative fury? Frank Auerbach has enormous energy. He is not afraid to destroy work that he is doubtful of – indeed, his signature gesture is 'scraping away' the picture surface and beginning again, building with the traces remaining of earlier work. Tusa asks if he is aggressive, and he agrees that he is: 'I've always felt myself to be aggressive, and perhaps I am.' Confronting one of his collaborators late in the afternoon, he experiences a sudden charge of fresh energy: 'It gives me a charge of energy; you know you've got to work, there they are, and I think somehow one gets a charge from the presence of another person.'

For Auerbach, the new work finally emerges 'as a gift', an intuition, a 'calling'. He says he has no idea how he behaves at such a moment. Except that there is 'aggression' in it:

If things are going really well, I feel that it's almost as though something arose on the canvas of its own accord – you know, the various attempts one's been making come together and an image seems to call to you from out of the paint – when I'm actually in pursuit of this, I really haven't the faintest idea what I'm doing and I may behave somewhat excessively and mutter.

(ibid.: 46)

It would be hard to imagine a more powerful evocation of the fury of Wood – the sense of simply being carried away, of uncovering, being gifted, being summoned by the image that is already becoming the painting to be. On the other hand, the feeling of empathy is also at work, connecting the artist's decision-making to his sense of what works and what does not, what might be true and what might not – and, when unease creeps in, there is nothing to be done but to destroy it and begin again among the ruins. This is authentic, formative judgement, born of the habit of art. 'If one feels a slight unease, even if the thing seems plausible and presentable and nobody else might notice that it's no good, one's got to destroy it.' So, at this critical point of the creative cycle, passion (Wood) must be informed by formative judgement (Earth). Summative judgement, on the other hand, belongs to the phase of Metal. Formative judgement (what we have been calling 'reflection-*in*-action') makes possible the moment of recognition (Gadamer) and the gift can be accepted. Without this element of discovery, Auerbach says we would be talking about handicraft, not art. He says he is impressed not so much by how clever Velazques is but by his 'innocence' (Earth). Paintings that are 'fresh and radical' are done 'in response to feeling'. Feeling, for Auerbach, is innocent, and so to be trusted, uncontrived, uncalculated and incalculable. All this is eloquent of the Wood phase of the Syncretic Model. Earth, of course, is influential at every phase of the cycle.

I am also intrigued to discover, in the Auerbach interview, evidence of Witkin's 'holding form' – and, as we shall see, Auerbach is not alone in this. It will be remembered that Witkin saw the 'holding form' as the first approximation of the image to the artist's desire: the first intimation of the emergent work. For Witkin, this would often take the form of a preliminary outline, sketch or gesture made in an attempt somehow to capture (hold) the essence of the impulse propelling the expressive act. But it could equally occur as the moment of recognition, of the surprising gift that presents itself, almost despite the maker's deliberate action. Auerbach repeatedly speaks of the creative process as a journey or a quest – an idea, of course, that entirely corresponds with the role of Metal in our model. Here he describes the 'holding form' as a crucial step along the 'experimental journey' – through the Wood. I shall quote this important passage in full.

I also had another art education – all sorts of intelligent people taught what was generally taught. What Bloomberg taught was that whereas the drawings that one

did in other classes were a sort of addition of various parts – a piece here, a bit
more there, try and fit them together so that it becomes coherent and true – he
had this idiom that allowed one to go for the essence at the very beginning; to
adumbrate a figure in ten minutes and then to redo it, and then to find different
terms in which to restate it, until one got something that seemed to contain the
mind's grasp of its understanding of the subject. Firstly, the gestures could be very
large; secondly, it could be totally incomprehensible as anything but an abstract.
And it never was an abstract – its essence lay in the fact that the balance and the
rhythm were exact; it was an experimental journey.

(ibid.: 35)

Moving on to Harrison Birwistle, we come across the 'holding form' again. For
Birtwistle it often occurs as a single chord. He improvises, and he comes across a
chord that he 'likes' – 'that was directly from my unconscious state'. (This is, incidentally, my own preferred way with a class – simply to set the materials in motion – to
begin with the act of 'displacement', on the lookout for something that takes one's
fancy, something potential in the moment.) Having found his chord, Birtwistle commits
it to analysis to see what can be made of it, where it might take him. 'I find a way of
thus proliferating the situation, a method of composition if you like.' He then goes on
to qualify the notion of the compositional element – again, in line with Auerbach's feelings of openness to chance, almost (see Aristotle, who claims the artist thrives on the
accidental). 'I would hate to think that I have a method of composition because it is
something that happens, it is ephemeral, what I do.' The idea he wants 'sort of creeps
in, the way I do things' (as in Ted Hughes's iconic poem about his own creativity, 'The
Thought Fox'). After a while, Birtwistle will return to the original chord, to realize 'that
it was a sort of modality, which was to do with situations which have increments, which
have more of one thing than another'.

In the case of both these artists, it seems they are talking about recognizing the
emergence of the so-called subject (see Gadamer's *tessera hospitalis*), and having
found the subject, giving the expressive impulse direction and particularity – intimately,
personally felt – is what the phase of Wood is essentially about. Like Auerbach,
Birtwistle rejects the idea of working to 'pre-compositional' schemas. He is talking
about living with uncertainty, with hope, working spontaneously, recognizing that a
composition might only emerge in its finished form after what he calls 'one, two, three,
four journeys'. Paula Rego counts her approximations on her fingers. And with each
journey (what T. S. Eliot calls 'each new beginning') 'you've got to sort of keep your eye
on the ball, I think. That's the risk I'm taking,' says Birtwistle. Composing music, as we
have seen already, is 'the most terrifying thing' he does. It can feel like 'having no control
over the thing'. I sense the shade of Dionysus.

Anthony Caro gets his subject for a work, a specific creative idea, from a variety of
sources:

It comes from thinking about art. It comes from looking at art. It comes from a conversation you have. It comes from the last work you did. It comes from what the architects are doing. It comes from a painting you saw. It comes from seeing two bits of steel on the ground together, or it comes from coming across something and saying, 'That's a start, now wait a minute, what does it need?

(ibid.: 76)

With Caro, his newly discovered subject is a form with possibilities: a 'start' in the sense that, within a particular idea, might lurk a 'potential object'. The making then becomes the process of the realization of that potential. Insofar as both Auerbach and Birtwistle describe feelings akin to loss of control, of entering an almost trance-like state of concentration or absorption in their quest for the potential object (feeling form), they would seem to be referring to the 'potential space' (Winnicott) itself. Caro describes himself having several goes at a piece before handing it over to his collaborators to 'finish'. Getting going, however, often means 'messing about', just working because 'you can't help it'.

You start by messing about and in a little while you are enjoying it so much that you are working away.

(ibid.: 78)

Pleasing yourself tells you that you are being serious. We seem to be talking here of Wood and Earth at the back of consciousness, sensing, judging, offering approval, keeping the work on track and sustaining it with joy and affection no matter how 'terrifying' (Water) the risk may seem, how vulnerable it may make you feel.

Tony Harrison is another artist who finds his inspiration (not a word any of these artists is comfortable with) in the actual process of working. For Caro, it feels like 'messing around'; for Harrison:

All my life I always spend a lot of time every day working. I don't always write anything, but I'm always working around finding the occasion when the writing becomes possible.

(ibid.: 157)

Tusa suggests that the idea for a poem must force itself upon the attention. Harrison agrees:

It does. It's sometimes in a phrase or an image. I always have a notebook with me and I still work in notebooks rather than on a computer. I still work with pen, and then I type, then I correct on a transcript…It's a very layered thing which comes out of often months of putting down phrases which I'm sure will lead somewhere. And actually to find out what the context of that phrase is, is finding the poem.

(ibid.: 158)

Each of these artists speaks about composition as a kind of journey of discovery, an uncovering. They are alert for early signs of life in the subject, finding a holding form or idea and then keeping its development, its disinterment, 'true' (Birtwistle's 'keeping one's eye on the ball'). It's as if they were referring to a process going on below the level of consciousness, as if some activity of the mind were proceeding at a level beyond either direct observation or calculation (Aristotle): a secret life of the mind yielding gifts to perception for us to praise and endorse – or reject. The metaphor of the 'journey' signals the passage of time that has to be allowed to accommodate that secret life, which may be neither predicted nor commanded, and yet which might be encouraged to pick up pace under the influence of an approaching, internal deadline. Its time will come. Perhaps nothing is ever finished; it is simply stopped, or runs out of steam. It moves from inner to outer reality, and continues growing. As if to endorse what I have just been saying, Tony Harrison identifies his creative writing as 'absolutely feeling-driven': this is where the expressive impulse (emotion expressively charged) has to be understood as working creatively within the oldest part of the brain, in the right brain below the surface of consciousness, as the secret life of the mind. This is the minding that makes for art. All these artists claim that 'enjoying' their work is a sign of the creative impulse alive and well, deriving from the Water phase and impelling the quest for a particular work. Wood defines it, giving it 'a local habitation and a name'.

Muriel Spark's is another account of the Wood phase's fury or frenzy. In her prime, beginning as a writer so late, she had several novels at a time in her head, circling around waiting for her attention. 'I left it so late in life that everything was bursting out and I'd do two novels a year', writing twelve hours a day. The novel composes itself in her head; all she has to do is 'clear the decks and then I can start'. Her 'holding form' comes to her as a mental concept of the book as a whole. She has to 'get it down and then flow on'. The impression, once again, is of considerable hard work done on the basis of a gift – which might be a way of speaking about serving one's talent. To fall in love, it is said, you have to be ready to do so: half in love already. 'Excited' is the word Elliott Carter uses. He has to feel a surge of excitement at the prospect of writing for a particular set of instruments or for a specific band. 'That's the first thing. The second thing is that there are certain types of thing that I like to do and there are other things that I don't like.' The Water or appropriation phase seems to determine his likes and dislikes in general terms: Wood, with its circumstantial specifics, defines the particularity of the work as like *this*. Once again we have the process of discovery, the journey, accepting this and rejecting that, and the excitement all the while gathering in intensity. 'Once you've gotten focused on the thing, let's say the excitement of writing, it becomes more and more important as I write the piece.' The so-called fury or rage of Wood is none other than this state of intense creative excitement. The 'excitement' of the potential (the compositional) space may be at one and the same time enjoyable and painful – but the end of creativity is joy (Fire).

Fire: summer, publication, joy, love

We have been able to draw deeply upon the evidence of the Tusa interviews to lend the substance of the artistic creative experience to our account of the Metal, Water and Wood phases of the Syncretic Model. These aspects of creativity, the origins of these artists' creative impulse, and details of their working practice, loomed particularly large among Tusa's interests in creativity, and he interrogates them sensitively and in depth. He seems rather less concerned about the contributions to that process made by our remaining phases: the social aspect of sharing as the work nears completion (Fire), and the judgemental phase of critical reception and enculturation (the return to Metal). It is, of course, one of our central claims in this book that we envisage a more complex account of, a wider trajectory for, the creative impulse than has traditionally been the case with writers theorizing creativity according to a linear, hierarchical pattern. We claim that each of the five/six phases bears equal weight in the totality of the artist's experience, carries equal responsibility for the guiding principles of empathy and authenticity, and is probably operating simultaneously with all the others as elements of a complex network or web. It will therefore be important to conduct further such interviews, giving full weight to each phase. This means, in terms of the evidence available to us, that we shall fare less well with the remaining phases than with those already covered. (For the purposes of this analysis I have seen the Metal phase as both the beginning and the end of the cycle, so, to be absolutely exact about it, there are six phases, and five elements.) None the less, evidence there is. Against the odds, Paula Rego, for example, with whose interview we shall conclude this analysis, fully takes the hint with respect to these remaining phases and provides powerful corroborative evidence of Fire and the return to Metal from her own experience.

Something that has, I have to say, rather surprised me, reading these interviews, has been the sociable aspect of the creative process of many of these artists. The stereotype of the artist struggling alone, sequestered from the world, is certainly not borne out by this set of witnesses – and this has helped me to think again about the Fire phase of the cycle. I have always understood it to have a strong social character, and this was no problem when I was focused on the function of publication: the finished work is shown, published, exhibited, shared. However, with Fire continuous in some degree with the creative fury of Wood (Fire has its own fury), bringing the intensely private early making phase into an increasingly more public arena, I was uncertain about the dividing lines between the two. I now feel that, by allowing the making phase to span both elements, it makes perfect sense to see a shift in attention by the artist from an early inwardness towards a growing sense of the work's ultimately public destiny. Feeling isolated or forbidden the consolations of publication – I think of the poet Gerard Manley Hopkins – can put a huge strain on the artist.

I think it is possible to follow this trajectory in the testimony of many of the artists we have been studying. Auerbach, for instance, has his chosen, intimate group of collaborators, turning up late in the day, to help move the work along or provide a fresh impulse. As we shall see, Paula Rego also has very 'special people' to serve as companions to her work. Birtwistle enjoys the dynamic and close relationships offered by working in the theatre; Tony Harrison likewise. Performing, for Tony Harrison, serves a similar, socially interactive function – his audiences are never merely inert, passive receivers of his work. He certainly doesn't see them so. Anthony Caro works, initially, on his own before passing the work on to his trusted collaborators, with whom he is then in continuous conversation. There would not seem much room for companionship in Muriel Spark's 12-hour day, but, who knows?, she might well have a muse, a best receiver, an angel, hidden somewhere, if not actually in the house, then hard by. No such question-mark hangs over Elliott Carter, who invariably takes his cue from the musicians he expects to be writing for. My take on this social aspect of the creative process is that it counter-balances the intensity and unavoidable isolation of the early, private work of the Wood phase, helping to steady and ground the psyche by providing human perspectives and drawing upon other human sources of energy. Artists whose working practices are weak or unbalanced in respect of their Fire element are likely to find their creative fury more difficult than it might otherwise be to live with, and the later phases of the cycle could also prove problematic: sharing, letting go, remaining confident at the prospect, and in the actual face of criticism, and so forth.

So Fire is about completing the making – perhaps finally more concerned for the form than the subject (with the subject becoming more a matter of form) – and about 'having something to show'. We should not underestimate the strength of the desire to show, the need to have the work in circulation. It stems from a deep desire to be known, to open up to others, to be seen and to belong. As Lewis Hyde (1983) points out in his book *The Gift*, it is the business of gifts to circulate: and they do so, more often than not, in the context of mutual intimacy, trust and friendship. If receiving a work is a gift for the maker, passing it on only confirms the economy of the gift. Being like-minded is to share fellow feeling – as we shall be arguing a little later in connection with 'kindness' and the imaginative identification with others that defines empathy. And even if 'letting go' can be a struggle, and is only finally achieved at the Metal phase, showing, for most artists, seems something of a basic instinct. It certainly seems to be a healthy one.

The impulse perhaps arises in what Winnicott describes as our need to have our experience, our mind, 'reflected back' to us. Without reflecting back, says Winnicott (and he has in mind the client's experience reflected back by the therapist), there can be no creative growth, no moving forward and moving on. All those various companions, collaborators, first receivers we have been noticing, fulfil this essential function of acting as reflectors back, and in doing so are assisting in the difficult labour of birth, and of making the work a separate, independent entity. Is it OK? Will it do? Does it work? What do you think? The maker somehow doesn't need to ask for this reassurance and won't necessarily be taking advice from anyone – but it is instinctive, and it helps, when you are most alone, at your most vulnerable, to know that another also 'sees' it. So Auerbach, by his own admission not a prolific painter, needs the support of others if he is ever to have something good enough to show.

Birtwistle describes the more formal Fire phase as a long hard slog – concentrating on the formal possibilities inherent in the original idea. He speaks of building 'the superstructure of the piece', of 'the journey of the piece'. The earlier period of spontaneity now gives way to a different kind of energy – the more systematic, comprehensive, even ruthless, application of Fire.

> The actual amount of time it takes is the opposite to spontaneity. Because the initial thing is that you might want this gesture, but then you have to start with your Lego and then you build it up and build it up and build it up. And so consequently, the next bit of spontaneity is a long way from the last one. I mean just look at that piece of page there. It takes about ten seconds to play and two days to write!
>
> (ibid.: 64)

Anthony Caro describes the process as letting go of privacy. Affection for the work plays an important part in the making process itself, but you get over it. The work must move on, must move out there, not least because of what we have been saying: the psychological importance of its being 'reflected back'.

> I think it's very important that we have a response. I think that it's very tough on an artist who paints his pictures and makes his sculpture and has no means of showing it, he doesn't put his works into shows. What's he done? He's just turned it to the wall and I think it is like talking in the dark or talking to yourself. And it's a very unhappy way of going about this thing because we need a response, we need it!
>
> (ibid.: 80)

We have opened a window onto our soul and it isn't enough: someone passing by has to look in on us, come in for a cup of tea. With his reference to happiness, Caro touches on the emotional character of Fire: joy and love. The reflecting back we have been talking about, for all the tensions and difficulties along the way, should eventually give rise to mutual celebration. Caro gives a touching example of the Fire phase:

I've got some people working with me. They have been students. They're a delight. I happen to be lucky. I've got really nice people and we talk about all sorts of things in our tea breaks and we look at art together. We look at my art and I say, 'What do you think about this? Perhaps we should change this end. Do you like the colour of it?' I mean, I talk to them like that and it's very open, it's very nice. I don't think I'd accept somebody out of the blue, no.

(ibid.: 86)

This significant companionship Tony Harrison finds in his public readings.

Earth: late summer, authenticity, empathy

For Muriel Spark, the fashioning of a novel has a musical impulse; she is aware of a musical or poetic spirit shaping the emergent form. The musical shape of the piece will tell her 'when I'm coming to the end and what I should do, and various things like that'.

Our artists speak of knowing when they've got it right, of having to be ruthless in destroying what doesn't quite work. They seem to possess an inner confidence as to the integrity or their work – as highly successful and accomplished practitioners they should know. But they have their moments of doubt and confusion. How much starker these moments for the inexperienced and aspiring maker, who must, never-theless, have access to an inner sense of conviction without which authenticity is simply impossible to achieve – and nothing worthy will come of inauthentic work. Authenticity, as the refusal to compromise their sense of having a voice of their own as well as having something of their own to say, is of paramount importance to these artists, and authenticity becomes the 'ear' they apply in testing the work: it is the perfection of their pitch. This ability, this inner resource, is indispensable to the origi-nality and creativity of the work; which is why the Syncretic Model has Earth not only at the centre but also implicated at every stage of the cycle. Auerbach speaks of visit-ing the Giotto chapel in Padua, where he was struck by the painter's 'radicalism'. The 'root' of Giotto's work is 'feeling' – and it is feeling that determines its authenticity – its quality, or power, or virtue. Of Giotto's paintings:

I think they're done in response to feelings, so that the gesture would not be done with any view of correctness firstly in view. But if someone touches somebody gently, or the cherubs are blubbing because of death, it's done out of feeling. It seems to me that these are fresh and radical paintings done in response to feel-ing.

(ibid.: 41)

Tusa suggests the word 'innocent' in this connection. Auerbach accepts it readily.

Yes. But then, in a sense, there's a sort of element of innocence in great art. There's an element of innocence in what was perhaps the most sophisticated painter who ever lived – that's Velazquez. And yet if you see a portrait of Philip IV – I think, 'There he is.' You don't think this is Velazquez being clever. It's just he's ingested it and made this marvellous image.

(ibid.: 41)

Auerbach could not be more accurate here in identifying the quality he is interested in with 'ingestion': one of the two organs associated with the Earth element is the stomach.

He puts the same point slightly differently talking about his own work, and the work of fellow painters 'trying to do something new':

When the dust has all blown over, it finally comes down to spirit and quality and perhaps human quality, and nothing to do with the idiom in which people work.

(ibid.: 42)

Empathy – for Earth is indeed about 'spirit and quality and perhaps human quality'. Empathy is Earth's intelligent feeling. I take him to mean the artist's being in tune with the work, but also being emotionally in tune with himself – and with his fellow artists. It's the kind of attunement that Stern writes about in his account of the emotional understanding between mother and infant; it is the intelligence of feeling. The 'human quality', if we admit to the implications of the model, pervades the whole creative cycle, even when having to share emotional space with powerful and often contrary characters such as Fury, Fear, and Grief. Empathy says we feel these things too, we know this experience within ourselves as makers and within those whose art-making it is our business to nourish and enjoy and cherish.

For Harrison Birtwistle, authenticity (Earth) means keeping faith with his musical intuitions, his deepest artistic impulses. He enjoys the challenge of working in the theatre. But his instincts are musical, so he inclines towards the opera. As a composer working in the theatre (the National Theatre), he says,

It's not simply a question of thinking of an interesting story to tell. It's really an interesting story to retell and something where I can deal with my preoccupations as a composer of pure music in the theatre. So the same journeys that I make through a piece of music, I can make in the theatre.

(ibid.: 67)

There's an interesting, almost throwaway, line in the Caro interview in which the sculptor responds to Tusa's question about new work 'bubbling up inside':

> Quite a lot of things are bubbling up inside me but odd things too. I do have some plans to make some art and I don't want to kind of spoil my luck by talking about them too much now.
>
> (ibid.: 84)

Caro seems to have this powerful intuition that 'talking about' would interfere with the mysterious activity of creativity deep below consciousness: left brain bears right brain down. Authenticity and fertility cannot be put at risk at such a delicate and sensitive time. He couches his intuition in a little superstition.

Tony Harrison believes it is a primary function of art to stimulate and provoke human sympathy. (As we have already said, D. H. Lawrence makes a very similar point speaking about literature affecting the way our sympathy flows.) Harrison cites Nietzsche: we need the kind of art that is 'open-eyed about savagery and darkness and blood', and yet refuses, as Nietzsche says, 'to be turned to stone by experience'. Kindness is like love in this respect. So the nourishing of 'the human quality', of empathy, becomes central to his impulse to art. He tells of a casual meeting ('when I was very young') with an old woman on a train in Ireland, going to Galway. She said to him: 'What do you do? What are you? What do you do?' I said, 'I'm a poet.' 'Well, that's a grand trade to be in'.

Muriel Spark brings fresh insight to the notion of completion, of the journey being over, the work done, perhaps the possibility of peace – for the moment. All this also belongs to Earth.

> It can't matter if you finish, because we die in the middle of something, usually. And it can't be an obligation to finish anything. But one hopes to finish things, complete things. Yes, I feel I've realized myself but I'm never happy, you know. I want to finish something else, a number of things.
>
> (ibid.: 238)

So much, then, for our sampling of the Tusa interviews as an exercise in mapping the creative cycle of artistic experience on to the Syncretic Model. I hope I have, even with such a tiny sample, gone some way towards convincing the reader that there is not simply a match, but evidence of matching in a plausible degree. More to the point, the patterns we have discerned in the analysis support a richer account of the creative process than is customary – a process that is natural and holistic rather than technical and linear. We shall wind up this analysis with Tusa's interview with Paula Rego. Bearing the Syncretic Model in mind, hers is remarkable testimony.

Paula Rego

We shall now apply the model to analyse a single Tusa interview taken as a whole. It is clear from what we have just done that the model is implicit in Tusa's line of questioning, and that it can be amply illustrated in the answers he elicits from his artists. It will be interesting to see to what degree it is also evident within an artist's experience of her creative process considered as a whole.

Metal: autumn, conventionalization, grief

Paula Rego was born in Lisbon in 1935 – coming to study art in England in the early 1960s. She describes herself as a much loved, spoilt child, living in a strict home but 'with few rules'. Rego's sense of artistic identity is very strong: for all her apparent readiness to defer to the judgements of others, she knows what she likes and is sure of her work's value to her. Her 'habit of art' has deep and secure roots. She was actively encouraged to draw as a child and was fed 'the stories I liked to hear'. She trained at the Slade in London, where several 'oddballs' inspired her – in particular her beloved husband-to-be, Victor Willing, a fellow student. Her time with Willing, up to his early death, constituted the most formative period of her artistic life. Willing was 'the biggest influence, possibly the only influence. I mean copying-wise; I didn't want to do pictures like him because we're such different people, but the things he told me I still remember.' Going on alone after his death was extremely difficult – she had to learn to rely on her own judgement, 'to distance myself'. 'And I was very scared that when he died I wasn't going to be able to work. But I've done my best. I don't know how brave I've been, but I hope so, yeah'.

Water: winter, appropriation, fear

Rego's imagination fed on the stories told to her by her Aunt Egeria. 'The stories I wanted to hear.' She enjoyed being frightened. For her, the real world was a world of 'mystery and enchantment'. Drawing, in such a world, was both comforting and assertive – almost, perhaps, to use Seamus Heaney's term, a form of 'redress'.

> I always drew, ever since I was really small, as children do. They just scribble away, and I did that. I loved drawing, you see, because drawing is incantatory, and it also brings you peace, because you rock backwards and forwards when you're drawing, and there's something sexual about drawing. And there's a great deal of comfort in it as well. It was just the point of the pencil. And when the point of the pencil scratched on the paper, it was utterly thrilling; and then I'd make a noise, I'd go 'uuunnnn'. That's how it was incantatory, you see, the 'uuunnnn'. And I went into a kind of, not a dream, but somewhere else. And I became completely absorbed in what I was doing. I'd sit on the floor and draw hour after hour.

(ibid.: 204)

Drawing, then, became established early on as a compelling expressive language – and the power of drawing was almost ritualistic for her, carrying her, not into a dream, but 'somewhere else'. Her 'song' made her space special. I think we can safely assert that she is speaking here of the potential space (Wood), the space of transformation. But this obsession had something transgressive as well as comforting about it – taking off into story (story-making was, and remains, her driving impulse) could make her feel guilty, ashamed. 'Ashamed of pretending, ashamed of being found out, ashamed!' We are very close here to the Water phase of emotion: fear. Rego insists she always knew she wanted to become an artist. She describes the powerful influence upon her imagination of Gustav Doré's illustrations for Dante's *Inferno*, with which her father used to frighten her when she was small – the 'frightening' character of some of her own work recalls Doré – 'full of black and full of nauseous images, very nineteenth century nausea'.

People are her basic subject matter, her enduring focus of attention – setting up a particular scene to draw in the studio, using collaborators (models) dressed up and in role, and arranging scenery and props, is her way of discovering a particular subject for a work. Such scenes capture and evoke the mood she is interested in – the meaning seems to be in the mood.

> I use figuration because it is the only way that I can put the mood across – through figures, because I like drawing figures, because I like drawing people. I'm very interested in people; I like people above everything else.
>
> (ibid.: 216)

There are hints of aggression, as with Auerbach, in her approach to drawing – she thinks of herself as a man: 'Well, I stand aggressively in front of the easel, and I walk from one foot to the other with my hand in my pocket. And I swagger like people do in operas.' Here is Wood, strutting its stuff. If we are looking for the key to Rego's sustained creative energy, the flame of her creativity that has never been allowed to be blown out, then it seems to be the child in her, gathered and waiting like a folded concertina, like a tune in her waiting to be played.

> Well, you can't really get rid of it. It's that the child is concertinaed into you, and it pulls out at every instance – even in the most posh places, in the most awesome situations, this lilt comes out. And it's the bit that saves you really. It's not a bad bit, it doesn't mean you're going to do something really rude, it means you have more a sense of yourself.
>
> (ibid.: 220)

Here comes Earth: the sense of authenticity; here, too, her instinct for publication (Fire). If her Portuguese childhood is the enduring flame at the heart of her work, it is embodied in the Portuguese language:

There's a part of me, the part that speaks in Portuguese, brings memories back that I don't have if I speak in English. But as for poetry, for instance, I understand the language in English rather than Portuguese. In literature I get on better in English than I do in my own language. And to talk about pictures, for instance, I find it immensely hard to talk about them in Portuguese; I cannot. So English is for the grown up more, the Portuguese is the childlike, which also comes into the grown up and is totally precious, because without that we cannot exist.

(ibid.: 219)

Wood: spring, transformation, fury

Rego has already described moving into the potential space ('not a dream but somewhere else') and the incantatory ritual that would carry and keep her there – something she still does when circumstances allow. Once there, she begins 'a series of approximations to a resolution', to use Witkin's expression: 'You can only do four. Any more is self-indulgence, and also it goes off. The first one, you're grasping for what you want. The second one, you get it. The third one, you get it very, very well. The fourth one is decadent already.'

For Rego, the process of discovery is 'fraught with danger' – with risk. Her Water aspect is fully alert to this. She describes it as a thrill that you might go over the edge into some area which is fraught with danger and risk of total embarrassment; doing something that is going to reveal unspeakable things. I don't know quite what but that's the risk of it.' But a risk that must and will be taken. Creativity cannot be reduced to a method, she says. 'Method stinks.' She embarks in hope. I think Earth is hope – empathy. Hope is everywhere in the creative cycle.

Rego is another of our artists who chooses to work creatively with other people. She says this of her special Portuguese friend and collaborator, Lila:

Well, we work together and it's a collaboration. She's able to interpret what I want. By now she seems to know what it is that I want and she falls into positions that I find just right. I work through her, she's like a medium for me. Through her I can tell a story, I can do a picture. We really started with my *Dog Woman* when I realized I had to have a model because I couldn't do it without the information that I needed from another human being to copy. And she put herself in that position and it was so marvellous. Then after she was the sleeping dog; then she was the bad dog; then slowly we began to understand a language together and now she can interpret all sorts of things for me. It's always different.

(ibid.: 214)

This extract beautifully suggests the way raw materials are transformed into symbol, into expressive 'media' – into the substance of signing. Her 'holding form' arises, not from some prior conception but from within the act of drawing itself: 'from drawing from my head on a piece of paper – where you're actually bending over this piece of paper and things pour out of your head straight into it through your hand. Then if you like it, you try to set up a scene…'. And with Rego there can be no half measures with Wood's fury: 'If you go into a picture, you go the whole hog, you know, and there it is – phwar!' To be able to go the whole hog she had to move from repressive Portugal to liberal England, where she finally felt free.

Fire: summer, publication, joy, love

Working with Lila and with her other collaborators, Rego's making becomes a social and companionable practice. She loves doing pictures that mean something to her: 'that's terribly good really'. For Rego, art has indeed become a habit – she seems to have taken Aristotle at his word. 'I paint because I just do one picture and then another one. And I got the habit, thank goodness. It's got to matter to me somehow!' The forward drive of Nature, experienced as the Water phase, seems to amount to what she calls 'caring', to a mindful, heartfelt, spiritual commitment to her own art. With Fire, love comes into the equation, as we would expect it to. She needs the love of others, too; their companionship and endorsement. When Tusa asks Rego if she can 'justify' her work, she replies:

> It's not up to me to claim such things; it's up to me to do them. It's up to other people to claim for me. I can't claim, you see, I have no potential, I don't know. But other people may claim if they think it's right. You know, I do them…
>
> (ibid.: 219)

Earth: late summer, authenticity, empathy

'Going the whole hog' means not simply surrendering yourself to impulse; it also implies knowing for sure that the project is grounded, rooted, earthed; that it is propelled and guided by an energy that is completely authentic, absolutely right and true – for oneself. Here, right being or virtue, as an artist, is the result of unstinting and sustained application. Rego has acquired 'the habit of art' – as it means and counts for her. It is this pervasive sense of the good habit that informs every phase around the creative cycle, and that constitutes its hub. We have seen that 'habit' does not mean 'method' for her. Earth is central to the habit of art, and this seems to be what she means when she refers to the aesthetic dimension of the work, to its 'formal correctness'. 'If it's formally pleasing to me, then the story has to be right.' Judging the rightness of the story – of the work's emotional impact, or meaning or significance – becomes, finally, an aesthetic judgement based on formal values: in Rego's case, visual values. When she says the story is right she is affirming that its look pleases or satisfies her. Form authenticates feeling. A musical story must sound right; a piece of theatre must 'play' right; a dance must move right. Rego's eliding of form with story here is akin to Yeats's elision of the dancer with the dance: the one is the other. They cannot be told or held apart. This same principle of trusting the language of form finds its emotional counterpart – empathy – in Rego's tender, even passionate, understanding of herself as an artist, and in the intimacy of her relationship to drawing, to her medium and her model – beautifully expressed in her account of her working relationship with Lila. In Rego's words, we have the clearest and most poignant account of the role of Earth in the creative cycle of art.

Conclusion

And so we come to the end of this brief analytical excursion into the realm of the case study – courtesy of the enterprise of John Tusa and his collaborators. My purpose has been to look at the Syncretic Model through the testimony of these expert witnesses – to test its relevance and the extent to which it was able not only to accommodate but also to illuminate their witness. I believe the model has convincingly passed the test: each of the artists studied is conscious of participating in a sustained and demanding process that goes well beyond either a 'method' or an account of working practice. We have seen how important has been the enduring sense of self-belief, and of confidence in and commitment to personal authenticity (Earth). We have seen the importance of early support for their talent, and then finding powerful teachers and masters to help shape and resource their project as it develops (Metal). We have heard them spell out the burning expressive impulse that propels the work and endlessly renews and powers the creative effort (Water). I come away from this analysis with a much richer sense of the making process itself, from the essentially private early phase, reaching out after a possibility, to the often more social circumstances attending its final stages, and the beginning of its independent public life (Fire, Earth and Metal revisited). This often vivid and powerfully articulate testimony from such a range of experts suggests to me that we can have confidence that the Syncretic Model really works as a way of understanding the 'habit of art'.

Quite clearly, as a set of case studies, this tiny sample has to be seen as a very modest inquiry indeed. It suggests that further such testimony could usefully be collected – and from different sectors of the artistic community. Tusa's interviewees are all experienced and successful professionals with established reputations. It would be good to invite informal artists to speak about their experience, including representatives of the constituencies that are most specifically the focus of this book: students, clients in therapy, artists from other cultures and members of the wider public, both makers and receivers of art. Audiences could also have their own evidence to give – not least because so-called reception theory proposes a creative role for the reader/listener/viewer. My strong guess is that the usefulness of the Syncretic Model as an analytical instrument and as a way of theorizing creativity in the arts will only be further endorsed in the testimony of such witnesses.

There is something else. We have restricted ourselves to testing the descriptive power of the Syncretic Model in respect of the creative process. I think it would not be unreasonable to imagine a much more personal form of analysis, using the underlying principle of the Five Phases of Change, to reveal the elemental make-up or inclination of a particular artist, identifying blocks, imbalances and weaknesses (or excesses) within the system. For artists experiencing, say, 'creative block', or suffering from 'creative illness', it might be possible to identify the possible cause or causes and propose a remedy based upon a re-balanced practice. I'm certain that Five Elements medical and therapeutic intervention (including acupuncture) would also be beneficial – but that is another matter. My point here is that it might be possible on the basis of a more detailed understanding of an individual's elemental profile to make helpful adjustments to practice, i.e. to retune or rebalance the cycle with some precision. In the meantime, the model gives us a map by which we can keep track of the creative project and intervene as mentors, teachers and therapists to nourish and cherish the work in progress. It will also serve as a useful framework for individual reflection and for the reflective conversation with another.

Part 2

Practical

7 The irresponsibility of an art teacher

Jolanta Gisman-Stoch

Where I address practice through the Syncretic Model, I make the assumption that the difficulties many professionals have in becoming true participators in the other's creative process arise as a consequence of their being unable to think about it effectively. Jola's, on the other hand, is a more pragmatic offering. For her the creative teacher is trapped in a dilemma: the issue is not so much conceptual or procedural as moral. The creative teacher is wedded to the principle of student autonomy and individuality; the education system is, by definition, an instrument of cultural conservation, subject either to the light or the heavy touch of a political administration. The problem facing the creative teacher is how to be faithful to what Jola calls her students' 'hope', whilst at the same time fitting them to take their place within a publicly sanctioned profession.

Malcolm writes:

Writing this book I have always wanted to have Jola's voice and her testimony at the centre of it. Jola is a uniquely creative artist and teacher. Positioning her thus reflects my esteem for the quality of both dimensions of her work, and also my indebtedness to her for a rich conversation, in practice and reflection, over almost 20 years. My regular visits to Poland during that time to work with her cultural animation students have sustained my continuing commitment to the arts in education: without that connection with Jola there would have been no question of my writing this book now. Having said that, I have gone my own way in this writing, and although Jola has long felt comfortable with Harré, and been happy to contribute her own link to the Gilgamesh myth cited earlier, she has no personal stake in the Syncretic Model – may indeed have reservations about it. I've had to suspend my visits to Poland in order to do this writing, so we have not really gone there yet. Nevertheless, she has read the manuscript and given me invaluable help in making it publishable. For agreeing to contribute this paper of hers I am deeply grateful.

From the perspective of the book itself, I wanted her personal credo as inspiration, for that is what her chapter means to me. The book broadly sets out to map a living encounter between two creativities: that of the teacher and that of the student; that of the therapist and that of the client. Within the realm of cultural animation in which Jola now, for the most part, works, these two creativities are those of the animator and the individuals and groups he/she works with in a wide range of community settings. Unlike the UK, where cultural animation is only now beginning to find its feet in some of our larger towns and cities, in Poland the practice has a long and honourable tradition. To gain a qualifying degree can take up to five years of full-time education.

Introduction

The traditional lecturer has knowledge to share with others, or rather to transmit to her/his students. I have nothing of that sort. I possess nothing of myself. My thoughts, my ideas are born in a dialogue, and I am who I become in mutual contacts with things, animals, books, people and trees. I have agreed to write something only because I am going to write about the irresponsibility of an art teacher. I would like to question our assumptions about what it means to be a 'responsible' art teacher – something generally understood as so obvious and so transparently a good thing as to be beyond the shadow of a doubt. I have some doubts.

I shall refer to the thinking of Janusz Korczak, doctor, progressive educator and writer, who died, with the children of the orphanage of which he was the director, as a victim of the Holocaust. I would also like to introduce some of the ideas of the contemporary Polish philosopher, Józef Tischner, whose writings I find very pertinent to our theme. This is the context in which I shall speak about the irresponsibility of the art teacher.

I am not sure if it is possible to 'teach' art. A teacher is traditionally thought of as having knowledge, skills and understandings to transfer. There is no one definition of art. My knowledge about art may be useful to one person but useless to another. There is nothing I can do for someone that will guarantee that they become a successful maker of art, art critic or art lover. I have nothing useful to give, nothing for someone simply to take away and use. I can try to awaken something you have inside you; and I can be with you, be present as a witness; but I cannot make an artist of you.

Art for me is connected with such notions as 'readiness', 'openness', 'vigilance'; the ability to listen and respond in a vivid, lively way; the ability to improvise in a dialogue and conversation. The art teacher I want to talk about is not someone who teaches routines in art (though he may teach rituals in art). Neither is my kind of an art teacher perfect. Rather, I have in mind someone who still looks for, still asks questions – questions for which she or he may not be able to find answers; someone who doesn't have the answers because the answers only come one at a time and as particular responses to particular problems. The kind of teacher I have in mind accepts that some questions must go unanswered – though not without a response.

As an art teacher I have nothing someone could simply take away from me and use as a recipe or formula for making art. I do not have the know-how that would be either sufficient or exact enough for the art that each of my students wants to make. There can be no such instruction from outside the creative act. When I say that I cannot be a teacher of art, it doesn't mean, of course, that you can learn nothing from me, or that I cannot happen to you as your art teacher, or that I don't have a lot I can share with you. Being with you, I should happen to you first of all as a different being in whom somehow you can find a reflection of yourself. I can be with you, be present as a witness – and bear witness to you, if you find me worthy enough to share your truth. It is you to whom I bear witness of what I know as truth. And this is the truth I know, I believe in, I am a witness to in my being with you. I express what I know, not to be rid of it but as an invitation to a conversation with you. An invitation extended, addressed to you personally. Let me point to some of the problems we face as art teachers.

Art for me is a way of knowing, by which I mean that art has the unique power of bringing together our experience of truth and beauty. Everyone engaged in the adventure of art must find her or his special way of knowing in art (or through art). An art teacher can only say: 'Maybe because of my presence you will come to find and recognize your particular way of knowing in art, just as your being here will help me to discover (or encounter) mine.'

Each work of art – we might say each work *in* art – needs its own instruction, has its own system of rules. The instruction, the system of rules, must be born in personal freedom. Making art is a unique ability to make choices in profound personal freedom. Choices in art are always made in mutual acts of response. To make a choice in profound personal freedom means always to sacrifice, to resign, to give something up and to make something sacred (chosen and special). I can show my students what I value, how I make choices, how I confront what I find different and strange, how I struggle to make my choices authentic and faithful to what I understand as the truth, how I give meanings, living at the edge, at the 'front line' – how I live in the place where personal and cultural (individual and shared) meanings are being born.

I teach by example, but that doesn't mean that I expect someone to follow my particular effects, gestures, pictures, shapes, patterns or practices – my particular decisions. That means not only that there is a way of being that I embody and that might be useful for you to understand and perhaps emulate, but also that I can become a resistance as well as something to follow. In being with me, my student must be allowed, and be enabled, to confront my truth. Being a 'teacher' means for me, *being with the other*. Being with the other means to converse – to ask and to answer. Sometimes, also, to speak together in attunement. It doesn't mean that my pupil is the one who asks the questions and that I am to provide the answers. The exchange of questions and answers is mutual, a reciprocal engagement. The questions we cannot answer are a source of learning; they teach us respect for the mysterious. By questions and answers I do not mean the exchanging of notions. I am not talking merely of language; I mean a way of reciprocating, of mutual encountering, that preserves infinity; as happens sometimes in poetry; as happens sometimes in the 'face-to-face' encounter described by E. Lévinas.

Six questions

1   Making art and its receiving are very intimate experiences. Between the artist and the work, very intimate ties are being established. The question is: What do we need the other person for in this process? What do we need an art teacher, a cultural animator, an art therapist, for?

   Being a very intimate experience, art is always a creative act that happens within the social and cultural context – the individual creative act of art work is, at the same time, an effort of taking part in the bigger conversation we call culture. I think art can be thought of as essentially social when we see it as 'facing the other'.

2   As an art 'teacher', I understand my task as being with my student. That means that at the centre of my interest is the other person. My interest in the work is an aspect or extension of my principal interest in the student.

   What does it mean to 'be with' another person?
   What kind of experience are we talking about?
   What kind of person do we need to be, to be an art teacher?

   As a teacher of teachers, I must discover how to release in my students the capacity for a deep and comprehensive understanding of the other. This means the capacity for saying the basic word 'I-Thou', the basic word that, as Martin Buber says, establishes the world of relations. Such an understanding is essential to 'being with'. A capacity for a deep understanding means readiness, openness, vigilance, an ability to give and to receive. Every utterance of our student especially her or his art work – demands our response, the expression of our seeing (feeling) or understanding. I do not mean the collecting of information about a student. I mean establishing a relationship, the apprehension of a person, much as we apprehend a work of art. To be with a person means also to be able to reflect on human nature, on the human condition as we experience and understand it. We have to become real people for our students, come into being, come into relation with them – as we might say, in relation to the world they find theirs.

3   Herbert Marcuse has said that art is 'the cosmos of hope'. As an art educator I understand my task as working with my student's hope. What does it mean to work with somebody's hope?

   To have hope means, to me, to act heroically. First, perhaps, we should ask ourselves where we place our hope. In response, the Polish theologian Jozef

Tischner says that some of us place our hope in the wisdom of history and put our heroism into it, believing in the justice of its judgements. Some of us feel abandoned by the gods, by other people, and say, 'I can trust only myself. I shall look straight into the face of my death and simply accept the condition of humanity'. This heroism lies in not seeking to escape into a world of fantasy – it means to face profound existential human tragedy. Some of us place our hope only in God, whom we place far from us just because we do not trust other people at all. And this hope is also a kind of heroism.

Tischner proclaims the hope that I find to be mine also: he calls it a 'Gospel' heroism.

> Not the abstract rightness of history; not myself in my loneliness; not a social class but a man, this man, this woman, his or her heart, his or her freedom. I look for the heart of this man, this woman, to put into it a part of my heart – my heart full of hope.
>
> (1992: 100)

It is a kind of heroism to trust my students, to place my hope in them, and I do not find it easy. They do not find it easy either because it is not easy to live knowing that someone trusts you, has placed their hope in you. But it is possible, and each act of trust restores our hope.

4 There are many reasons for hope, but following Tischner, I would like to focus upon a specific one – important in the I-Thou relationship – the hope for an ideal love. How might we build, or rebuild, such a hope inside another person? How to elicit or evoke the other's hope for such a love?

There are many words and gestures of love but they must be addressed individually. This is a question we each have to answer for ourselves at a particular moment. The answers are being born as our personal responses. We can probably prepare ourselves to receive love, though love may simply find us out. Again, it is not a question of participating in an unthinking (perhaps daily) routine.

5 Every day we struggle to have the right to our own inner truth and at the same time to be accepted and understood by others. We experience two contradictory demands: to take care of what we find as our truth and what makes us unique, and to share what we know. The risk we run is that as unique, living testimony of what we value, we might not be understood, or that in the attempt to share what we have, we might lose what we most wish to preserve. Following Tischner, we ask: How is it possible to preserve our authenticity as the unique, living testimony of what we value, and at the same time take care of our dialogue with the culture?

6   Sometimes we feel that we cannot at the same time serve the institutions of
     culture (educational or cultural institutions) and the individual student – the other
     person. So the question arises: How to be at the same time a proficient official
     and a faithful partner, an expert and a reflective practitioner? Our social and
     personal responsibilities are experienced in contradiction yet again.

     All these problems and contradictory demands define the conditions in which
     we work. Our situation often means that we experience conflict, frustration and
     pain, but we have to go on struggling to legitimize ourselves in the place where
     we have chosen to work. This is the price we have to pay, working on the border
     between two worlds. Perhaps such conflict is inevitable: the aims of educational
     institutions can often be at odds with those to which art teachers feel committed.
     Educational institutions are charged with preserving the social order, with the
     reproduction of the dominant cultural values. Individuals need to be with another
     person, not an institution, in order not to feel lonely. Social (institutional) and
     personal needs are often felt by arts teachers to be in contradiction.

Upbringing and education

In his writing, Tischner makes a clear difference between upbringing and education
(understood as an officially accepted process of teaching embodied). Upbringing
begins, to me, with the sacramental: 'I let you be', and 'I am here with you'. Then a
promise: 'I will bring you up. I will be your support.' In education, the promise seems
not to be necessary. In the educational process it is sufficient to inculcate in the other
a definite, specified, precise structure of being. This is what the institutions of education usually are obliged to do. That is why the institutions require efficient
functionaries to take on the responsibilities of the institution, to be loyal to the institution's task. Such functionaries are concerned rather to wring (or extort) a
disciplined response from their students. Isn't it a kind of treason to be responsible
for the institution rather than looking after the hope in another's heart? asks Tischner.
Certainly, a responsible art 'teacher' must be responsible for the institution in which
s/he works, but where there is a conflict of interest, our duty is to the hope of the
other person.

I feel such conflicts are inevitable and intrinsic to the situation of the educational
institutions in our culture. And probably our 'profession' (our 'vocation') is *to be in
conflict*. This is 'the reality that hurts'. What I am suggesting is the necessity of questioning once again the basis of our educational institutions. There is a 'hidden
curriculum' embodied in them. They teach aggression, that being stronger means to
be right; they teach totalitarian thinking; they teach knowledge in a selective way; they
teach (by example) infidelity, lying, how not to accept personal responsibility; that
everything outside or contrary to the official curriculum is wrong. Nothing has
changed much over the years, only that the tools our culture uses to manipulate

people are more efficient, and the values our culture proclaims are more dubious and questionable, because the same culture, in practice, acts against them.

As professionals, with some understanding of human nature, we have to be attentive to our students' needs, to what they value, what they admire; and using our imagination we can help them understand who they are and what is their virtue – not simply what their social usefulness might be. As art teachers we should be in the very moment where the culture is being born in individual and shared experience, where values are challenged and established. It demands from us an understanding of man, and knowledge about the culture we live in. By knowledge, I mean here everything that builds our wisdom. We have to be the first representative of the culture for our students and the trustworthy guardians of the virtue of the individual person. We are to preserve the infinity of the culture, not its closed (finished) forms, as well as the infinity of the person. The ways into that infinity are the ways through which we transcend what makes us closed and finished as persons, communities, nations, religious fellowships, political parties, groups of artists, and so on. Infinity is always *between*; infinity opens to us in relationship.

It seems to me there is and always will be an inherently irreconcilable difference between the interests of social institutions (closed forms of culture, the cultural establishment) and the legitimate work of the art teacher as I understand that work. The art teacher can be the first representative of the culture for the child in his/her experience of art. If we want to preserve the sense of infinity the child has as a natural tendency, and to preserve our culture against its own death inside the closed form of itself, we must be present where it is confronted – in the encountering of the other person. I would want to say that to be an art teacher is not necessarily the same thing as teaching the art subjects (music, art, dance). Institutions, social as well as cultural, prefer experts who protect them rather than reflective practitioners who continually question their assumptions and *raison d'être*. Institutions prefer their functionaries to suspend their personal responsibility in the interests of the institution; to exchange a personal for a social responsibility.

The responsibility of the artist is the responsibility of someone in their deepest, personal being.

Andrej Tarkowski, the Russian film director, says that the artist tries to destroy the stability society tends towards, because the artist tends towards infinity while society's aim is security.

Is it possible to be an artist and a teacher at the same time?

It is difficult, if not impossible, to separate radically the two passions of our one life: the passion for our making art and for our 'teaching' art. They are both immersed in the same style of our being in the world, of our being in face of (what we find as) the other.

Isn't it a kind of treason to be more responsible for your own art than for your student's hope? Many art teachers use their students as live material to fulfil their personal artistic ambitions and ideas rather than being with the other in their creative artistic process. It causes a dilemma in our practice. Can we separate our own artistic responsibility from that connected with our students' art?

I was talking about a certain tendency in our culture: that the institutions of education are required to reproduce the culture in its present form. But there is also another tendency to reproduction that lies at the root of the pedagogy of totalitarianism – the pedagogy, which, as Józef Tischner says, gives the educator the right to make himself the ideal model for his student.

Maybe someone has said to you at some time, 'Work on your own character, your moral life; perfect yourself and your art and when you are the right kind of person, the right kind of artist, you will be fit to become a teacher.' In due course you entered the profession. Perhaps you see yourself as a model for your students to emulate. As a consequence of such thinking you will feel free to impose your own vision, your own way of thinking, your own way of working in art, the style of your art, on your students. At the same time you will deprecate, in a clear or a hidden way, their vision, their way of thinking and seeing, their style of life and work, even their way of holding a brush.

Janusz Korczak used to repeat that it was the right of the child to be allowed to be themselves.

It is not easy to accept, in practice, the natural individuality of each particular child; his or her world, full of wonders.

If you make yourself the centre of your students' interests, then you set yourself up as an art 'master'. Maybe you are a perfect person. Perhaps you are an ideal artist. But, as Tischner says, there is surely a kind of megalomania in making the imitation (or reproduction) of the teacher a basic principle of education. Any disagreement is construed as an attack upon your dignity. And you start to be anxious; you are afraid to lose face, to compromise yourself in your students' eyes. Being with a student in an informal situation, in unstructured time and place, becomes a disaster.

An art teacher who understands his or her professional commitment as working with somebody's hope must not feel too responsible for the ideal image of themselves.

Tarkowski

I understand my task as revealing the truth about our common existence to people, in the way I see and understand it, because of my own experience.

(1991: 133)

Our task as art teachers is the same task that Tarkowski speaks of. It is the artist's responsibility extended to include giving the other the chance to own their own truth and to share their truth with us; to discover what is important to them. I am not sure whether artists are able to accept those truths that have been discovered by others and are different from those chosen by themselves. Maybe artists cannot be so tolerant. In his diary, the Polish writer Witold Gombrowicz has written that something an artist cannot stand is another artist nearby. As art teachers we have to stand other artists nearby constantly.

I do not think totalitarianism in education is a result of a teacher's bad will. It seems to me, rather, that it is sometimes the result of an excess of responsibility, the result of a feeling of responsibility in excess. The totalitarian teacher wants to control reality totally: 'I want to know everything about you. I want to know your thoughts. I must possess all your mysteries so as to use them in the educational process, so as to have them under my control.' Korczak, on the contrary, says that we do not possess a child.

What does it mean to indoctrinate in art education?

For Tarkowski, a work of art should express the idea of human freedom, but freedom in art is not a free-for-all, understood as the absence of rules or discipline. The rules and the discipline of art are different from those that are obligatory in our social life. An artist, for Tarkowski, must be responsible individually and personally to the rules of art, and those impose their own particular discipline.

To indoctrinate in art education means that a teacher is not able to suspend his own artistic ideas and ambitions in formulating tasks for his pupils, as well as in assessing their achievement. Sometimes an art teacher is 'so creative' that the work a student has started becomes, in the end, the teacher's work, and, while the teacher may well feel satisfied, the pupil does not recognize his or her own ideas in it at all. There are art teachers who want the art work of their students to be authentic and honest, but the last word must be theirs – as the 'master'.

My task is to provide the conditions, to set up a situation in which my students feel free while being fully present – even if they find it painful, and very often they do. But this is not the end of my obligation, the sum of my responsibilities. Freedom is a runway not a resting place. Freedom offers us a foretaste of infinity, a promise. Possibilities are infinite, but we have to make choices, decisions – and merely to be free is neither to choose nor to decide. Freedom is but the vestibule of the infinite. When the individual must choose, must come to a decision, this is the moment in which the rules governing this particular piece of work are being established. The question at the moment for me is: How can I help them deal with the horror of freedom? Then: How can I help them reflect upon the consequences of the choices they have made? In helping them with the horror, I do not take away their responsibility for responding to the freedom. In helping them reflect upon their choices I do not usurp their right, their responsibility, to choose for themselves.

'You can do it, dear friend, and the awe you feel is right, right for you. You are more than you know. I will not help you to respond, but I will not leave you. If you want to escape, that is your choice. Once the choice is made, you have taken the first step.'

My task, as I understand it, is teaching them vigilance: the ability to listen and to respond. If it is a dream, it must be a light dream, a kind of freedom. And hopefully *my* vigilance is able to put *them* on their guard. I am speaking of that vigilance that is a kind of tenderness or, rather, sensitiveness, a keenness, a readiness. To be tender does not mean to be sentimental. Sometimes I offer my students a way out, so they can escape for a moment if they need to. But I try to make it clear that this is really only an emergency exit. They cannot, in the end, avoid taking responsibility. They have to manage both freedom and rule. I think an art teacher should not be too responsible for the art work of her/his students.

Our professional duty is also to show what we appreciate and value in the culture. Knowing how things are selected as valuable by our culture, I doubt if being faithful to the values of the culture is always to be truly responsible in the way I have been speaking about. What should an art teacher do if those truths and values discovered individually by his/her students are not on the list of cultural treasures, and those which can be found there do not find confirmation in the students' experience? An irresponsible policeman of culture will say: 'You have got a right to your personal, private history of art.'

To indoctrinate in art education means also to present content selected by the culture as the only valuable content, at the same time denying the students real contact with works of art, either by simply talking about a picture or presenting a reproduction. The people we work with have to be given a chance to come by the truth, the force in art, in an intimate, subjective way – to see how something manifests or reveals itself between them and the form of art they face. An irresponsible guardian of culture will say: 'You have a right to an unofficial, informal and even historically unaccepted interpretation of the art you experience and the culture you live in.'

The student teachers and cultural animators I have been working with say that beauty demands two contradictory actions: to share the joy, to share the experience, to tell someone we trust about it, but also to keep it a secret, to be careful not to tarnish its mysterious character. The beautiful tends to disappear as we speak about it. At the same time it fills us with such power that we feel we must share it, shout it out, sing about it. We want to give testimony, to bear witness. Is it really possible to share it? Being with the other in art education means sharing the most intimate knowledge – of this one moment that increases our store of wisdom: this knowledge that one can only tell someone in confidence. You confide a secret; the other confides a secret in you. Such knowledge has the power to rebuild us – rebuild our hope as well as our mode of perception – completely, not just to change the way we think or increase our store of information.

In my opinion, our vocation as art teachers is first of all to be vigilant witnesses: to be present to those truths that are uncovered individually by our students in subjectively important experiences. Our work also means to take care of the authenticity of our own life, of our own being, of the testimony we ourselves give, and of the quality of our being with the other. Facing infinity is an awesome experience. Such an experience needs our presence, our vigilance, our responsiveness. Our work is to build these possibilities in the lives of our students, and the only way to do so is to be with them, to join them in the world between, 'in the twilight'.

But first of all we ourselves have to be present. So often we are lost in the past history of objects (sometimes they are called art objects), or we become frightened of the future because we fear the destruction of what we ourselves value. Such an anxiety betrays our own lack of faith in what we claim are lasting values. It is probably true that art provokes individual revolutions. It is born in response to reality. Gombrowicz used to say that reality is something that hurts, something that resists us. A real human being is somebody who feels pain.

Art is not simply the making of a finished (finite) artefact. The cultural heritage is not merely a collection of finished (finite) artefacts. Art has to be perceived. The act of reception consummates the artistic act. A gallery full of pictures is only potentially an art gallery. To free the bird there must be someone who opens the cage. Each work is at the same time an end and a beginning. Perhaps this is what distinguishes the arts from ordinary language – which so easily ceases to be contemporary. Art lives in perception and when it lives it can only be contemporary. No matter when it was originally made, it is 'finished' anew in every act of reception. A work of art is a potentiality.

'Here you are!' What does it mean to present, to be present?

Janusz Korczak speaks of the child's right to the present day.

> Many of us seem to be thinking: 'A child is not an artist – he/she will be. A child doesn't know art – he/she will know art. A child cannot do art – he/she will do art.' 'Mark, you are almost!'
> 'I wait and wait. When will my time come?'

So often we treat children as half-beings – as unfinished people. Your time is always *now*, at this very moment, even though your time of being is sometimes also a time of waiting. And you are none the worse for not being an adult. Your *now* is important, and if being an adult means for some people being finished, you had better stay a child. In the Gospels, Jesus says, 'Be like children'. Maybe he is saying, 'Be unfinished: take care of your infinity.'

The problem of 'presentness'. What does it mean for art education? I like the English expression, 'Here you are!' We do not have a similar form of words in Polish. When I say this, giving you, for example, a cup of tea, I feel you are here, as I am also. I feel our common presence. Here and now.

Tibetan sand mandala

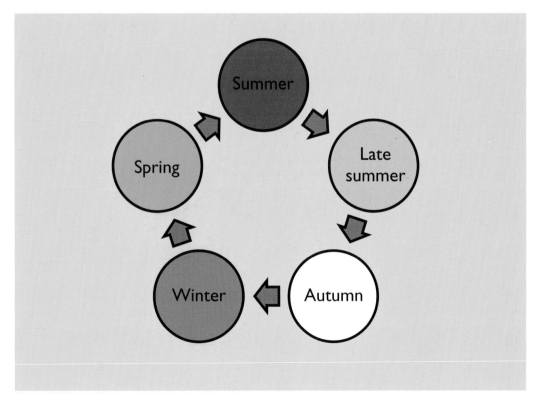

Figure 2.2 Cycle of the seasons

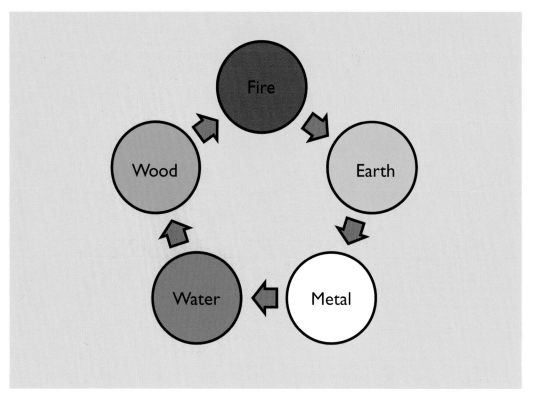

Figure 2.3 The *Sheng* cycle

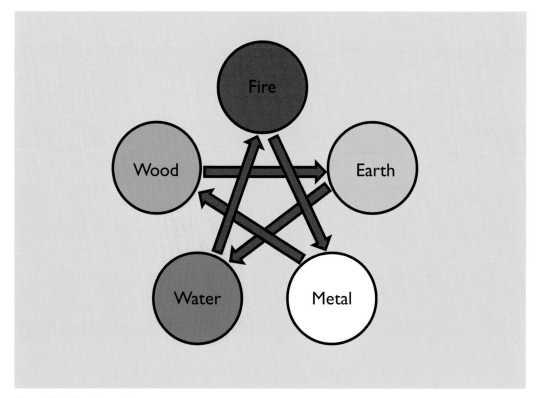

Figure 2.4 The *Ke* cycle

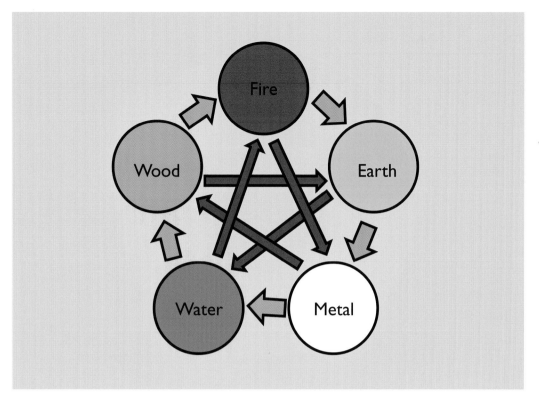

Figure 2.5 *Sheng* and *Ke* cycles

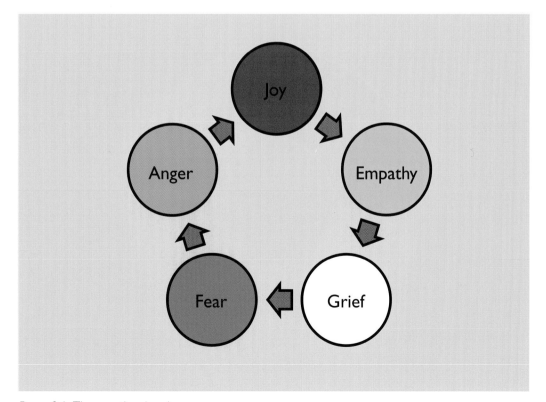

Figure 2.6 The emotional cycle

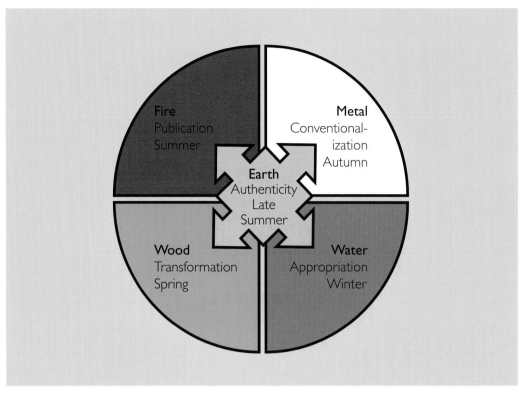

Figure 3.2 The Syncretic Model (original)

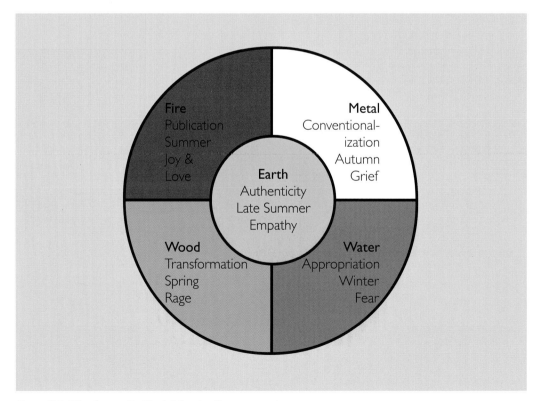

Figure 3.3 The Syncretic Model (revised)

According to Józef Tischner, mature hope is not the hope that loses itself in dreams and recollections, which overrates the past or the future. A mature hope allows a profound experience of actual reality (of what is now and here).

If we want to be now, we have to be prepared to 'kill our memory'. By this I mean we have to be able to look at the present moment innocently, free from a sense of obligation, without expectations, without making plans and predictions. We should find value in the way the world surprises us. You can respond sincerely to your reality only if you can be present in it. Vigilant presentness is open to grace. Grace is a gift that is not at my disposal. Grace is a 'present': something addressed precisely and uniquely to me, something delivered correctly to me, like a properly addressed letter.

So often we understand our responsibility as an opportunity to possess a world. When I encounter another person in the present, I do not want to take responsibility for them, or for their world. I can be responsible only in the sense that I can be vigilant enough to respond to what is given freely, making no demands, entertaining no expectations for myself. If you believe that the world sometimes comes to you as an act of grace, you must expect to be surprised. Being responsible in such circumstances cannot constrain you. Responding to what surprises you makes you present (forms bonds between you and with what happens now and here).

I understand the creative process in art not as a plan for changing the world but as an ongoing dialogue, a reciprocal relation between two separate and different states of being. Carving a piece of wood is like dancing with the other. Sculpting in stone or touching a tree is like making love. If you are not actually in love, this is a kind of prostitution. The creative process in art is always a shared creative act, and it starts with acceptance: it is wonderful that you are. It is wonderful that you are different. I allow you to be. I will respond to you in acts of love to let you know yourself, to know myself, and maybe the mystery of our being will open for us.

Similarly, being with the other can be an art; two separate, different worlds full of wonders and sharing the hope of an ideal love – an ideal communion, the miracle of communion. Janusz Korczak says we should get to know the child so as not to make too many mistakes. There must be mistakes. But we shouldn't worry. The child will correct them with his/her astonishing vigilance, if we have not already destroyed the huge capacity they have for self-preservation.

A reciprocal election

Talking about their aesthetic experiences, my students said that experience of the beautiful took them into another world – a sacred world of a different time, into a space of enduring presence. They did not wish to speak of the different 'phases' or 'stages' in aesthetic experience. They did not wish to use the words we use to speak of our usual experience of time. Similarly, Edmund Leach and Mircea Eliade write of the experience of sacred space and time.

The experience of beauty is a reciprocal election. One of my students, describing his experience of beauty, told a story about a stone. There were hundreds of stones in a hill of stones, but he chose one particular stone as beautiful. He had not seen all of them, but, having seen this stone, he stopped seeking. He said that the stone had chosen him.

In our present day experience of the other, something very important has broken down. We are afraid of the other, afraid of 'each' other. We do not trust the other any more. As Tischner says, 'We live in a space tainted by treason', perceiving the other as someone who can betray. Only someone or something I have placed my trust in, confided my hope to, can betray me. Treason makes it impossible for someone ever again to trust or confide in another person. After such an experience, we place every-one under the shadow of suspicion. We begin with suspicion and not with faith. We are afraid to face the presence of the other.

I was recently talking with a ten-year-old boy about a family of dogs living close by. Jacek told me that what makes them all different from each other are their levels of anxiety. He said that this was on account of their different experiences. The greater their experience (father and mother dogs) the more their anxiety. The puppy is not afraid at all. We need each other. However, afraid of betrayal, we subject others to some kind of formula that we hope may protect us. We look not to the individual person but to some contract, some artificial structure to protect us, to guarantee his/her fidelity. Sometimes we establish bans and orders and we put all our energy into protecting that system.

What does it mean to be responsible for the other?

Sometimes I wonder why children like so much to play with adults who are not their parents. Could it be that parents easily become too weighed down by the burden of their 'responsibility', by their anxiety for their child to do well, to find success, to be safe?

Janusz Korczak wrote that a child had a right to die. He also said that sometimes we had a tendency to tear a child away from life in our anxiety that death might tear the child away from us. How savage a reply to this thought was the answer of the reality that Korczak had to face later in his life.

The loss of a possession is always painful. But a child, the other, as we have seen, should be no-one's 'possession'. How does Józef Tischner understand our responsi-bility for others? Responsibility, he says, is our enduring presence, one with another. Responsibility is an aspect of human faithfulness. It is not only in our shared memo-ries that our faith rests; it always rests in our shared hopes.

The supreme experience of hope and of faithfulness is when two people commit themselves to each other, intimately, heroically; when someone has entrusted, charged, confided, committed to me their hope and all of themselves is held in this hope (the essence of their existence, the mystery of their life), making me their human support, and I have committed myself to them, making them my human support. In such circumstances, as Tischner says, being responsible for someone's hope means being responsible for their dignity as a human being. Janusz Korczak was told he could leave his orphaned pupils in the German Fascist's ghetto and be helped to escape – an offer he did not accept. His death in Auschwitz was such an act of heroic responsibility and faithfulness.

Malcolm writes:

In the next two chapters we return to the Syncretic Model to explore its application in the fields of arts education and arts therapy. The big issue of the moment for arts therapists is public credibility. Serious efforts are being made to establish a research centre capable of generating, among other things, the 'evidence base' the profession is deemed to need. The whole field of therapy and psychological counselling is under siege at the moment from authorities looking to impose codes of practice that are seen by practitioners as threatening to the philosophy and integrity of their profession. Here again, as with education, there is a growing sense of embattled positions being taken between dedicated professionals on the one hand and, on the other, the authorities representing the wider society on whose sanction and support they depend. Jola's paper speaks to them as well as to creative arts practitioners. Before moving on, I want to quote from an unsolicited email written to Jola by one of her culture animation students following the latest research camp. These camps take place every year and are residential weeks 'in the field' – often quite literally, set in some remote spot. Sometimes students work alongside schoolchildren or adults from the local community; sometimes they focus more exclusively on this unique opportunity for sustained creative work on their own account. The camp in question took place on an isolated beach beside the Baltic Sea in September 2010. The student writes:

> *Thank you for*
>
> - *your gift of seeing;*
> - *making it possible to hear the roar of the waves in our ears in September;*
> - *a sea of possibilities;*
> - *the story of Gilgamesh;*
> - *conversations opening eyes and souls;*
> - *help in carrying stones;*
> - *waking up our imaginations;*
> - *good advice and wonderful ideas;*
> - *the opportunity to work on our own ideas;*
> - *new perspectives of seeing;*
> - *warm words of encouragement for our work.*

8   A note on creativity

Keith Sawyer's recent book, *Explaining Creativity*, is a functional take on creativity as a useful and trainable personal asset in today's entrepreneurial world. Despite their genuine concern for wisdom and trusteeship, Craft and her colleagues seem rather shy of looking radically to shift the grounds of the creativity debate. Lewis Hyde on the other hand, in his book *The Gift*, celebrates the creative human impulse of 'gift exchange'. For Hyde, the arts illustrate the universal, sacred or 'gifted' character of human creativity, an idea that closely mirrors this book's concern with its cognitive character, and with the artist's pursuit of enlightenment and un-concealment.

> But it is more salutary for thinking to wander in estrangement than to establish itself in the comprehensible.
>
> Martin Heidegger (quoted by Veronique M. Foti, *Heidegger and the Poets*)

Creativity and the science of innovation

Early in his book *Explaining Creativity: The Science of Human Innovation* (2006), Keith Sawyer sets out to dispose of what he calls the 'myths' that have grown up around the notion of creativity and provide a 'fully scientific' explanation with which to replace them. He is a collaborator and follower of Mihaly Csikzentmihayli – an equally firm advocate of a multi-disciplinary 'systems' approach to the subject of creativity.

In brief, Csikzentmihayli sees creativity arising within a system comprising the personality of the individual, the domain or discipline in question, and the field of its application or practice. This sociocultural model is preferred to the traditional approach concentrating exclusively on the psychology of creative persons, on what makes a person or personality creative. He acknowledges the central importance of individual psychology but refuses to give it exclusive status, seeing it operating within a powerful, sociocultural matrix, as one element in an integrated system. Sawyer is at one with his mentor in preferring an interdisciplinary approach involving psychologists, sociologists, anthropologists and historians.

Sawyer defines creativity (2006: 33) as 'the emergence of something novel and appropriate, from a person, a group, or a society'. He claims that by studying creativity 'scientifically', he will be able to explain 'how creativity really works'. He proposes two fields in which creativity operates: the arts and what he calls 'the everyday', where the everyday seems to mean business and science. He aims 'to move beyond creativity myths and to develop a science of human innovation'. I shall take issue with Sawyer's attachment to scientific certainty, and with creativity understood as a mental technique to be perfected rather than as a natural force to be watched and waited upon, as a 'gift'. That said, the Syncretic Model, like Csikzentmihayli's model, functions as a multifaceted, integrated system, and there are clear connections between what we understand by the Metal and Water phases and his notion of domain; and by the Wood and Fire phases and what he intends by field.

'The science of human innovation' seems to mean understanding or theorizing the *mechanics* of innovation: so it comes as no surprise to find Sawyer concluding his book with a chapter entitled 'How to Be More Creative'. It seems that the science of human innovation is to be very much an applied science, an acquired technique. It will be about getting better at creativity. The better your technique the more creative you will be. Creativity = productivity. Sawyer joins many another creativity expert in the field of self-help, e.g. the 'lateral thinking' school of Edward de Bono. Sawyer's first advice to the would-be-more creative person is to abandon the false thinking embedded in the 'myths'. Here are some of the myths he wishes to challenge:

Only special geniuses are creative.
Creativity is only found in the arts.
Creativity is only found in crazy people.
Creativity is fun (he prefers the idea of creativity as a hard slog).
Creativity is a burst of inspiration.
Creativity is an individual trait.
Creativity is a rejection of convention.
Creativity is for everyone.

From what we have been saying, it must be clear that some of his targets are ours also. But there are key points of disagreement. Our argument essentially favours the 'myth' that everyone is creative, and comes pretty close to endorsing the Archimedian principle of the burst of inspiration. We are perhaps less convinced by the efficacy of the hard slog than Sawyer is, but, as we have already observed, Tusa's artists all seem to be committed to hard work and to practise their art habitually. By way of replacing the myths with 'scientific' truths, Sawyer offers his own 'sociocultural advice for creativity':

Choose a domain that's right for you.
Choose a field that's right for you.
Turn your gaze outward instead of inward.
Market yourself.
Don't try to become creative in general: focus on one domain.
Be intrinsically motivated.
Don't get comfortable.
Balance out your personality.
Look for the most pressing problems facing the domain.
Collaborate.
Don't worry about who gets the credit.
Use creative work habits (e.g. work hard, multi-task, take time off).
Be confident and take risks.

Towards the end of his book, Sawyer offers a mild recantation, thereby demonstrating a piece of advice he didn't give, but might have done: 'Don't be too dogmatic'. He reasons with himself that not all of the myths might be so bad after all. Maybe a bit of what he calls 'belief' (as against science) wouldn't hurt. He admits to being a back-slider himself sometimes.

Why do I cite this book? Firstly, because it is representative of much of the material coming out of creativity studies and research departments now – we need to have the measure of this sort of thing in order to position ourselves somewhere else, as we must do if we are persuaded, as I am for example, by Lewis Hyde's arguments on the subject (more of which later). Secondly, the strong endorsement of Sawyer's book by Csikzentmihayli must give us pause for thought. Is the sociocultural approach a real advance on the myths Sawyer indicts? Are the myths the enemy and is science what is called for to deliver the answer as to 'how creativity really works'? I suppose neuro-science might. I clearly endorse the principle of the 'systems' approach, but our system is a richer, more complex, more open-ended one than that proposed by either Csikzentmihayli or Sawyer. We make much in our own advocacy of the *dynamic relationship* between the Five Elements or phases. We characterize their distinguishing features as separate and independent systems of their own, but also draw attention to the interrelated workings of the larger system (e.g. the workings of the *Sheng* and the *Ke* cycles). On our account here, human creativity includes the idea of innovation but sets generative thought within a wider cognitive/affective system that speaks to the whole of human life as the human brain's expression of nature's cycle of creativities, of the Five Phases of Change. We tend to agree with the point made earlier by Joseph A. Goguan that the bulk of creative processing probably occurs beyond or below the level of consciousness. The really interesting questions, then, become how to nourish and control it.

Creativity, wisdom and trusteeship

Sawyer's account of creativity as 'the science of human invention', and his advice on making oneself more creative, would, in some ways, seem to represent just the emphasis from which the authors of the book *Creativity, Wisdom and Trusteeship* (2008), referred to in my Introduction, might wish to distance themselves. Admittedly, Craft *et al.* are focused upon the future of education, but they all seem agreed that the prevailing dominance of market theory not only within Western societies but increasingly across the developing world as globalization takes command, needs to be resisted. Craft is deeply concerned about the cultural and ethical damage being done by what she calls the 'blind' promotion of the market-based idea of creativity as 'profitable innovation'. She points out the specifically Western flavour of the individualistic and self-assertive character of market values that underpin the now-dominant view of creativity, and contrasts these values with those more typical of the East, which she describes as more 'inward' and 'spiritual', where 'creativity involves a state of personal fulfilment, a connection to a primordial realm, or the expression of an inner essence or ultimate reality'. (Craft is here quoting from Lubart, 1999). She complains that the Western capitalist model might be 'inappropriately assertive over other values' and asks how we are to use our creativity wisely and 'who are the trustees of generative thought in a globalized world?' She assesses the cultural impact of 'market-hinged' creativity, and, because of its dismissal of continuity, tradition and what she calls 'frugality', sees its possible connection with intercultural conflict and terrorism. The job of teachers, in her view, with respect to creativity, is to 'nurture wisdom and an orientation towards responsible stewardship, or trusteeship, of ideas'. Craft favours a 'multiple perspective' account of creativity.

Despite her strong concerns, however, Craft seems uninterested in rethinking the notion of creativity itself. Rather than do so, she counsels increased awareness of the down side of market creativity, and hopes to see steps taken to ameliorate the worst of its cultural and ethical ramifications. Creativity (as 'generative thought') seems to find its legitimate expression in projects like Gardner's Good Work Project and Sternberg's WICS (Wisdom, Intelligence and Creativity Synthetized) Project. Sternberg's project 'attempts to show how successful leadership involves the synthesis of three qualities: 'wisdom, intelligence and creativity'. For Sternberg, good schooling is about developing 'these three attributes working together' – it does not just teach facts. According to the Sternberg model, successful intelligence is defined as 'one's ability to attain one's goals in life'. In other words, his idea of the creativity project is still pretty strongly pragmatic or technical, and his own preference is for teaching problem-solving techniques. Wisdom comes into the equation alongside intelligence and creativity as balancing one's personal 'interests' with those of others. The final purpose of the project remains 'to adapt, to shape and select environments', presumably, as he has already said, 'to attain one's goals in life'.

Gardner's project began as a joint study with his colleague Mihaly Csikszentmihalyi to investigate whether it was possible for an individual to be 'both creative and humane'. Since its inauguration, the project has changed its focus and is now called the Good Work Project, and is a study of the creative performance 'of high-level professionals'. Gardner seems to be looking for ways of reconciling job satisfaction among high achievers with working ethically and responsibly – in other words, the reconciliation of notoriously contrary impulses; namely, the desire for profits, personal and corporate, and the wish to behave decently to others. At a time, according to Gardner, that has seen the decline in public life of significant figures giving a moral lead to the country – what he calls the loss of the 'traditional trustee figure' – he would like to see a renewal of the trustee spirit 'among quality people running for top positions'. So the public need is clear: good work must mean profitable work but also work that somehow passes the ethical test. Gardner and his team are promoting 'education for trusteeship'. Meanwhile, there is no evidence of radical rethinking about creativity here either.

For fellow editor Guy Claxton, whereas creativity and wisdom might be very similar in their cognitive aspects, 'wisdom has moral, motivational and social aspects with which creativity does not concern itself'. Creativity, writes Claxton, is primarily a matter of pragmatics rather than morals. Innovation is again the defining idea. Like Craft and Gardner, Claxton counsels wisdom to soften the worst effects of market creativity: he proposes the idea that wisdom might constitute 'advanced creativity' – a spiritual form presumably superior to its other, more workaday, varieties.

Whilst displaying serious concerns over the crisis of values now plaguing Western society generally and Western education in particular, and seeing as at least partly responsible the relentless pursuit of creativity as profitable innovation in the market-place, the authors of *Creativity, Wisdom and Trusteeship* are not, it seems, ready to reject market creativity altogether as inherently corrupting and as an impaired and inadequate reading, preferring instead to look for ways of softening its impact, limiting the damage it does and trying to redress the balance through the reconciliation of more spiritual concerns (wisdom and trusteeship) to pragmatic ends ('the ability to attain one's goals in life'). In my Introduction I confessed to a strong sense of kinship with the authors and I am indeed grateful to them for their commitment to exposing the damaging effects of the new, market-driven education policies all around the world, systematically promoting the training of 'creative' marketeers, all of which reminds me of the first frenzy for creativity in schools prompted in the USA by the launch, on 4 October 1957, of the Russian *Sputnik*. But I am disappointed, in the end, to find too little to choose between their accounts of creativity and that of Sawyer, already discussed.

To oversimplify, I do not think the problems they have identified will be resolved by the addition of yet another subject to the school curriculum, called, perhaps, Advanced Creativity or Comparative Wisdom Studies. Creativity – creativity proper, that is – has to determine the whole *modus operandi* of a school – as it did at A. S. Neil's Summerhill, alluded to admiringly by Guy Claxton in his chapter. And this, of course, is where I see the authors providing me with the opportunity I need for my own project. Craft discovered what she calls two 'blind spots' in the way we tend to think about creativity in the classroom, which she then sets out to explore and redress in her own paper. I see yet another one. Sawyer in his book distinguishes two realms of creativity – the arts world and the business world. What is missing from the book by Craft *et al.* is the dimension of the creative arts, more particularly the idea of art as wisdom and trusteeship. When Craft writes about her understanding of the Chinese 'contemplative' tradition, she comes close to what I mean and closer to the position I take in this book.

In a way, what is missing from this otherwise interesting book is Lewis Hyde's account of 'how creativity transforms the world' – including the personal world of the individual. Hyde makes great play of the arts. His book, *The Gift*, is a surprising omission by Craft *et al.* – although having been around since 1983, it didn't appear in Great Britian until 2006. For Hyde, the arts belong to the culture of gift exchange rather than the marketplace, to the realm of *Eros* rather than *Logos*. Hyde is interested in what he calls 'an economy of the creative spirit'. What is missing from Craft *et al.* is the lived, at root unconscious, activity of the creative mind, rather than a calculated strategy for improving one's chances in a world of sales executives. We are talking about a different quality of experience, an experience situated in the inner, imaginative and feeling world of the subject, in the contemplating soul rather than in the calculating brain. Even Claxton seems wary of the intelligence of feeling when he describes empathy and compassion as 'kinds of objectivity'. None of these authors adequately considers the likely contribution of market creativity to what the philosopher R. G. Collingwood calls 'the corruption of consciousness'. When Craft closes her paper asking whether there might not be some 'profoundly humane framework' within which creativity could be stimulated and celebrated, I want to thank her for her question and boldly offer the Syncretic Model.

Hyde's discussion of the tension between the values of the marketplace and our more tender, more generous human impulses of creativity, is pivotal for the model of creativity being offered in my book. We have already alluded to him several times and we should now briefly glance at his basic proposition. He opens his book with a quotation from Joseph Conrad: 'The artist appeals to that part of our being…which is a gift and not an acquisition – and, therefore, more permanently enduring.' Is this so very different from the position taken by the neuroscientists in Chapter 5?

Hyde describes himself as a sort of 'scholar without institution'. When he wrote his book he was trying to make his way as a poet and translator. He sees the dilemma of the creative artist in the contemporary world thus:

> Every modern artist who has chosen to labour with a gift must sooner or later wonder how he or she is to survive in a society dominated by market exchange.

And if the fruits of a gift are gifts themselves, how is the artist to nourish himself, spiritually as well as materially, in an age whose values and whose commerce consists almost exclusively in the purchase and sale of commodities.

(1983: xv)

A gift, says Hyde, 'is a thing we do not get by our own efforts. We cannot buy it; we cannot acquire it through an act of will. It is bestowed upon us.' He uses the idea of the 'gift' to cover both what we usually mean when we speak of an artist's (anyone's) 'giftedness' – their 'talent' – and the gift as something given. It is the given talent in Sen's formula: talent + opportunity = capability; it is also what cannot be bargained for. He reminds us that we speak of both the artist's inspiration and their creative output as 'gifts'. He means here the sense the artist has of being in receipt of his idea and the work that embodies it: that somehow it is not merely the fruit of her/his labours, the reward of talent and its dutiful application, but that the germ of the work's truth and originality has arrived fully formed as a gift from beyond the conscious, industrious and responsible self. Without such a sense of being 'gifted', there can be no creativity; simply hard work, ingenuity and applied imagination – and where art is concerned, none of these is quite sufficient. When *poiesis* deserts us, we cannot expect to be able to make do with *techne* instead.

Traditionally, creative inspiration has been attributed to some form of divine intervention – the muses, the gods, are held responsible. It is a well-documented experience, and has been variously called a vision, a revelation, an epiphany. It is invariably accompanied by a sense of the 'uncanny' (with its etymological roots in knowing, conning and cunning). Doubtless the now familiar devices of lateral thinking and brainstorming, complemented more recently by corporate training courses to promote leadership, team-bonding, partnering and risk-taking, can all help prepare the mind for the disclosure it must finally make for itself, the moment of recognition described by Gadamer in his story of the *tessera hospitalis*. But, against all that, I want to insist upon the notion of 'bestowal' and its moral as well as practical implications.

If Hyde is right and creativity is a form of bestowal – not simply a talent we are expected to invest but a capability we have for engendering and recognizing the new in whatever sphere we happen to be expert – then, on his understanding, the rules of the gift apply. What we have been saying in this book is that we are all invested with the capacity for creative perception – it is a feature of the brain and one of the tricks intelligence is continually playing on us. Bestowings, in this context, are not a once-in-a-lifetime experience, like receiving the Nobel Prize for literature. They are certainly not to be had for the asking – nor for the brainstorming. They tumble about us continuously, as meteors shower in the heavens. It's the way cognition works, it's what our brains do when they are not over-exposed to the light of day or switched to auto-pilot. The sense we have of creativity's being a gift derives from two factors: (a) the delay and sense of disconnection experienced between conscious deliberation and the moment of insight, and (b) the suddenness and surprise – even drama, as in 'blinding flash' – of its arrival. It would seem that, appearances to the contrary, the default condition of the brain is vigilance. Where art is concerned, Hyde maintains that without this 'uncanny' moment there can be no way forward for the maker and no fulfilment for the reader or viewer. These moments are radically transformative (Wood).

> The art that matters to us – which moves the heart or revives the soul, or delights the senses, or offers courage for living, however we choose to describe the experience – that work is received by us as a gift is received. Even if we have paid a fee at the door of the museum or concert hall, when we are touched by a work of art something comes to us which has nothing to do with the price.
>
> (ibid.: xiv)

And for what we have so received we thankfully put our hands together – rather than merely in our pockets. It is as if we are not free to trade our gifts. Hyde describes 'gift exchange' as continuous: the gift is never used up and somehow remains in circulation. This is part of the mystery of 'art proper', as understood by Collingwood: that it is never used up, that it never exhausts the desire it provokes but, like Shakespeare's Cleopatra, keeps us perpetually subject to its charm, vulnerable to its appeal and in pursuit of its mystery.

> We may not have the power to profess our gifts [note he doesn't say we have no gifts to profess] as the artist does, and yet we come to recognise, and in a sense to receive, the endowments of our being through the agency of his creation. We feel fortunate, even redeemed.
>
> (ibid.: xiv)

The urge to creativity proper is the dark life-hunger itself: is the cyclical rhythm of the waxing and waning of the life-force deep within each one of us. It occurs as naturally and as continuously as the cycle of the seasons, and, I believe, is actually determined for us and influenced in some significant measure by that cycle. In which case our task, as inveterate creatives, is to attune ourselves to nature's cycle of change and adapt our own energies to it. Like the parable of the lilies, we simply have to wait upon their being. But we do have to wait. We are required to watch. It won't do to be fussing about on fools' errands and taking too much heed of the morrow. Where we have a project, it might help to use the winter months, quite literally, to muse and vegetate, to write wanderingly and gather ideas, and then, with the onset of spring, to catch the surge and set sail. 'There is a time,' says the Ecclesiastes prophet, and Shakespeare says so too. Why should we not believe them? And even if you do choose not to wait for *Kairos* (qualitative time, the opportune moment, deep time, a time in between) and stick with *Chronos*, each creative brain project must be allowed to follow its distinctive emotional and energetic cycle and will benefit from being managed on the model of the Five Elements with its counter-rhythms of the *Sheng* (nourishing) and the *Ke* (challenging).

As is evident from the testimony of some of the artists interviewed by John Tusa (see Chapter 6), arts colleges and conservatoires are not always the seed-beds of creativity proper, any more than professional artists are always themselves 'creative' in the sense for which I argue in this chapter. We need 'creative artists proper' in schools and as therapists not because they somehow have mastered the techniques of lateral thinking, but because they are intimates of that realm of the uncanny, of the inspirational, the epiphanic moment; because they operate within the economy of the creative spirit and know no other way but the way of the gift. We need them in our schools, and communities and health centres, for the gifts they bring – and for the opportunity they give others to use their hands and voices to express heartfelt gratitude and love, feeling fortunate, 'even redeemed', perhaps blessed (Fire).

> The daily commerce of our lives – 'sugar for sugar and salt for salt,' as the blues singers say – proceeds at its own constant level, but a gift revives the soul. When we are moved by art we are grateful that the artist lived, grateful that he labored in the service of his gifts.
>
> (ibid.: xv)

Postscript

The Syncretic Model maps the habit of art – when it has an expressive mission rather than merely representing change. It shows the partnership between culture and nature, between the individual psyche and the collective soul, between *poiesis* and *techne*, between hand and brain. It is neither fatalistic nor deterministic: it is (as is the case with Chinese philosophy generally) about partnership, about working with, rather than despite, the forces of nature: the given. Plato's husbandman does this. Teachers, therapists and artists do this if they know what's good for them. Thinking of Amartya Sen's formula for human capability: talent + opportunity = capability, the artist has to be her own opportunist, capable of receiving opportunities as gifts and of recognizing them when they come along, but of leaving no stone unturned where opportunities might just be lurking. Adapting Donne: 'Send not to know for whom the opportunity knocks; it knocks for thee.' The derivation of the word 'opportunity' is very interesting for us. The *Shorter Oxford English Dictionary* gives the following definition:

> L. *opportunus* (orig. of wind) driving towards the harbour, (hence) seasonable (cf. *Portunus* protecting god of harbours), f. Ob- 1 + *portus* harbour, PORT sb.

With Sen's formula in mind, I think it would be perfectly reasonable to align the central phase of Earth with what Sen calls talent (and Hyde might call gift), whilst thinking of the other four phases as 'opportunities'. Talent + opportunity = change. The force we have spoken of as characteristic at each phase of the creative cycle seems beautifully captured here in the image of the friendly breeze that brings the ship safe to harbour. Think of Ithaca. The Syncretic Model as a systems model of change (capability) marries talent with opportunity.

The Syncretic Model also reconciles the twin principles of *techne* and *poiesis*. *Poiesis* is Wood and Fire, *techne* is Metal and Water. *Poiesis* is yang; *techne* is yin. The Syncretic Model reconciles stability and motion in the single principle of change. Earth, of course, combines them both.

For Hyde, *Eros* is the principal force at work in the gift economy and is distinguished from *Logos* (the force of the market). *Eros* animates Gablik's call for the re-enchantment of art: to which we might want to add the re-enchantment of education, of therapy – of creativity itself.

9 Cultivating the arts in education

This chapter looks at some of the practical implications of the Syncretic Model for teaching the arts in schools. It begins by identifying Plato's notion of education as 'illumination' and Aristotle's idea of the 'habit of art' as principles central to the project of the book. It then provides a phase-by-phase account of the arts curriculum with accompanying participatory pedagogy, giving a practical account of the arts teacher's partnering of the student's creative process. The chapter concludes with an assessment of the emotional dimension of the partnership of co-creation.

> There is no writing of mine about these matters, nor will there ever be one. For this knowledge is not something that can be put into words like other sciences; but after long-continued intercourse between teacher and pupil, in joint pursuit of a subject, suddenly, like light flashing forth when a fire is kindled, it is born in the soul and straightway nourishes itself.
>
> Plato, *Seventh Epistle*, Section 341

Plato and illumination; Aristotle and repetition

In January 2010, I presented the Syncretic Model at a symposium of arts teachers in Athens, at the invitation of my friend Hari Alexaki. Towards the end of the conference, following a workshop, I was in conversation with Magda, an art teacher with a degree in psychology. She asked me if I knew Plato's *Epistle VII* ('To the Friends and Followers of Dion'), because she was sure it would appeal to me. Once home, I managed to track down a copy, translated and with initial notes by Glenn R. Morrow (1962). The book arrived – exactly on cue where the writing was concerned. Wherever my own thoughts had been leading me, I was grateful to find Plato's short digression on the theory of knowledge. Plato's ideas on education as 'illumination', I have to say, came as something of a surprise. It was a shock to find him apparently arguing against over-reliance on argument, reasoning and the primacy of discursive language in approaching 'last things'. Plato, in his letter, insists that serious learning can never be simply a business transaction between one who knows and one who doesn't. All true learning, he argues, occurs as a moment (a gift) of insight or illumination in the mind of the learner – of fusion between the learner's capacity and temperamental inclination to know, and what presents itself in their *experience* to be known. Such a moment can be strategically anticipated and even, to some degree, prepared for (e.g. through the dialectical encounter between student and teacher), but in the end it is something that the learner achieves for themselves, and thereafter – and this is the most surprising thought to me – *it nourishes itself.*

The Syncretic Model is a metaphor of just such self-nourishing. My preoccupation in the early part of this book has been with the role of the teacher as participant in response to this spontaneous impulse of self-sustaining energy. Perhaps, like the arts therapist's, the arts teacher's role amounts to trouble-shooting more than anything else. Where self-nourishing seems to break down, enter the teacher and the therapist: the teacher to focus on artistic problems, the therapist to focus on expressive ones. As part of the argument, Plato makes clear what he calls 'the limits of verbal reasoning' in the acquisition of true understanding. At best, he claims, words, illustrations, models and diagrams can take us only so far in the pursuit of knowledge, whilst true knowledge always and only occurs as revelation, as a profound apprehension pervading body, mind and spirit: it is a metaphysical and aesthetic transaction rather than a purely logical one.

Implicit in such a view of schooling and learning lies the total rejection of what John Cheever calls 'the ceremonies of marketing' (our target in the preceding chapter on creativity). Morrow's commentary – it is his 1962 edition I have been reading – on Plato's dialectical theory is, itself, illuminating, and I take the liberty here of quoting from it at length.

> But dialectic at its best is only preparation of the mind for an 'illumination' (*eklampsis*). Without this experience all preceding labour is in vain; for the knowledge of the ti – or as it is now put, the knowledge of virtue and vice, of justice and all other forms of beauty – will not be attained. The meaning of the doctrine of illumination is not necessarily to be found in mystical insight. It was the problems of the teacher that were probably in the forefront of Plato's attention here. No thought is neatly transferable from one mind to another. Every acquisition of knowledge by a pupil comes as a result of his own effort, and culminates in an insight whereby the preceding labour suddenly assumes significance, and he 'sees the subject', as we say. And real knowledge is easily distinguished from 'language behaviour' ... by the fact that it feeds itself, to use Plato's own phrase. What Plato calls illumination is essential in all real learning; but it is especially important in the apprehension of ultimate realities (i.e. of 'the sacred').

Here the learner must be something of a mystic; his soul (Plato is talking about 'the soul's quest for the Good') must possess more than quickness of grasp and tenacity of memory; it must be akin to the object, because of some divine quality which it possesses… Such a vision of absolute reality cannot be communicated in words like other knowledge. It must be acquired by the individual himself, and the task of the teacher is limited to finding well constituted natures, and giving them the preliminary dialectical preparation for the vision.

(1962: 77)

We have already touched upon the idea of the reader 'inscribing' themselves in the text they are reading. I think we have that notion again here, in what Plato is saying. The step the child must take for themselves in the act of learning is this act of self-inscription within what is to be learned. Counting themselves in means writing themselves in, means finding a way of recreating the subject, of enacting it. It has always been the way of the arts. But even in the arts it has been long out of fashion in schools, which is all the more pernicious if, like me, you take the connection between the arts and the sacred to be just that, i.e. sacrosanct.

Morrow again:

Plato is here, as always, an uncompromising rationalist; but he never believed that the goal of knowledge is a set of logical formulas. The ultimate object of the soul's quest is the Good, whereby he meant not simply the subordination of knowledge to morality, or science to human welfare, but the complex contentment of the whole man – reason, imagination, and emotion – with the ultimate scheme of things… To such illumination Plato would not dare refuse the name of knowledge, for the reasoned and impartial pursuit of truth through dialectic is the only way the soul can be prepared for it. *And yet there is something in this experience that goes beyond logic and language* [my emphasis].

(ibid.: 78)

Morrow concludes his commentary on Plato's digression into knowledge by comparing what he says in *Epistle VII* with a passage in the Phaedrus (275d–278d) conveying much the same message, namely that the relationship between teacher and pupil must be dynamic and interactive, rather than 'expressive' on the teacher's part and merely 'impressive' on the pupil's. Plato's notion of learning as a shared act of mutual co-creation is embodied in his theory of dialogue. Plato has no patience with the traditional, academic 'lecture': for him the language of education must be vividly alive and interactive. Plato constantly draws on the 'tending' (rather than 'forcing') metaphors of husbandry and cultivation in his educational thinking. A final comment from Morrow:

The written word, says Socrates, is dumb and helpless before its questioners. It is only the image of the intelligent word written in the soul of him who has learned, the counterfeit of the living writing which feeds itself and constitutes real knowledge. Such living knowledge can be produced only by the trained husbandman, who will choose not the hot-house method of written exposition, but the slower method of dialectic.

(ibid.: 81)

If this book of ours were to carry only one message it would be: Slow down! Interestingly, Plato himself warns against trying to write about any of this – any of this that I am trying to write about. Someone choosing to do so, he says, is mad: 'the gods have taken his wits away'.

Having adopted Plato's notions of 'husbandry' and 'cultivation' as appropriate in describing the practices of the arts teacher, the relevance to the Syncretic Model becomes immediately apparent. The model is rooted in nature and the natural cycles of the seasons, the elements, the weather, the earth. Its energies are natural, as are its logistics. The creative development and the autonomous progress of the student follow a natural cycle of growth and decline, of nourishing and structuring – both at the macro- and the micro-level – and it is the teacher's task to align herself with this cycle, position herself as the one responsible for the student's 'cultivation', able to connect at any given point of the student's self-developmental trajectory in ways that are both nourishing and challenging. In what follows, we shall be characterizing each phase of the creative process in Five Elements terms and exploring the teacher's role in providing the student with expressive opportunities and resources, keeping the creative flow moving, while at the same time supplying the restraints, resistance and controls that will test and probe the student's grasp, potential and resources. The relationship of teacher to pupil is understood as a partnership in cultivation, not only between them as individuals but also between the twin forces of nature and culture themselves. Teachers, as with husbandry everywhere, are partners with nature in the project of cultivation – the Syncretic Model represents a bid or a challenge to return to much older (slower) traditions and much older (natural) metaphors for the re-enchantment of schooling.

Might it be such a wild idea literally to tune the work of one's class to the cycle of the seasons? For those of us impressed by Five Elements theory, it makes perfectly good sense to time our students' creative cycle by the annual clock of the seasons. We should be exploiting the traditional shape of the 'academic' year: beginning in the autumn (Metal) and concluding with summer (Fire and Earth). As Magda, in a letter from Greece following the Athens symposium, reminded me, Aristotle insisted that education depends upon 'repetition' – and repetition that is not merely a slavish reiteration but a deepening and embedding is what the creative cycle is about. She particularly referred me to a section in *The Nicomachean Ethics* where Aristotle makes the point that repetition means 'habit': it is here that I found the first expression of the idea of the 'habit of art'. It is by means of good practice (good repetitions, good habits) that we acquire and perfect the potential practical skills and understandings that nature embeds within us, without actually herself supplying. And, for Aristotle, art-making, for all its 'contemplative' character, is a form of action, a practical business. He finds no contradiction. All this he proposes in Book II Section 1. Later, in the same text, Aristotle defines art-making as a form of what he calls 'coming into being'. In terms of the Syncretic Model, he seems to be speaking in particular of the phases of Metal and Water (yin). In another of his writings, *The Poetics*, he gives us the complementary aspect of art (yang) when he writes of 'imitation' or *mimesis*: art's symbolic or expressive aspect; so, *techne* and *poiesis*. No account either of art or of the aesthetic is to be entertained that does not, in effect, feature feeling as meaning, or that would divorce *poiesis* from life, or, apparently, from chance (the idea of the gift again). According to Aristotle, 'Chance and art are concerned with the same objects. As Agathon says, "Art loves chance and chance loves art."' (1980: 105)

At Appendix 1, the various meanings of 'habit' are explored further.

Here, in Sen's terms, we are talking about not only talent but also opportunity. In so many ways this writing of mine has been a chancy business, and all the better for it. Meeting Magda was a case in point. And there have been countless other such meetings along the way. Similarly, I have been aware that the journey I have been on has found its own rhythm despite my intentions to the contrary for it – its seasonal force has been irresistible. The Syncretic Model is a holistic model: no phase is self-sufficient or may be extracted from the whole, omitted or reversed with impunity. For all its restless and impetuous cross-referencing, the habit of art is an integrated, dignified and slow cycle of repetitions, with authenticity and empathy holding steady at the centre. Culture follows Nature.

Arts education and the Syncretic Model

Metal – autumn – conventionalization – grief

In partnering the student around the model, we can, of course, begin at any point. But there is some sense in starting with Metal, with the cultural guardians and the treasures of the cultural heritage, of customs, conventions, wisdom, collective myths, the established repertoire, cultural meanings and values. It is into precisely this world that every child is born – a world going its own way despite the new arrival, and yet morally charged with every child's care and cultivation. The element of Metal gives clear indications as to the character of the world at this point in the cycle of change. The essential features of Metal are its inspirational and aspirational sides, together with its conserving and protecting roles; its commitment to the search for and reverence of a society's ultimate values; what we have been calling 'first and last' things. Metal inclines beyond the pressures of the everyday to a consideration of the essence of individual being, of what defines the best in a person or in a society. Hence the predominance of a sense of authority, of judgement, a passion for clarity and quality. This passion is coloured, according to Five Elements theory, by a sense of grief, of loss, as if the signs of (tragic) decline that are the inevitable badge of autumn speak too insistently of our mortality, of the irresistible forces of decline and decay. Beauty is one of the supreme values in the arts, and yet deep within the moment of enchantment lurks an intuition of sorrow – we call it poignancy. The Christian saviour was 'a man of sorrows'. Beauty brings tears to our eyes; but beauty is also one of our most potent sources of inspiration. It is as resistance to this sorrow that the guardians require our allegiance to what is best, to what Iris Murdoch has called 'the sovereignty of the good'. Plato, it will be remembered, sees man's deepest longings in just such terms. Rothfeld and Levert (*The Acupuncture Response*) summarize the character of Metal in terms of purity, perfection and a commitment to values. Sadness over missed chances and the transience of relationships is moderated by the presence of a strong father figure (complementing the maternal force of Earth), and the feeling that the sovereignty of the good in our lives can lift us above our tragic destiny.

Metal's energy fuels the impulse to education and training: the student must be prepared for hard work and lots of practice in acquiring the skills, inspiration and understandings she needs. The quality of the teaching is crucial at the 'immersion' phase. When Metal is depleted or fatigued, life, including the life of study, can feel unrewarding and pointless. And, uncontrolled by Metal, the self-centred element of Wood can threaten to overwhelm everything in its rage. Furthermore, with Metal under-functioning, the next phase, Water has nothing to feed on, no tradition worth appropriating. The artist's sense of personal character, of having a voice and a set of tastes of her own, and her underlying desire to express herself creatively is threatened.

As we have been saying, we may choose to consider the Metal phase of the creative cycle from the macro or the micro point of view. There will be times in our lives when our sense of life's meaning feels clear and affirming, when our own values seem secure and securing, when we feel at home in, and in tune with, the mores and aspirations of society itself. On the other hand, allowing ourselves to retreat either into a kind of fortress or a complacent sense of self or society ('resting on our laurels'), idling in uncritical assumptions or grieving abjectly over the 'degeneration' of one's community and of public life in general, are all signs of Metal imbalance. A lack of self-esteem, a tendency to doubt oneself, are also signs of Metal fatigue in the sense that Metal strength is needed if these qualities are to arise in the Water phase. Equally damaging is the blind and severe presumption and assertion of an unblinking authoritarianism. To remain healthy within the phase of Metal means, on the one hand, drawing nourishment from Earth's authenticity and empathy, and on the other being cheered up by the spirit of festival and sociability and celebration of Fire. Fire (its *Ke* partner) reminds Metal that at the heart of appraisal beats the impulse to praise. At the micro level we may see a specific creative project in precisely the same terms. The newly completed work is placed in the context of the culture or tradition as a whole, and is judged by it. More personally, in Earth, we ask ourselves whether it is worthy of our own hopes of it. Given the distance the project has come from the Wood and Water phases, from the creative rage that drove it and the seed lying dormant within, what do others say we now have, in cool, detached, consideration? Fear of how it will stand up in the public domain, speaks to the rigours of Metal.

At the level of the tradition itself, as a context for our own future creative work, we immerse ourselves in Metal's treasures, apply ourselves to grasping the culture's history, its schools of thought and practice, its meanings and conversations. Equally, we range more widely in our cultural travels, familiarizing ourselves with, and finding ways of savouring and valuing, cultural landscapes other than our own, some kin, others utterly strange, even alien. These forays and adventures may form part and parcel of our own productive work; on the other hand they may stand alone as voyages of discovery, as exercises in enculturation. So we enlarge the scope of pleasure and inspi- ration, and we advance our own skills and understandings in discrimination and connoisseurship, together with our capacity to judge and refine our own making. Here are the treasures of the cultural 'Earth' and our expeditions bring us all the bounty and wonder of encounters so awesome and sublime as to dwarf our more homely pleas- ures. We need the 'giants', as we call them, of the cultural mountains to help us to a sense of proportion, a true vision or apprehension of the scale of the imaginative land- scape.

It is, therefore, I believe, entirely counterproductive to offer children and young people (to offer anyone, in fact) 'short' or 'lite' versions of the classics in the misguided pursuit of 'accessibility' or 'new audiences'. We must allow the novice to grow into the more extreme cultural experiences by training on the slopes, acquiring a head for heights – and yet never entirely conquering the sense of awe and reverence that accompany art's highest and most profound exertions. To persuade children that *Hamlet* is just a ghost story, framed in a whodunit? is to defraud them of a particular moment of illumination and to foist on them the lie that nothing need be beyond their grasp, held in awe. The same tendency is to be observed in the, again misguided, project of modernizing and popularizing the rubrics and the rituals of the Church. When reverence, awe and a sense of being 'beyond understanding' are thrown out to accommodate a juvenile hankering after the cozy, the familiar and the sentimental, you can say goodbye to worship altogether. All compelling religious faith has Metal, if not at its core, then in its soul.

In the Metal phase we are concerned with the way arts institutions work to conserve the heritage and invest in the cultural future. We study the role of the curator, collec- tor, exhibitor; the way the art market works; how art values are determined; notions of the true and the fake; art crime; the repertoire, the canon; art criticism; the story of art; the philosophy of art (aesthetics) and the great seminal texts of the culture; the inter- face between art and entertainment; the role of the media; state funding and other forms of patronage; arts education and training. We are all, to some degree, members of the arts wedding and the guest list is continually growing: it now involves colleagues in neuroscience and psychology. The Metal stage is the great hinterland of arts information, opinion, values and judgements; it is also the project of stocking and managing the storehouse and seeding development. To be endured, the orgy of the arts prize-giving and the arts sales pitch, the dry academic squabbling, the hype, the snobbery, the pretentiousness, the self-regard. But without a strong and healthy Metal element a culture loses its shape, its confidence, its sense of identity – both at the level of the collective and of the individual. Metal is the public aspect of the creative cycle at its most rigorous and unforgiving. But it mustn't be allowed to get out of hand – again either at the level of the individual or the collective. To be intimidated by Metal – to fear public exposure and possible 'failure', to be brow-beaten by the experts – is to endanger the creative impulse itself (Wood), perhaps even to chop it off altogether. Wood holds nothing back, nor must it be inhibited from doing so.

The teacher as empathic companion knows how it feels to be at the beginning, totally dependent on others, and at the end, once again denied absolute control. She will do her best to convince her student of her reliability as the student's companion and of her confidence in her student's future. All shall be well, despite the frustrations and the difficulties, because the cycle begins anew, the process is self-propelling; the wheel turns. These same qualities will be to the fore as the creative project reaches the end of the road. Empathy rules.

As the one responsible for nurturing the students' experience of Metal, the teacher will hold them as they acclimatize to their cultural surroundings and master the rudiments of the cultural life. She/he will embed them in the culture with tact and respect, helping them to assimilate the demands of convention and tradition. She/he will do this through empathic identification with the students' needs, but also as someone whose authenticity guarantees personal meaning in terms of the culture they inherit – increasingly, a 'global' phenomenon.

The teacher will bring their own joy, love and praise to challenge the students' dismay at the severity and solemnity of real-world values and judgements, and to soften the strangeness of the new for them. At the Metal phase of the cycle, the teacher's clarity, stillness, absolute integrity and command of the subject make for a reassuring and inspiring presence. The teacher's focus in Metal is to hold, to inspire and to instruct.

Water – winter – appropriation – fear

For Rothfeld and Levert (2002), the characteristics of the Water element are power, wisdom, sexual potency, fear, but also courage, remaining young in spirit (and also looks), flow, depth, reserves of energy. Imbalance produces the opposites of all the above – a retreat into isolation, cynicism, inflexibility, occasional rashness, even harshness. Healthy Water is the essence of life. Life cannot be sustained without it – much that lives is composed almost entirely of it. The desert is barren, drought destroys – but then so does the flood, the tsunami, the mudslide. Water has an awesome power of determination, holding the fate of the future, ensuring the renewal of the Earth, keeping the cycle going – or, losing faith, allowing it to grind to a halt. We are told that in the worst scenario of climate change, the next round of global conflicts will be the water wars. We are already seeing huge migrations of people driven from their homelands by drought and famine on the one hand and flooding on the other.

In the cycle of artistic creativity, the phase of Water has to do with the appropriation of resources to the project of one's own self-determination, the achievement of independence. It is about identifying those aspects of the culture, the tradition, the storehouse that speak to us, that hold for us the inspiration, the resources, the possibility of our own making, of our self-renewal and self-definition. So it is a time of deep nourishment, for waiting (hibernation) upon the propitious moment, for the gathering of strength, for allowing the incubation of the seed of regeneration. It is a time for making ready. The resources of the collective are there to sustain us and keep us going, for the flow of water must never be allowed to give out. Above all it seems to be a time in suspension – self-contained, confident, full of faith, but biding one's time, gathering strength. Water people seem both to respect and to relish adversity: what threatens and dismays others, they approach playfully, stoically and sometimes even recklessly. They love play and are often given to its more extreme forms. Winter is Water's season. Winter has its joys as well as its hardships. It comes as a period of enforced respite, of sheltering, of taking care: and of challenge, of course, for the brave of heart. And if one looks at the demands made upon us by the phases comprising the rest of the cycle, it is a time to be profoundly grateful for. We can take an invigorating break on the slopes, while waiting for the warmth to return, with its call to be up and doing once again. Meanwhile we must keep faith. Above all, we must care – Water people tend to make good carers. And because we care so much, Water can heap cares upon us, make us anxious, make us afraid.

The teacher as empathic companion respects and may even have to insist upon her student's winter-time. So here is an opportunity to reconnect with the collective, to visit galleries, museums, cinemas, concert halls, for nourishment and for keeping her spirits up. That well-stocked storehouse of culture must be raided for what it has to offer to this particular student – one has to be selective as well as imaginative, tempting as well as challenging. It is important for the teacher to remember that the creative cycle includes this substantial period of lying fallow, of self-communing, self-nourishing and self-defining. With time to spare, and perhaps hanging heavily, Winter is also a time to keep fit through play. Lacking the focused pressure that comes with Wood and springtime, this is a time for playing games, because, as Winnicott has said, it is through playing that we become most fully ourselves, and the Water phase is about identification through appropriation. The teacher will encourage a playful approach to art-making and, above all, the gradual emergence of the child's sense of self-determination and worth as a developing artist, an artist with a creative future. Here the latent seeds of self-belief and self-realization are nurtured and prepared for full expression. If, in terms of Winnicott's analysis of the mother-infant relationship, the Metal phase is the time of 'holding', then the Water phase is the time of 'handling' (of the mother's experimental playing with and for the child).

My favourite Water/winter poem is Kathleen Jamie's 'Dipper'. In its way, it beautifully captures what we have just been saying:

Dipper

It was winter, near freezing,
I'd walked through a forest of firs
when I saw issue out of the waterfall
a solitary bird.

It lit on a damp rock,
and, as water swept stupidly on,
wrung from its throat
supple, undammable song.

It isn't mine to give,
I can't coax this bird to my hand
that knows the depth of the river
yet sings of it on land.

Water is the time for sounding one's own spiritual depths. Our 'undammable' song, telling of our loves and our hopes, can only be sung in the material world. Our song *nourishes itself.*

Water is nurtured by Metal – the storehouse of culture filled by the twin processes of harvesting and sorting for quality. The teacher will have provided for the student's reaping and gathering. She/he will also be attentive to the student's strength as a potential author, as the potential author of their own truth and of their empathic feelings for themselves and others. The student's confidence in their personal being, their sense of identity, will play a crucial part in containing and controlling the more dangerous forces of Water. Winter's glooms and depressions need to be resisted by powerful self-belief and the knowledge that an awakening is in the offing, which means keeping faith with the past and finding inspiration there, making ready for the future, as the huntsman makes ready, for the physical, mental and spiritual challenges to come. Winter stands between the old and the new: it looks both ways. Winter holds the key to the future and stands freighted to bring it on. The teacher's focus in Water is playfulness and empowerment.

In drawing this section to a close I recall an image in Annie Dillard's brilliant *Pilgrim at Tinker Creek* (1998):

After the flood that year I found a big tulip tree limb that had been wind-thrown into Tinker Creek. The current dragged it up on some rocks on the bank, where receding waters stranded it. A moment after the flood I discovered that it was growing leaves. Both ends of the branch were completely exposed and dried. I was amazed. It was like the old fable about the corpse's growing a beard; it was as if the woodpile in my garage were suddenly to burst greenly into leaf. The way plants persevere in the bitterest of circumstances is utterly heartening. I can barely keep from unconsciously ascribing a will to these plants, a do-or-die courage, and I have to remind myself that coded cells and mute water pressure have no idea how grandly they are flying in the teeth of it all.

(1998: 164)

Wood – spring – transformation – rage

Towards the end of his book *The Wild Places*, Robert Macfarlane writes:

> As I moved south, my own understanding of wilderness had been altered – or its range had been enlarged. My early vision of a wild place as somewhere remote, history-less, unmarked, now seemed improperly partial.
>
> It was not that places such as Hope and Rannoch, the last fastnesses, were worthless. No, in their stripped-back austerity, their fierce elementality, these landscapes remained invaluable in their power to awe. But I had learned to see another type of wildness, to which I had once been blind: the wildness of natural life, the sheer force of ongoing organic existence, vigorous and chaotic. This wildness was not about asperity, but about luxuriance, vitality, fun. The weed thrusting through the crack in the pavement, the tree root impudently cracking a carapace of tarmac: these were wild signs, as much as the storm wave and the snowflake.
>
> (2007: 316)

Wood, the element above all others most obviously designated 'creative', the agent of transformation and regeneration, is characterized by precisely the kind of energy Macfarlane identifies here: 'luxuriance, vitality, fun'. It is about animal spirits, puppydom, being wildly optimistic, letting rip, having a go, going for broke. In short: wild. As I look out on my solemn little garden – it is 28 January – only the grass looks healthy. The flowerbeds are waterlogged and a tumble of decaying browns and blacks. The miniature box hedge looks as if the persistent heavy frosts might have killed it; all its 'evergreen' leaves are a dry, a dismal grey. Even the usual gloss of the camellias has been dulled – there are as many brown and yellow leaves as green. The ivy hangs doggedly to the wall, sullen and subdued. But the sense of patient waiting is strong. Very soon there will be a stir of energy, and then, before I know it, a huge surge will bring the daffodils into bloom and star our little wood with primroses. We have already used 'fury' to describe the energy of spring. For the creative writer, artist, composer, dancer, this phase of the making process can indeed feel like a sudden burst of anger – rage is in the air, and the will to make, to grow, to be is irresistible. Such is the testimony of John Tusa's interviewees. Such, too, is the impulse of the child at school – if not blighted by an oppressive curriculum or teacher. The wild of small things is every bit as impressive, as Macfarlane discovered, as the wild of the sublime. If the creative project doesn't get its explosive shot of transforming energy here, then our hope for it will be still-born.

The strength of every element in the cycle has its corresponding weakness. Fire's enthusiasm, over-taxed or under-funded, quickly turns to despondency. Water's life-giving flow can freeze over or dry up. Every phase of the cycle depends upon what is going on everywhere else – the twin processes of nurturing (*Sheng*) and controlling (*Ke*) must be doing their dynamic work. Acting as the student's empathic companion at the Wood phase means the teacher must be fully acquainted at first hand with what it feels like to be initiating an arts project and being driven by the rage to make, to create, to express. This rage, incidentally, may take many forms – it is not simply a matter of splashing paint about, going OTT in a drama improvisation or tossing countless sheets of A4 into the waste-paper basket. Maurice Sendak's lovely children's story *Where the Wild Things Are* vividly captures the force and the fun of this world that opens up when the spirit of transformation takes over the child's mind and imagination. Being someone's companion among the wild things requires huge resources of empathy, and not a little wisdom – to say nothing of having the technical know-how to supply the student's voracious appetite. (If appetite is not 'voracious', there's something badly wrong.) And you must have been there, and be still in the habit of going there, yourself. As for its more carefree moments, Wood translates as a certain kind of abandon, but also as taking a tea break 'on the job', much as Anthony Caro describes when talking to John Tusa about his creative life with his friends and collaborators in the studio (see Chapter 6).

It is perhaps worth reminding ourselves again (we have touched on this earlier) of a useful pedagogical strategy devised by Robert Witkin for his book *The Intelligence of Feeling*. He recommended that the student at the first phase of the creative process attempt to make what he called 'a holding form'. This is how Witkin describes it:

> The holding form is merely the seed of which the full expressive form is the flower…the effectiveness of a holding form depends upon its complete simplicity, its 'minimal' character. Its purpose is to encapsulate only the essential movement of the sensate impulse and to hold that movement for the duration of the expressive act.
>
> (1974: 181)

Witkin argues that the sensate life of the mind is extremely volatile, and that unless a particular expressive impulse can be captured or fixed, held in consciousness in some such way as he suggests, then it will rapidly degenerate and dissolve – move beyond one's conscious grasp. This device, whether it takes the form of a rapid sketch, a defining gesture or movement, a particular rhythm or musical riff, perhaps a neat working title (for a poem or a story or a book like this one), can indeed prove absolutely crucial in converting the expressive impulse into form, transforming materials into media, feelings into symbols. It is the move into the symbolic order of experience. Virginia Woolf is very strong on the idea of the defining rhythm of a piece, seeing its discovery as the basis of all good writing. The point about the holding form is that it marks the beginning of the process of transformation – of the embodiment of feeling in form. Only material understood as media can serve as signs – and making meaning and fashioning signification in the arts is a symbolic project, i.e. it is the making of signs. We shall later argue that the presentational symbol (Langer, 1967) is the medium of affective knowing. An empathic companion in the making of signs will understand what a slippery process this can be, and will have an eye for the potential of the holding form. Given success at this stage, the student can comfortably move on to developing and elaborating the work to embrace more and more of its expressive potential and their expressive desire. In the best cases, that development and elaboration will seem to take care of themselves (*nourish themselves*) – constantly checked against the maker's intuitions of authenticity (Earth) and desire (Water). Teachers tempted to supply their own answers, to touch up a child's painting or put the finishing touches to a poem, risk aborting and invalidating the student's authenticity and outright ownership of the project.

We can now look at the teacher's nurturing and controlling roles in respect of the student's Wood phase. Wood is nourished by Water, which means that the student's creativity must be powered by what Witkin, in the passage just quoted, refers to as as kind of inner turmoil, a restlessness for release, a 'sensate disturbance'. Put another way, the student must be motivated by a deep sense of wanting (caring) to speak. What Wood adds to this diffused agitation is specificity, an expressive particularity; an impulse to say a particular kind of thing, as yet unclear. There is an inevitable sense of mystery and uncertainty surrounding these often tentative beginnings. The urge to write or paint or dance is barely strong enough to cope with the fear and anxiety to which uncertainty and risk-taking can give rise. The Wood phase is where the artist must give up the safety of balance deliberately to court the uncertainties of unbalance, the sap of inspiration rising to power the work. Losing or forfeiting one's balance is one of the most exhilarating but also one of the most daunting aspects of the creative moment. The good-enough teacher will be alert to the student's stress at this time.

In the *Intelligence of Feeling*, Witkin describes the creative process in art not so much as a cycle but as a sequence, a step-by-step operation. Concerned to position the teacher firmly astride the student's project, Witkin urges the art teacher to 'set the sensate problem' – implying that this can be effected somehow, much in the way her maths colleagues might set a mathematical problem. He goes to some trouble explaining how this might be done. My own preference, however, has always been to begin with the student rather than the teacher and to allow the student to 'set' their own problem, either as just described – following their nose, and then, as a teacher, trying to catch up and identify it. It's a question of allowing Ted Hughes's 'Thought Fox' to slide into the creative space from just below the window of consciousness, the poet catching the whiff of its rank scent as it passes, and setting out in pursuit, or, where no such chance inspiration is available, by following Paul Klee's practice of 'taking a line for a walk'. This is an invitation to doodle, to play, to improvise, to have a conversation with materials, to be thought of simply as 'activating the medium' (Witkin speaks of 'displacing' the medium).

Given that the phase of transformation is not yet fully under way, we should be talking about 'materials' rather than 'media', transformation means the conversion of materials into the media of sign-making, which is to say a transition in the artist's perception from materials to symbol, from handling to meaning. Very often the best way of identifying the hidden seed of creativity is to begin working with the materials blind, open to possibilities. It is in some respects like the elk hunter's dance (see the Valediction chapter): the creative idea will disclose itself to formative consciousness, if we are sufficiently well prepared, if we are fully attentive to the possibility and capable of seducing it into revealing, disclosing, unconcealing itself. Here is Plato's moment of illumination. This is the connection we are looking for. Our expressivity is with us always – it is like a cup full to the brim, ready to spill over at any moment (Water). All it takes is a little nudge of the elbow. It is a case of knowing, with total confidence, that if we seek we shall find. From the dark forest, the quarry emerges into the clearing of consciousness, where it will find a holy habitation and receive its name. We have direction and are purposefully focused. The hunt is on. More particularly it is *our* hunt and has been from the very beginning – as, of course, it must be if authenticity is to retain its sovereignty at the centre of the work. Meanwhile we look to Water for the impulse to go hunting at all. All this, as I say, will become clearer in the story of the Yukaghir soul hunter, told at the end of the book.

Water holds the key for Wood (the nourishing *Sheng* influence). And Metal says there are rules and conventions to be considered (the controlling *Ke* influence). A sonnet should have 14 lines and must rhyme either this way or that; a haiku should contain 17 syllables, neither more nor less. The poet Tony Harrison enjoyed all this. Conventionalization rules: the quadrille, the blues, the epic, the fresco, the pathetic fallacy, the stream of consciousness, art for art's sake. All are the ways and means, the business of the habit of art within our culture. But Metal also speaks of judgement and of Judgement Day. Both in public and in private we shall want to get it right, we shall want it to be good enough to satisfy the strictures for what passes muster, unless, of course, we are determined to overturn or ignore them (as Virginia Woolf was). In the creative rush to make, the exuberance to express, the impulse to remain faithful, we may need reminding of the constraints imposed by the materials we have chosen to work with, and of the assumptions and expectations attaching to particular forms, including their fitness for purpose. And this will make formidable demands not only on the teacher's expertise and judgement but also on the thoroughness and depth of her/his education and training. An audience of arts therapy students suggested to me recently that they needed to know relatively little about art since therapy rather than art was their expertise. I think not.

The teacher's focus in Wood is tending – tending the student's creative energy.

Annie Dillard, in *Pilgrim at Tinker Creek* describes the frenzy of creativity – the rage of the Wood phase. The vital spirit can be frightening.

> The driving force behind all this fecundity is a terrible pressure I also must consider, the pressure of birth and growth, the pressure that splits the bark of trees and shoots out seeds, that squeezes out the egg and bursts the pupa, that hungers and lusts and drives the creature towards its own death. Fecundity is an ugly word for an ugly subject. It is ugly, at least, in the eggy animal world. I don't think it is for plants.
>
> (1998: 163)

Fire – summer – publication – joy

Fire is the yang phase at its most dramatic and sensuous. The sun, the heat, joy, laughter, festival, celebration, making whoopee, making love; Dionysus at full throttle. If you can't stand the heat, you know what to do.

The important lesson of the Fire phase is the impulse to publication, to sharing, to celebration and love. Exposure is a *natural* tendency of the creative process, especially where that process, as in the arts, has a strongly 'expressive' force – i.e. where, as Harré would have it, the impulse is towards identity or, in Maslow's terms, towards 'self-actualization'. This is why, for many authors and artists, the creative project is a conversation, an exchange of gifts. Many authors and artists admit to having a muse, someone whose being acts as a stimulus or incentive for the work: someone conceived of as the *perfect receiver*. Much creative work is overtly directed towards the good-enough other, is offered not simply as evidence of affection or admiration or worship, but as a bid for symbolic fusion, the intermingling of souls. Here is another sense in which we might discern the spiritual dimension of the element. Famous partnerships between authors/artists and their muses, or best receivers, include Vincent and Theo Van Gogh; Wordsworth and his sister Dorothy; Beethoven and Elise; W. B. Yeats and Maud Gonne; Tennyson and Arthur Hallam; Benjamin Britten and Peter Pears; Margot Fonteyn and Rudolph Nureyev; Virginia Woolf and her husband Leonard; Sylvia Plath and her husband Ted Hughes.

To work in front of the bland reflection of the mirror can never be enough – even for a dancer. In as much as every creative work is a work of love, its function is to serve as a love gift. The reception it receives, or might hope to receive, therefore, is absolutely critical. Within the phase of Fire, love gifts are exchanged in the spirit of love – more detached and exacting rules apply, as we have seen, when Metal, later in the cycle, exerts its sober authority. But the first impulse of the maker is to express her love for her muse, her perfect receiver – and even when that perfect receiver is abstracted to the receiving 'public', the response has to be one that respects the loving impulse that prompts the making and giving of every *authentic* work. I stress authenticity here because the rules only apply upon that condition – and in our examination of Earth we have seen how central, how fundamental that principle is. What Collingwood calls 'pseudo' art doesn't actually count as art at all, let alone a love child.

A passage from E. L. Doctorow's novel *Homer and Langley* (2009) well captures the essential themes of Fire. The narrator is describing the summer camp he attended with his brother – 'in our youth'.

> I was in the fullness of my senses then. My legs and arms strong and sinewy and I could see the world with all the unconscious happiness of a fourteen year old. Not far from the camps [the boys camps and the girls camps] on a bluff overlooking the ocean, was a meadow profuse with wild blackberry bushes, and one afternoon numbers of us were there plucking wild blackberries and biting into their wet warm pericarped pulp, competing with flights of bumblebees as we raced them from one bush to another and stuffed the berries into our mouths till the juice dripped down our chins. The air was thickened with floating communities of gnats that rose and fell, expanding and contracting, like astronomical events. And the sun shone on our heads, and behind us at the foot of the cliff were the black and silver rocks patiently taking and breaking apart the waves and, beyond that, the glittering sea radiant with shards of sun, and all of it in my clear eyes as I turned in triumph to this one girl with whom I had bonded, Eleanor was her name, stretched my arms wide and bowed as the magician who had made it for her.

(2009: 9)

The student entering the Fire phase will be in the final stages of the creative project. The flesh will be on the bones, and already they may be seeking perspectives on its completion other than their own, including their teacher's. It's often difficult to know when enough is enough, and easy to go too far with a piece – as Paula Rego reminded us earlier. The Wood phase is always over-productive – not least because it has to be if the impulse to make is to be allowed its head. Of course, it is natural for it also to lose its head and must be reined in – but only when the time is right, not before. I can't believe how much of my writing for this book has had to be shed, at the prompting of those closest to me. But it was so necessary at the time. The notion of the unfinished work has much to be said for it. Perhaps all creative projects simply stop, with a sense that they might still (always) be 'in progress', rather than ever absolutely over and done with. On the other hand, the student/artist may simply have missed the potential yet to be realized, through just a little more perseverance – and here the teacher's, the lover's judgement can be helpful. Many artists return to their 'finished' work time and again – and it is very usual to leave a work to 'mature', to 'settle', so that coming back to it in a different frame of mind (at the Earth phase), with a clearer head, the artist or author is able almost immediately to grasp what else might need to be done, what cut, what doesn't work and what calls for further attention. All this is allowed for in the phase of Fire, as friends gather round and the piece moves into its own space, onto its spiritual homeground. Here the work finally lowers its eyes, having so faithfully and for so long suffered to 'return our gaze'.

The teacher as empathic companion and practised artist will know all about the Fire phase – its rigours, excitements, uncertainties, satisfactions, vulnerabilities, temptations – and, whilst ensuring the student makes the most of the sunshine, will be mindful of sun stroke, burn-out and exhaustion. Above all, this is a time for bringing everyone together, stepping out of the sea and towelling down. It's a time for sharing not just the thing made but also the whole adventure of making with the rest of the creative team. We need to know not only that our work has been seen, but also that we have been seen as its maker as well. It is a time for making an exhibition of ourselves and for not running away, because we need company at this stage. Quieter, less insistently sociable, more personally reflective moments lie ahead. Now is our moment in the spotlight, as the proper centre of attraction and affection. We need it just as the body needs the sun, as the infant needs her mother's smile – to help us recover from the over-committed, exhausting and high-risk actions of the Wood phase. We need it to build up our courage to let go, to separate ourselves from the work that may have cost us too much and for the future of which we can do no more, no better than hope.

All this, the empathic companion will know, and will have developed coping strategies for. The *Sheng* contribution for nurturing Fire comes from Wood. For the Fire element to be strong it needs a constant supply of creative Wood. This would suggest that the springtime of the creative project should be vigorous and highly productive. The transformation of materials into symbolic forms will have been thoroughly established and the artwork will be well on the way to completion. Spirits must be high if we are to have something to celebrate, some confidence in arranging a party. The teacher will have done her best in encouraging and containing the student's creative fury, supplying thoughtful advice and technical support – and the occasional cup of tea. Above all, it is a time for keeping morale high, but also for keeping expectations and ambitions realistic, so the project remains securely grounded and bounded – as well as joyful. Teacher and student must understand each other.

The controlling (*Ke*) influence on Fire is Water. The creative artist who loses all sense of fear is likely to fall victim to foolish risk taking and reckless over-extension. But Water as corrective, as structuring agency, has a subtler task, which is to keep personal expressive desire alive at the heart of the creative process. We have called it 'caring' – caring enough. In the fury of a particular making, it is all too easy to break the subtle bond to the deeper, personally defining desire. That connection ruptured, the work loses its integrity and becomes another instance of 'pseudo art' – an empty, or merely exotic, form, like so much 'quality' West-End theatre these days. This is where Water's questioning and Earth's integrity come in. So the teacher will have an eye open to such a possibility and may want to refer the student to the work's 'holding form' (see Wood above) since, thus formulated, the link between general and particular desire was clear. Here we get a vivid sense of the dynamic interaction of the different elements in sustaining and structuring the particular project: Fire needs Wood to sustain it; Wood to be of any use must be nourished by Water; Fire needs Water to discipline it, Water to be useful needs to have been controlled by Earth and nourished by Metal. Tracing problems with the Fire element might require a careful working through by the teacher of the different phases of the history of the project in order to find the root of the difficulty and come up with a strategy for restoring balance and unblocking jams.

The teacher's focus in Fire is praise.

Earth – late summer – authenticity – empathy

In every way, Earth is the ground and centre of our whole scheme. Earth is, of course, our only home, and with the grim prognosis of the climate scientists of the damaging consequences of our lack of care for the planet, we are being made painfully aware of its vulnerability and of our absolute dependence upon its wellbeing. We are gradually learning to listen to Gaia. Equally, conserving and nourishing the element of Earth in the constitution of our personal lives, and at the centre of the cycle of creativity, becomes of the utmost importance. Here, somehow, we find the essence of our sense of self, of what Harré calls the Identity Project. Here is the fruit of our work; here is our song. Donna and I chose to endow Earth with the pivotal value of authenticity and to adopt from the Chinese its defining emotion of empathy. Empathy comes as close as makes no difference to the Greek idea of love as *agape* (Latin – *caritas*). Earth functions at every phase of the creative cycle as the organizing intelligence, the intelligence of feeling.

When our Earth element is under-performing, we feel neglected, even disowned by ourselves – there is no use or goodness in us, nothing of authenticity to turn to in making decisions or judging for ourselves. Every impulse around the cycle of creativity is authenticated against the core of our being, which speaks for what is good and right about what we are doing (Earth is an aspect of every phase of the cycle). Call it our moral centre, our conscience. Call it the intelligence of feeling. We ask of the expressive desire itself, is it good? Of the impulse that fuels the making process, is it good? Of the intuition that carries the work to completion, and of the finished work itself, is it good? Of our estimation as to the work's final standing, is it true? How crucial, therefore, that we should have cultivated the habit of authenticity, and have developed both conscience and sensibility to the point where we have confidence in our own answers. Imagine the distress of children forced to lie, repeatedly denying their own truth, their own authenticity.

We should now consider the three aspects of the participatory pedagogy, as they relate to Earth. As the student's empathic companion, our commitment is to reinforcing her sense of personhood, of identity – this entails understanding the student's personal identity project, her life within the cycle of creativity and the phases of change, as they influence her as an author. We have to work towards a deep, compassionate understanding of that personality; of her characteristic strengths and weaknesses; her fears and scruples; her passions, pleasures and sorrows. All this amounts to a powerful commitment to trust and confidentiality. We have already pointed to the line of correspondences between empathy, *agape*, love and faith (faithfulness). Those we cannot love will never take us to their hearts, nor should they. The struggle to authenticity, to self-belief and the feeling of self-worth, is harder for some of us than others – our role as a good-enough companion can be absolutely critical in fostering the emergence of the confidence to be, to be oneself. Our focus of attention is not their private affairs but their 'fruits' – their expressive projects of self-realization through their chosen medium: dance, writing, painting, music. Our concern is for the integrity of that work, for its fullness and finish, that it might be a source of joy and a vessel of living knowledge. So we build their confidence, boost their resources, increase their know-how, protect and nourish their creative flame, reward their courage, recognize and apprehend their authenticity, love them that they might love themselves the better, celebrate and praise their achievements, offer them the honest criticism that our different, trusted perspective allows; wonder and rejoice at their illumination.

Earth is always in play, informing each phase of the cycle. But it has a moment all to itself, (as Donna insisted) and we need to authorize such a moment for a student who might not know how important it is. It is a moment of reflection, a moment almost of self-nourishing and self-cherishing. 'I did all right.' 'I can go on from there.' 'If x or y backs me, likes what I do, it can't be that bad.' This moment needs to be made room for in the course of the reflective conversation. Authors are people – and the wellbeing of the person makes a difference to the wellbeing of the author. So we draw upon the joy and love and festive spirit of Fire to strengthen, fertilize and enrich Earth; our self-belief grows under the liberating influence of the summer sun, and the delight in life itself is heightened as we enjoy the fruits of the season in the company of loving companions. Again, it is part of the nourishing role: to ensure our students have rich and memorable experiences of Fire, of its passion, its freedom, its laughing energy. The Fire phase includes the final emergence of the finished work – there is the joy of achievement, of having something to celebrate, to party about. All this belongs to the nurturing *Sheng*.

For the controlling *Ke* dynamic, we look to Wood. Wood binds Earth together, prevents an artistic mudslide, resists emotional erosion. Wood, the original impulse to make, to give form to feeling, places great stress on respecting and working in part-nership with materials – the ego, the self, cannot simply have its own way, overwhelm the medium through which expression is to take place. Earth must be strong to hold and resist. For all its ferocious energy, the creative impulse of Wood has to be well-disciplined, well-organized. Where Wood has been effective in furnishing the creative project, it will also serve to maintain Earth's self-belief, to counter the effects of erosion and exhaustion. If the teacher has been able to ensure a strong Wood phase, the student's authority and capacity for empathy and authenticity will have been secured, will have been stabilized. If there are weaknesses or blocks where the student's Earth is concerned, the teacher looks not simply at Earth itself, but also, in remedying the situation, at the quality of the student's Fire and Wood energies and experiences.

The teacher's focus in Earth is to be the student's empathic companion and part-ner in the reflective conversation: in soothsaying.

Summarizing the teacher's repertoire of skills in the cultivation of the student's habit of art we have:

Metal (1): to inspire and to instruct
Water: to play and to empower
Wood: to tend (attend)
Fire: to praise (appraise)
Earth: to co-create the reflective conversation
Metal (2): to judge.

The Syncretic Model and the emotions

I may not have said enough about the emotions associated with the five elements and what part they play in the cycle of creativity, or indeed about the account to be taken of them by the teacher. We have already identified the 'basic' emotions of which the cycle is constituted. Here they are:

Water: fear
Wood: fury
Fire: joy; love
Earth: empathy
Metal: grief (gravity)

Teachers of the arts, therapists working with or through the arts, will recognize the rele-vance of the basic forms of emotional excitement in connection with the creative process. The fear associated with the beginnings of any creative project, with nothing achieved and sometimes almost nothing to go on; the fury or frenzy that must be expected and accommodated as the headstrong author allows her inspiration to carry her away; the joy and love that emerge with the safe completion of the work; the pervasive ethos of interpersonal empathy that characterizes personal authenticity; the grief (or sense of gravity) that attaches to letting go and arriving at sober judgements. Teachers will prepare themselves as empathic companions to stay with their student (client, patients) as they handle these emotional states and respond to their distinctive forms of intelligence. They will also recognize their nurturing and controlling possibilities.

Responding to existential grief (the Metal phase as beginning) means the teacher must summon the student's inner supplies of empathy and self-belief. She/he will also help the student temper that grief with joy and love from her Fire element. Helping the student understand and cope with grief means their recognizing and savouring grace (Earth).

Coping with Water's fear and accessing her reserves of courage means nourishing with the strength and sober authority of Metal, and challenging with the empathy and authenticity of Earth. This becomes a demand for specific emotional responses from the student, over and above either fear or courage: her own moral authority, her own empathy, in nourishing and controlling her fear. Good fear, complemented by courage, suggests an appropriate level of caution or vigilance and springs from the intuition of having something of the utmost value to protect – and to realize.

Feeding Wood's fury means bringing the student's fear energy to bear (Water) – her calculating of the risks involved and confidence that they can be handled. Caution and deliberation will come into the equation as the student's Metal element: her concern for standards and respect for convention. Here the teacher's guiding and steady hand in managing the emotional dynamic of the situation will be very important. Empathy from the teacher means understanding what this dangerous phase feels like and being there with support and encouragement to enable the student to stick with its surge and ride the rapids.

Coping with Fire's highs and lows means the teacher's helping to bring the creative project to fruition and finding a strong, sympathetic audience for its reception – these first receivers must be capable of meeting the maker's exhaustion and apprehension with joy and love. The danger of disappointment will be reduced if the student's nurturing fury (Wood) for the project is sustained, matched by an element of caution and concern (Water) sufficient to challenge any loss of focus and concentration.

Feeding and affirming the student's Earth capacity for empathy and authenticity means the teacher's loving the student and helping the student to proper self-respect. These qualities in the student will be sustained by their own recent experience of shared joy and love (Fire), and stabilized with the help of their Wood element's furious passion to be.

Metal, considered as the end rather than the beginning of the cycle, is characterized by a sense of nostalgia, of loss and having to let go and say goodbye – so at this moment of being judged, the teacher will invest in the student's empathy and sense of authenticity (Earth), while at the same time steadying the student's grief with powerful injections of remembered joy and love (Fire).

As the teacher tracks and accompanies the student around the cycle, she/he will be watching for inappropriate emotional colouring: signs that the emotional imperative that should be driving the project at any given moment seems struggling to assert itself. For example, too much concern with Metal (judgement) can seriously undermine the passion of Wood (creativity), substituting a morbid misery for what should be exuberance. Lacking the strong emotional and social reinforcement supplied by Fire (publication) the maker may be unable to experience the empathy for the work and its maker (i.e. herself) that makes Earth a time to savour, a satisfying time of personal reflection and adjustment. Each emotion associated with each element is a manifestation of a quality of *caring*, a particular impulse of knowing. Each marks experience in its own distinctive and emphatic way. The emotional charges run the gamut as the creative project turns full cycle from grief back to grief again.

The teacher will pay attention to the student's emotional cycle of change as the ground of technical and theoretical support. Making art is a complex of intensely felt, personal experience, and is rooted in the earliest form of intelligence: the intelligence of feeling. Emotion is the ground of decision-making, in the creative cycle. Water is the source of our love of life, but winter holds life back: will the sun ever return? And what if it should not? Spring overwhelms us with its fury, throwing caution to the March winds, and Water's fear converts to Wood's anger. Fire welcomes what Wood heaps upon it, shedding warmth and light in all directions, bidding us throw off all restraint in a grateful festival of joy and love. But it burns itself out, as ash cools when the fire dies – and after the party comes a time for quiet reflection and a gentler display of compassion. For all the beauty of its dying, the year draws to a darkening close, and the lessons of the passage of time are melancholy ones. Beauty is a mixture of delight and grief, gravity and grace: the beautiful invariably moves us to tears with its poignancy, and we are hard-pressed to know why. But the harvest is in, the future is assured, and we may solemnly conclude that we are ready for what the winter may bring. We shall not cease from caring – and the cares that caring brings. As Hamlet said, 'the readiness is all'.

Footnote

No attempt is made in this chapter to work through either the implications for teaching arts reception or assessing student achievement. These topics have already been sketched in Chapter 1 and any further elaboration I judge to be beyond the scope of this book.

In the above detailed analysis of the creative process of teaching the arts embodied in the Syncretic Model, teaching arts appreciation will be understood as a kind of mirror image of the making process: where the one is expressive, so too is the other; where the one is projective, the other is the same; both are creative. Both entail the subject's inscribing themselves within a text/feeling form, whether that text/feeling form originated with them or with another. In receiving an art work, the student learns to place the work within their own repertoire of arts experience (Metal/Water); to open up to the work's creative energy and admit that energy into their own imaginative and emotional structures (Wood), thereby allowing the work to take form in their minds; to test the work against their heart's desire and participate in the public discourse generated by the work (Fire); to test its final impact upon their deepest personal sense of what counts as an authentic response (Earth). Learning to write art criticism is a function of Metal in its final aspect.

Teachers assessing their students might want to use the model as a structure of appraisal, and to develop their expertise in co-creating the reflective conversation, pioneered in *Assessing Achievement in the Arts* (Ross et al., 1993), and briefly illustrated in Chapter 1.

10 Cultivating the arts in therapy

In this chapter, the role of the arts therapist is described as repairing the expressive system and restoring the flow of expressive creativity in the client's life. The Syncretic Model is deployed to analyse the relationship between the good-enough mother and the child: the therapist is seen as surrogate mother on the one hand and as a promoter of expression through the arts on the other. Martha Nussbaum's concept of *eudaimonia* (fulfilment), and Semir Zeki's exploration of the splendours and miseries of the brain are invoked to point to art's uniquely transformative role in adapting the individual to their humanity. A framework of questions, derived from the Syncretic Model, provides a basis for troubleshooting the expressive dimension of a life of change.

A philosopher who has never studied and worked at natural science cannot philosophize about it without making a fool of himself.
R. G. Collingwood, *The Idea of Nature* (1960: 3)

When I consider every thing that grows
Holds in perfection but a little moment...
William Shakespeare, Sonnet *15*

Introduction

Reading Shaun McNiff's (2004) book, *Art Heals*, I was struck by the sentence, 'The creative arts therapies have yet to engage themselves about what we mean by "arts"'. I take him to be suggesting that it might be useful if arts therapists were to think some more about what it might mean to use the arts to therapeutic purpose: what might be the relationship between the practice of art and the practice of arts therapy. For example, the question arises as to the degree of competence in art deemed necessary to a responsible and effective arts therapist. There is a complementary question about the symptoms or difficulties the treatment is designed to address. Where do they lie? How do they manifest themselves? How reasonable would it feel to suggest that the focus of therapeutic intervention should be a client's actual or alleged difficulties in making and receiving the arts? I suspect, put baldly like that, such a suggestion might not receive immediate and unqualified support among arts therapists themselves. Surely it couldn't be right to tie the arts therapist to servicing a client's artwork in so direct and apparently restrictive a way? Therapy, I imagine, claims for itself a very much wider remit embracing the client's general mental wellbeing and quality of life. Making poets or painters of them, or passionate lovers of the opera or the theatre, might seem an indulgence and irrelevance in the face of the real-life anguish and disorientation that the therapist is asked to address.

And yet this is pretty much the case I wish to argue. No, I don't imagine therapists training budding painters and poets or converting the unmusical to a life at the proms. They might, of course, incidentally, have some such an occasional impact, but that will not be their principal focus. Having said that, insofar as art is an extension of our general expressive and emotional life, and the experience of art is a universal phenomenon in human societies, traditionally agreed to be serving vital, beneficial individual and collective ends, then it might indeed be reasonable to work with clients through the arts as a way of treating problems they are experiencing with their expressive and imaginative lives. I shall argue that many, if not all, of the issues with which arts therapists are familiar in their work might possibly be traceable back to blocks and imbalances in their clients' expressivity, if, as we have been arguing in this book, satisfactory expressive activity is the basis of the personal Identity Project (Rom Harré, *Personal Being*). I shall base my argument in this chapter on the proposition that it would be reasonable for arts therapists to understand their work as essentially supporting the client's Identity Project.

If this point is conceded, then it follows that arts therapists, like their colleagues in education, should receive significant training and experience in the arts as the ground of their professional work. *If art proper heals, and I believe it does, then the arts therapist needs to be a proper artist.* Therapists cannot be expected to deploy the arts to healing ends without first-hand knowledge of how art works and is an engine for probing and repairing the corrupt or malfunctioning emotional 'programmes of the brain' (J. Z. Young, *Programmes of the Brain*). The grasp I speak of will be rooted in their own deep, personal attachment to art, as art makers and art receivers. In which case, the Syncretic Model of creativity in the arts will provide the same theoretical framework for the arts therapist as it does for the arts teacher; whereas it is the arts teacher's job to cultivate 'the habit of art' in the student, to induct her into the ways and delights and satisfactions of art as an essential feature of the expressive dimension of her life, the therapist monitors the client's artistic performance as a way of identifying the source(s) of her emotional distress (her difficulties with self-expression), and cultivates the habit of art in her as a therapeutic treatment for difficulties within the expressive system.

To be able to work to improve or restore a client's emotional health, which I take to be the arts therapist's professional purpose, means, for the therapist, in addition to being well-grounded in the arts, having a fair idea of what the healthy emotional life looks like, and understanding what emotions are and how they work in the human body, mind and spirit to our weal or woe. Having said that, we must immediately enter a note of caution: we are not talking about delivering happiness or the good life or building the perfect relationship here. Rather we are saying that to be able to live a healthy emotional life means being able to cope effectively with the turbulence that emotions are *there to create*, because such turbulence is adaptive in a world governed by the principle of change. Emotions are understandings that upset our equilibrium; emotions experienced in the context of art have the same effect. Handling emotional disturbance in the arts is not only adaptive – it is deeply enjoyable and satisfying.

Martha Nussbaum (2001) cites Marcel Proust's claim that the emotions (he is writing specifically of love) produce 'real geological upheavals of thought'. Arts therapy, on my account, looks for blocks, weaknesses and imbalances in the expressive system colouring and qualifying daily life, and seeks to restore its healthy flow as either reactive or reflexive responses. Doing so will help the client to recover the sense that their feelings are manageable and their emotional information reliable. Most clients seeking the arts therapist's help do so because their feelings have become unmanageable, out of joint, often overheating, unreliable, and so forth – in extreme cases to the point where life itself is hardly worth living any more. Arts therapy seems to derive its remit from the belief that the expressive system can be repaired and improved, and the emotional life thereby achieve (or recover) efficiency. Where the expressive life is malfunctioning on account of some genetic chemical or organic disorder or accidental and irreversible brain damage, the arts therapist may still be able to offer palliative care.

On being needy and insufficent

Pretty much everything we do as professional educators, artists and healers inevitably draws upon and reflects the quality of a student's or a client's earliest experiences. In some measure, and by some means, we may wish to investigate those experiences for clues to inform our intervention. However, I doubt whether such an investigation is strictly useful. We might not need to go outside the art work itself for the clues we are looking for. It is not a client's history we are investigating or their story we are trying to reconstruct; our concern is primarily and exclusively with their artistic success, which is to say their aesthetic satisfactions. What does matter, of course, is that we will use the principle of the good-enough mother–infant relationship as a model for our relationship with our student/client: as teachers, healers and carers we must, at least to some degree, assume the role of the surrogate mother.

In Winnicott's famous phrase, we shall be trying to be 'good enough' in responding to what Nussbaum describes as the other's inherent 'neediness' and 'lack of self-suffi-ciency'. In other words we shall be following upon the earlier work done by the person's actual mother, building on what went well, even, if it seems to be appropri-ate, trying to make good or compensate for what might have been missing or done badly. The fate of every human being is to be needy, to be insufficient in supplying their own wants, to be dependent upon others to supply the companionship they desire – and often for practical help in getting by, in getting better. So it was at the beginning for every one of us, and so it remains throughout the course of a lifetime. Even the happy 'loner' cannot escape this predicament. No matter what sacrifices she has made to keep herself to herself, when she breaks a leg and cannot get out of the house unaided, she will hope for the empathic and generous help of others.

Our make-up determines that our human progress and survival as individuals is inseparable from the experience of pain and loss. Our default emotions are grief and fear. Of course, this is not the end of the story: pleasure complements the work of pain in steering us towards our satisfactions and clear of danger. Fear, as the Syncretic Model suggests, gives way to more pleasant emotions: joy, curiosity, wonder and love. But as human beings we must learn to live with what defines our vulnerability and our lack – and, as we slowly come to understand, the unavoidable bottom line of every life is death. Our very own particular death. Mortality dogs us like our shadow. Each of us has to find a way of making our deal with the Grim Reaper, whilst endlessly trying to outwit him.

Furthermore, the human body with its miraculous brain, and the heart's capacity for sublime attachments, is radically unreliable and subject to accident, assault, deteriora-tion and, finally, dissolution. And then there is our capacity for self-harm, for clumsily doing the wrong thing as well as for knowingly acting in hostile ways towards ourselves. Dealt such a hand by fate, it can be little wonder that we all struggle contin-uously to keep the accounts in credit – taking nothing for granted, for nothing is granted except the initial gift itself, and as the Polish poet W. Szymborska reminds us, even that, it would seem, is on loan and must be paid back. In our desperate straits, however, we are not abandoned. Nature supplies every one of us with a mother – and for every one of us, mother generally knows best and does her best: if not literally as a mother then as someone to do the mothering we need. And mother is simply the first in a long line of loved ones, lasting, if we are lucky, a lifetime. Where this doesn't work out, the risks, dangers and subsequent damage may be incalculable. But most mothers (friends and lovers) get it right – or at least do well enough for long enough. And as for that primal scream, most mothers these days take their babies in their arms to hold and comfort them. Where they don't or can't, they probably end up making work for the arts therapist.

The danger in this, however, lies, for the client, in the prospect that the therapist-mother offers of infinite regression into an unchallenged and unchallengeable infantilism, in which the comforts of the surrogate relationship create a parallel universe with little connection to reality. We have already touched on this issue in considering Stern's position on the therapeutic importance of the therapist–client relationship. It is at least arguable that the arts therapies, grounded as they are in the 'realities' of art, provide a degree of protection against this form of abuse. The habit of art has nothing to offer to those wishing to escape from life, since it is rooted in the handling of, and in conversation with, real materials, and has manifestly significant public consequences.

What might it mean to do well enough as a mother (friend, lover, companion)? We need to have some answers to this question since, in cultivating another's habit of art, we shall be facing the very same challenges in terms of our professional practice. Where mothers give nourishment, so must we. Where mothers touch, embrace and hold the infant, so must we be able to touch, embrace and hold those we are caring for, sometimes literally. Understanding how to nourish and 'hold' the needy and insufficient other is the beginning of being a teacher or therapist or carer. This is where our *empathic humanity* meets their need. I see these occupations in human rather than technical/servicing terms. If two or more humanities do, in fact, meet here, there is the desire for help and attention, on the one hand, and the equal and complementary desire to love and to care on the other: different satisfactions equally important to both parties. When a carer no longer feels empathy for the other, no longer cares, they can't be any use – and shouldn't try.

The Syncretic Model and the good-enough mother

I shall briefly explore good-enough mothering with the help of the Syncretic Model. I do so for what it has to tell us of the co-creative role of the arts therapist. In what follows when I speak of the 'mother', I wish to be understood, of course, to include the father and all other carers either carrying out or sharing in a 'mothering role'.

Metal: grief

Here we have the early days of the newborn child. The archetypal condition of innocence and purity. In this condition, the infant, we are told, already knows the feeling of existential completeness, of what is later described as the 'oceanic' feeling of peaceful union, stillness, clarity with the mother. It might well be the recollection of this blissful sense of completeness that survives in the human search for union with the other, and the drive to perfection and fulfilment that gives life its ultimate inspiration and meaning. Nussbaum (2001) has much to say about the experience of what she calls *eudaimonia*, meaning personal fulfilment, and we shall return to consider its importance in Water (below). Expelled into the world, following what must often be an acutely distressing process, the infant takes their first breath, utters their first cry and

162

experiences the grief and bewilderment of being, and the comfort of his/her mother's arms for the first time. This is the time of holding and being held, according to Winnicott. There's a lot of crying.

Water: fear

Personal dependency and insufficiency are impressed on the infant as they gradually become conscious of their new surroundings and slowly learn to differentiate between objects in the immediate environment. Mother is rapidly identified as the principal source of relief, satisfaction and pleasure: the infant turns to her breast to assuage the pain and fear of hunger, to discover the pleasures of gratification and find comfort and security in her arms and at her hands. With nurturing, protection and comforting established, the mother's next most insistent impulse seems to be to play with her baby and initiate the processes of empowerment and independence. Winnicott calls this the time of handling, and being handled. Relationship begins to assume a new dimension as the mother elaborates upon the theme of holding by introducing the experience of entertainment (from the same root word, *tenir* = to hold). So life comes to include mutual fun, and contact includes social give-and-take in a convivial (smiling) atmosphere that is loving, delightful and exciting. We call this activity play. The seeds of the child's potential for wonder, risk-taking, creativity and curiosity are sown here.

Working with the infant's innate curiosity is the key, somehow. The word derives from the Latin *cura*, meaning care: these playful exchanges with the mother give rise to the deepest sources of self-motivation – the desire to know, to care, to be, to become. This desire is the hunger for self-actualization (Maslow), for self-fulfilment or *eudaimonia* (Nussbaum). Where *eudaimonia* is weak, the client struggles to find the deep sources of their own ambition, their personal *élan-vital*. Curiosity will be little known to them. Fear fetters them. Success at this stage depends on the mother's capacity to attune herself to her child in a living, affective (affectionate) dialogue, to match her own playing to the playful, communicative impulses of the child. Daniel Stern has written convincingly of this process as building the store of resources for the infant's future expressive and creative life, including reserves of courage. The mother's presence and attachment make risk-taking bearable, learning a pleasure and self-assertion an early passion. Where a good-enough partnership is established right from the start, we shall see how crucial playing turns out to be for successful emotional, physical and social development. Fear, as we have seen, is the governing emotion of the Wood phase and play can be an occasion of fear as well as joy: 'good' fear for the most part is exciting. That Winnicott warned of the possible dangers inherent in play, and hence in the therapeutic use of play, is a point interrogated more fully at Appendix 2.

Wood: rage

The trajectory of independence is extended as the child is weaned, toilet-trained, encouraged to feed herself and play on her own, albeit under mother's watchful eye. As life becomes complicated by the child's increasingly setting their own creative agenda of makings and explorations, there arises the possibility of conflict: the child comes to understand and slowly to grant the mother's independent life, and learns their place within the scope of the mother's attention and caring. The child learns that her wishes and inclinations no longer carry priority status (that the emergency of emergence is over): that the world is bigger, more complex and much more interesting than they had thought.

Nussbaum writes of what she calls the 'ambivalence crisis', by which she means the child's experience of anger towards the one she/he hitherto had only loved and tried to please. Anger arises from frustration at having one's wishes thwarted. The child slowly learns that it is possible also to hate the one you love, and this conflict is deeply disturbing. They encounter the distress of guilt – and guilt has long been associated with human creativity (and curiosity). But, equally important, they learn that the hating can be made good: they learn of the relational possibility it affords of reparation or redress – and of hope. So the guilt is not annihilating where the mother's love remains constant despite the fracas.

Making amends corresponds with the infant's recovery of the self, with new energy and a will for further intrepid adventures. Pretend play and experimentation with objects lead to independent creation (this is Winnicott's time of the 'presentation of objects') and I see a significant developmental coincidence between the desire to negotiate the 'ambivalence crisis' and the creating and offering of gifts as a way of making amends and affirming ties. Sacrifice as sacred giving in atonement might lie close to the root of the impulse to artistic making, alongside more positive expressive impulses. Compassion comes to the rescue on both sides: hope is born in the space between the child's making amends and the mother's *acknowing* (I like this form of the word) of her child's absolute worth. Without hope, life cannot be lived. This is hope that is not mere wishful thinking but which is grounded in loving human interaction and celebrated in the exchange of gifts. Neuroscience, as we have seen, claims that the brain has a programme for it. It is the emotional imagination (empathy) at work at the heart of personal creativity.

Fire: joy and love

Solving the 'ambivalence crisis' through giving is an occasion of joy. The infant discovers many other such occasions as, by his own efforts and through his own creativity, he learns to change the world for the better, to fill it with the spirit of love and joy. Above all, the infant makes their home with others through regular acts of sharing good things, mutual caring, helping and collaborating, making amends and proffering gifts. The boundaries of loving and hating are extended, and the scope for hope and reparation likewise. Home is where the heart (hearth) is and the spirit of love and joy reigns supreme in the Fire phase. Spirit is the passport to happiness here. Attachments become commitments. At home in the world, the child begins to define herself as a loved and worthy individual, taking her own, sunny time, occupying her own space, welcoming feedback, a joy and a blooming pain to themselves and others. For the homeless and unhappy child, all this becomes problematic, and successful growing up is put at risk. Lacking praise, she/he will die on their feet.

Earth: empathy

It might not be too much to claim empathy as the crowning moment of emotional development, for upon the quality of our empathic responses depends not only our capacity for making loving relationships with others, but also the way others come to see and value us. The empathic person has access to the inner world of the other: our distinction as human beings lies in this inveterate openness to each other. This intuition or insight into another's mind and feelings provides the basis for intimate conversation and collaboration, for making common cause and solidarity, for giving and receiving succour and consolation, for creating a festive community. Its beginnings go back to the earliest experience of mother–infant mutual attunement. It fuels the impulse for making amends and offering forgiveness; it makes companionship possible and mollifies the negative impulses of suspicion and defensiveness.

Our capacity for compassion says we are right to hope. Where the infant earlier sought a sense of belonging and security in the arms of the mother, here they welcome the world with open arms; embrace it with love and joy drawn from their Fire element. Where all the emotions can be described as active, empathy is a formative, seeking, intelligent activity. Empathy is the feeling imagination. It has nothing to do with calculation; it is not about minding as reading but minding as feeling. As we shall see, empathy is the intelligence of feeling in action; as vital to the making of friends as it is in the composition of poetry, the decorating of a room or the negotiation of a peace treaty. In the Syncretic Model, empathy is linked to authenticity, and authenticity is sovereign in determining good-enough being. The lessons of joy and mutuality, of redress and companionship, of forgiveness and hope have been assimilated and the idea (ideal) of the good set firmly in its moral place as the antidote to pain and neediness. The good, like the earth, becomes the firm ground beneath our erring feet. Compassion, of which we shall have more to say later, is empathy with a piteous face. Coming to earth is the consummation of the expressive life, achieved again and again as the wheel turns, as the energy flows. Block, waste, frustrate that flow, and 'hark what discord follows'.

Implications

What are the implications of this brief resumé of the infant–mother relationship for the therapist? By examining each phase of the Syncretic Model for what it has to say about the mother's role in supporting the child's emotional development, we can discover clues, I suggest, to the different opportunities open to the therapist in co-creating a healing relationship with the client, and to the kinds of intervention appropriate to developing or restoring proper expressive functioning. Harré, as we have seen, builds his entire theory of the Identity Project on human expressive creativity. Insofar as the client-focused problems that arts therapists are called to address are essentially expressive or identity-based, then their remedy might well be found to lie in the creative and expressive opportunities offered by the arts. Furthermore, if my thesis that there is a direct connection between the making and proffering of the gifts of redress and the establishment of hope in the human heart is correct, then the actual making and sharing of proper artworks (as distinct from pseudo art) might prove to be a further opportunity for emotional/expressive recovery.

I claim that the Syncretic Model describes the healthy condition of human expression and creativity. I also claim that the model establishes a vital connection between art and emotional health. We cannot be fully human without the urge to sing, to play, to make and leave our mark, to create representations of our experience of the world we live in, and to share our stories with others and receive theirs in return. This is to cultivate the habit of art: i.e. to have a culture. This is why we are as adept at handling presentational as we are at handling referential (or discursive) symbols (Langer, Reid). 'The aim was song,' Robert Frost says in his poem of that title. As with the birds (and the winds), so with us.

Martha Nussbaum's intelligence of the emotions

It might, at this point, be instructive just to glance at Nussbaum's (2001) 'upheaval' account of the function of the emotions in the economy of the expressive life, and in art. The emotions, Nussbaum says,

> are forms of evaluative judgement that ascribe to certain things and persons outside a person's own control great importance for the person's flourishing. Emotions are here, in effect, acknowledgments of neediness and lack of self-sufficiency.
>
> (2001: 19)

Emotions as 'upheavals' are ways of knowing – Nussbaum's is a cognitive theory of emotion. Knowing what? Knowing as neediness and as lack of self-sufficiency, she says. Knowing as 'sensate disturbance'. Knowing that our circumstances are such that we need to be paying attention, to be vigilant, ready to change. At their most benign, emotions simply arouse us, and arousal, up to a certain level, is pleasurable – it feels good, it helpfully and pleasantly colours experience, it is what we mean by feeling alive: emotions make experiences memorable. They are responsible for Stern's 'vitality affects'. Moving beyond that level, in terms of disturbance, arousal becomes increasingly less simply pleasurable (though not immediately painfully so), and we are alerted to take action in our own interest: transformative action. From feeling mildly and pleasantly aroused we trip head-over-heels into love; from feeling a bit apprehensive we become chilled with fear. Next come the madness of love and the frozen sea of terror: by that time, we are out of control. Even the law recognizes that.

Where the expressive life itself is concerned, where art-making and the receiving of art are the focus of our attention, then higher levels of emotional arousal may also signal that there is a problem with some phase of the cycle itself. Emotion tells us about how we are coping with life; emotion may also signal, to a knowledgeable third party, how well our expressive system is working, how well adapted it is, how reliable is the information it generates. We have already noticed that we tend to participate in the arts to experience emotion as pleasure to be indulged rather than as a trigger to act in the world – or only indirectly so. The man who leaps to his feet in the stalls and shouts at Othello 'She's innocent you fool!' has made a categorical error. He is in the theatre. So what's gone wrong? The pleasure of illusion in art lies in the pleasurable quality of arousal: we have already characterized the activity of art as reflexive rather than reactive. I'd be tempted to explore his Wood phase, his capacity for transformation, for symbol use.

It is the reflexivity of the arts that makes them suitable media of therapy. Acute levels of emotion in their different ways are distress signals. They impose upon us – for they are very insistent. The state we seek to restore is one of positive equanimity: of feeling comfortable with ourselves, awake, engaged, energized, confident. In terms of the Syncretic Model, we are talking about balance and flow and harmony. There is an equation to be drawn between the severity of the emotional experience and the gravity of the underlying problem. The emotion, by and large, is not the problem; it is the, admittedly disruptive, symptom helpfully indicating where the problem lies and inviting or urging us to attend to it. Where emotion itself becomes the problem, enter the arts therapist. Art in this sense is not simply about the expression of emotion; it is about the probing of consciousness itself, about monitoring the shifting tectonic plates beneath the surface of being. In addressing serious problems in the expressive system, checking balance and flow and harmony, the therapist helps the client restore and enhance her feeling intelligence in the service of harmonious being. The subtitle of Martha Nussbaum's book is *The Intelligence of Emotions*. Since emotion points the way to change, emotional responses need to be adapted to trigger reflexivity.

According to Nussbaum, the cause of emotional malfunctioning is most likely to be a failure in the cognitive system more generally, leading to a false appreciation or judgement of the situation the subject is in: for example, to perceive a physical move-ment by someone else as a threat when it is entirely innocent; to fail to see that a remark interpreted as hurtful was, in fact, meant as a playful joke and thus to be entirely inconsequential; a failure to sense the increasing discomfort of a companion as one probes their personal life, 'meaning well', or seeking a closer, undesired rela-tionship. These things happen all the time – usually to no lasting ill effect, but sometimes getting it wrong emotionally generates serious problems.

Nussbaum argues that emotions arise on the basis of judgements made about how things stand with us in terms of our wellbeing and the prospects for whatever project we are embarked upon. Emotions work as 'upheavals', as provocations to change: in the arts they trigger symbol-making. Making sound judgements is the basis, she says, of getting reliable emotional information. Emotions are compound of mind, body and spirit, and sometimes it is difficult to decide at quite what level to address them. Opting for the arts as a therapeutic medium means opting for a holistic solution to an existential problem, a solution managed expressively by the intelligence of feeling. What is uniquely important about healing through the arts is that it engages mind, body and spirit as an integrated system of intelligences and influences, and tends to find its own best level of operation, guided by a growing sense of the rightness of the work as a symbolic form.

Whilst recognizing the importance of Nussbaum's analysis, our own particular empha-sis differs somewhat from hers. We assume that corruption of the Identity Project may arise not only as a consequence of the client's misreading of her situation but also from blocks and imbalances in the functioning of the system itself, and that these functional problems may lie at the root of existential anguish. Unable to process her emotional information, the client becomes subject to confusion and distress. Here the problem is not only an emotional one but also a practical one, signally suited to the therapeutic influ-ence of the arts. The intelligence giving rise to inappropriate emotional responses is, in fact, not the intelligence of the left brain but of the right: the intelligence of feeling. Failures at the Earth phase suggest some kind of breakdown in the handling of what Stern calls 'affective cues' – 'where the communication is in the performance' (2010: 129).

Empathic imagination

We must assume that arts therapy has its own particular rationale for addressing what we have been calling emotional and relational difficulties in everyday experience: which is to say that, as a practice, arts therapy will be more effective in treating some kinds of difficulties than others, will be more appropriate to some conditions of impairment than others. The position I have adopted centres on Harré's notion of the Identity Project and upon restoring and maintaining creative flow though the five phases of the Syncretic Model. Where this doesn't help, other forms of healing outside the arts must be looked for.

Arts therapy heals through the arts experience as it feeds and supports the growth and healthy functioning of the personality in her rightful pursuit of fulfilment – *eudaimonia*. In asking ourselves what that might mean, we could do worse than adopt Nussbaum's notion of 'taking pleasure in our vulnerability'. The human condition being one of neediness and insufficiency, of insecurity and difficulty, we are primed to be disturbed, one way or another, by the emotions to which our humanity gives rise. It seems we enjoy our emotions, where they are not too arousing. But emotional numbness (dumbness) is every bit as debilitating and disabling as emotional overkill. Whether the emotions concerned are of pleasure or pain, in acute forms they are dangerous in their effects. Therapists tend to see people whose emotional lives have become disabling. It is the mystery of art that through the process of creative expression our neediness may be made a source of pleasure and not merely a cause of anguish and illness, our insufficiency a route to self-knowledge and a means of redress against the curse of mortality, 'splendidly' (Zeki, 2009) converting that curse into a blessing.

If all men are indeed born equal, we are so in our vulnerability. If we seek to be united, it should be in pity and compassion for one another, in a condition of mutual empathy. Feeling with the other, what we call 'empathy', is, quite literally, central to the Syncretic Model as the intelligence that grounds us in our common humanity. Nussbaum calls it 'empathic imagination': also, 'the ability to take the perspective of the other'.

She has this to say about the redemptive power of the arts: 'It cannot be emphasized too strongly that what I am advocating, what I want from art and literature, is not erudition; it is empathy and the extension of concern' (2001: 432).

I am reminded, once again, of D. H. Lawrence's dictum that the arts 'direct the way our sympathy flows.' I am also reminded of the Water and Earth phases of the Syncretic Model.

Nussbaum continues:

> I believe that there is a *prima facie* and general correlation between artistic merit and the ability to engage the personality at a deep level. The fact that Sophoclean tragedy inspires compassion for human suffering and the fact that it is great and powerful poetry are not independent facts: it is the poetic excellence that conveys compassion to the spectator, cutting through the habits of the everyday.
>
> (ibid.: 433)

In her advocacy of the arts, Nussbaum concludes with a point of concern for her own agenda: good art, she wants to claim, makes good citizens. (We have been somewhere near here already with creativity, as understood by Craft and her colleagues.)

> If the sort of citizen we want participating in public deliberation has the robust and independent imagination of the lover of art, then we will need to protect the independence of the arts themselves from the interference of moralisms, both

religious and secular, that have always borne down upon them. This point was grasped as early as Periclean Athens. For Pericles, in his Funeral Oration, praised the love of artistic excellence for which his city was famous, and connected this love with the production of a certain sort of independent and passionate citizenry.

(ibid.: 433)

Evaluative judgements

It is important to note here that Nussbaum's intelligence of the emotions is not the same thing as Witkin's intelligence of feeling. Nussbaum's cognitive theory of emotion covers what Witkin meant by 'reactive' affective response. For Nussbaum, emotions are intelligent in the sense that they signal the need to act upon mental 'readings' (information) as to the situation or circumstances surrounding the subject for good or ill. They are tuned responses that stimulate us to act in our own best interests. 'Forms of evaluative judgement', she calls them: fear is generated by a perceived threat to our security; desire by sensory provocation. The intelligence of feeling is formative, is reflexive, is the way we resolve problems to do with form and quality and affective meaning, including the form and quality and affective meaning of our personal lives: so not simply an alarm system but a way of knowing.

When we say someone has a feel for something, an eye, an ear (some of this comes down to what we call 'good taste'), then we are speaking of the intelligence of feeling. It is what governs the work of the artists interviewed by John Tusa in their pursuit of authentic forms of expression, linking form and feeling. I also happen to believe that the good arts therapist, like the good arts teacher, uses her intelligence of feeling in her relationship with her student or client. Teachers and therapists have to be artists in this sense too. They have to practise the habit of art in the character and quality of their working relationships with people. Here, of course, we make contact with empathy again, at the centre of, and pervasive throughout, the Syncretic Model. Empathy is the intelligence of feeling at work, as it applies to the artist's handling of materials and feeling for form, and the teacher's and the therapist's sensitivity to 'affective clues'.

So wherein lies the pleasure in vulnerability, and why might it matter to the therapist? For Nussbaum, the pleasure of vulnerability available through the arts is the pleasure of knowing and growing, of having our sympathies enlarged and personalities enriched. Whilst in no way wishing to challenge her, I nevertheless want to suggest an additional reason. Art answers our most radical existential needs: for nourishment, for holding and for completeness. I think this is where Nussbaum's own idea of *eudaimonia* comes into the equation. As Warnock (*Imagination*, 1976: 46) argues in her account of aesthetic pleasure, what consoles and delights us in art is the scope it offers in satisfying our hope for completeness and cherishing its achievement. What was once merely physical holding has now gained a richer, affective dimension, as in 'holding dear'.

Art works are works of love: love-works. What is vulnerable about us makes us loving and loveable. There is no arts therapy outside of a loving relationship between therapist and client; there is no true arts education outside the loving of teacher and student. If play is the key to therapy, and if what Winnicott calls 'subtle inter-play' characterizes the healing conversation/transaction, then it is the play of equals, empathic in their vulnerability, but un-equal in their positions of carer and cared for. The trick for the therapist is to *attune* and *moderate* her playing, much as the mother does, to the emergent playing of the client. Eventually, they may be able to play as true partners, but by that time the treatment will be all but over, the client will no longer need the therapist. They will be making and receiving art together.

Zeki's 'splendors and miseries'

Semir Zeki (2009), in his book *Splendors and Miseries of the Brain*, describing how delighted we might justly feel by our brain's capability 'as a very efficient knowledge-acquiring or, if one prefers, knowledge-generating system', nonetheless points to a sometimes painful, even disabling, degree of existential grief associated with its very 'splendors':

> The misery that this splendid machinery entails is in fact the result of its very efficiency. The incapacity of our daily experience to live up to and satisfy the synthetic concepts that the brain generates commonly results is a state of permanent dissatisfaction. This does not much matter in many cases. It may be relatively unimportant whether a bottle of wine fits the concept of the perfect wine or whether a house or a symphonic rendering corresponds to my brain-constructed ideals of them. It is quite another matter when the concept of love or a work of art is left unsatisfied.
>
> (2009: 48)

What love and works of art have in common is their expressive realization of our personal identity, of whom we feel ourselves to be, of the basis of our sense of self-worth – and this is because, as we have seen, our authenticity is so deeply involved. If the brain's tendency to construct 'synthetic concepts' – also referred to by Zeki as 'ideals' – only serves to make us painfully aware of how life, and our own efforts, can fall so dismally short of them, then it is of little surprise that we feel miserable. However, it is how we are. Without this tendency to conceive of perfections, to imagine absolute fulfilments, then the life-drive we have associated with the Water phase would not be there to propel us beyond our fears; the creative surge of Wood would simply fail to give birth to the Spring; there would be nothing to hope for from the festival of Light (Fire); no ground beneath our feet in the struggle to be true to ourselves (Earth); no prospect of enduring truths and standards to build the good life around (Metal). Without this constantly shifting set of intuitions as to where our ideal love, our perfect work await disclosure, there would be no romance in our lives – and no art either.

Zeki sees this tendency toward perfection as a major programme of the brain selected and embedded to maintain the emotional drive to life itself. That it often brings misery in its wake is the price we learn to pay. Somewhere within this dialectic of 'splendors and miseries' lies the role of the therapist, applied to when the misery is too much for the 'splendor', when the pursuit of (expression of) the impulse to perfection gives way, perhaps, to misery. We have earlier referred to Plato's notion of the moment of illumination in education. Such a moment qualifies as the achievement of our hope for a perfection. (Perhaps all our perfections are gifts.) We say, 'That's perfect!' – and we are right. Fed on perfections (e.g. from a mother's love to a lover's), the good life regenerates and sustains itself spontaneously and autonomously, just as, in learning, once the breakthrough to understanding has occurred, according to Plato, if all goes well, learning is self-sustaining and irresistible. The therapist's help is needed where this natural capacity for the renewal and sustainability of hope breaks down.

Shakespeare, in his Sonnet 15, the opening lines of which are quoted at the head of this chapter, bemoans the fleetingness of human beauty, and the hopelessness of our struggle to protect our perfections from the toll time takes of them – a familiar theme with him. The poem concludes with the assertion by the poet that it is to poetry itself that he looks to defeat time, to keep his hope of perfection alive. The creative act of art is the way the artist asserts their hope, insists upon their apprehension of the beautiful, the good, the true, the perfect. The poet, at war with time, gathers his love into the timeless orbit of perfection, *sub specie aeternitatis*. Whatever more mundane ends the expressive project in us might seem to serve, it achieves its apotheosis in the arts, where, against all rhyme and reason, we preserve and cherish the possibility of new perfections.

> And, all in war with Time, for love of you,
> As he takes from you, I engraft you new.

Where Martha Nussbaum writes of our inherent neediness and insufficiency, Zeki writes of our splendid brains as the source of existential dissatisfaction and misery. Given the centrality of the expressive project to our book, I take both these writers to be giving us a clue about the nature of our work as teachers and therapists of the arts. I want to extrapolate from what Zeki is proposing here to say that impairment to our expressive system not only causes occasional, even sustained, dissatisfaction but can also escalate to threaten the very roots of happiness; indeed, may be so severe as to make life not feel worth living. It is to issues of such gravity – I say issues to do with the failure of the human expressive impulse and its resources – that the arts therapist is called to bring her healing gifts. Her art opens a splendid prospect.

What Zeki mildly describes as 'dissatisfactions' can thoroughly derail the Identity Project. He acknowledges the seriousness of the damage when he exchanges the mild word 'dissatisfactions' for the graver 'miseries'. One of the splendours of the brain is our capacity for interpersonal conversation, including the conversation of poetry – of the arts. Insofar as the expressive conversation of the arts probes and presents our feelings to the world, it serves a unique function in personal adaptation and relational satisfaction. To be inhibited from ready affective communion, either informally using the metaphorical resources of everyday language (both gesture and word), or more formally through the medium of the arts, is to know dissatisfaction of a very serious order – certainly one deserving of the term 'misery'. The poet Tony Harrison, interviewed by John Tusa and quoted in Chapter 6, describes just such a situation in his own family.

Therapeutic assessment

How might the therapist use the Syncretic Model to construct an account of a client's problems? What follows is purely speculative. It carries with it no authority whatsoever. I shall simply be asking myself the question, What forms of dissatisfaction might be associated with the different phases of the creative/expressive process with which we have been concerned in this book?, and sharing my tentative answers. The experienced reader will judge for themselves whether anything in what I say makes sense, and whether they might feel drawn to explore the model in similar terms, more intelligently and more authoritatively than I have.

Since, in earlier chapters, I have pretty thoroughly explored the role of the teacher in cultivating the emotional and technical aspects of the habit of art, using the Syncretic Model as a framework, I shall not be repeating that here. To the extent that the arts therapist must also be an arts teacher, then the two roles overlap. Improving the client's habit of art will mean, in many respects, adopting the techniques, skills and understandings of the arts teacher. The therapist's role seems to diverge from that of the teacher in as much as the therapist's client has traumatic, expressive – rather than purely technical and cognitive – obstacles in the way of satisfying their artistic impulses. By definition, these obstacles will have proved intractable to the patient, and it will be this very intractability that will have brought the patient to the therapist in the first place. Not that the patient will necessarily be aware where the cause of the problem lies, i.e. as a failure of expressivity. This should, I have been arguing, be the arts therapist's assumption and will provide the basis for the therapist's investigation, diagnosis and treatment through the arts. For the arts therapist concerned to identify problems in the expressive impulse, repertoire and effectiveness of the client, the investigation will fall broadly into the pattern suggested by the Syncretic Model.

1   Metal (1): To what extent does the client seem to be at home within the conventions of artistic expression, including her capacity to enjoy the arts? How extensive

is her acquaintance with the arts? How fluent is the patient's expressive behaviour? How effective is it? How does she understand her difficulties? How does she handle criticism and judgement? Has she ever had a loved mentor in the arts? What art works and which artists are an anchor, a bench-mark of excellence for her, or work as an inspiration to her? Can she handle tragedy?

2 Water: How well defined is the client's artistic/expressive personality? How play-ful is she? To what degree has she appropriated the conventions and repertoire of the arts and made them her own? What particular artistic language does she favour? Is it her true artistic home? How strong is her self-belief as an artist? Does she take easily to playing with her therapist? What is she afraid of that might inhibit her expressivity? How strong is her aesthetic drive?

3 Wood: How passionate is her response to an expressive opportunity? What makes her frustrated about her art? Is she happy to improvise, to take a line for a walk? How readily does she seize the expressive initiative? And once taken, can she sustain it and negotiate a living expressive transaction with others and with the world of objects and materials? Can she concentrate or is she easily distracted? How expert is she in negotiating the symbolic order of expression? How does she feel about working with private material?

4 Fire: Can she bring her expressive projects to a satisfying conclusion? Does she have expressive staying power? Is her expressive drive socially attuned? Does she welcome good expressive companions? Is she sought out by others and able to integrate into complex expressive transactions? Is she a good sharer? Is her artis-tic good will transparent? What does she know of joy and love in her artistic life? Is she comfortable with praise? Is she susceptible to wise advice? Can she be contained and protected from burning herself out, from going over the top?

5 Earth: Is she centred in some inner conviction about who she is as an artist, what her art is about, what she is worth, why truthfulness, honesty and authenticity matter? How strong is her empathy? Does she have the courage of their convic-tions? Are her feelings intelligent? How intelligent? Does she have strong aesthetic intuitions? How ready is she to let go of her work?

6 Metal (2): Can she bear to be judged? Has she respect for legitimate authority and tradition? What, for her, are the supreme aesthetic values? What are her ideals of beauty and perfection? Can she draw strength from the community of values, from the culture? Does she manage to maintain her integrity in her expressive transactions with the world? Does she see her contribution in art as making a gift?

Answers to these questions will come from direct interpersonal encounters and conversations in and around the work: via practical activities in the arts selected to disclose the client's quality of expressive fluency and, in particular, art-specific skills, satisfactions and motivations.

Treating the expressive problem

Having come to an assessment of the nature of the client's *expressive problem*, the therapist will treat it within the kind of intimate and supportive relationship described by Stern and his colleagues and reviewed earlier. It will be a co-created, inter-subjective conversation, with the therapist in a role modelled on the good-enough mother, providing emotional cover and unconditional love. Within such a relationship she will give knowledgeable support for the client's art in the role of the teacher: supplying artistic understanding, resources and techniques that will encourage full and satisfying subject-reflexive expression to take place. Earlier chapters in this book have attempted to cover what this might mean in practice. Additionally, the therapist will bring specialist insights and understandings from psycho-analytical theory to bear on her handling of her client, and in assessing the impact the arts therapy treatment is having on the problem(s) presented and within the broader context of the client's quality of life.

The arts therapist's overarching theory – their professional training as a therapist – will embrace the following understandings:

a   of the human experience of inter-subjectivity (empathy);
b   of human emotional development –including studies of the brain;
c   of human expressive behaviour and its relation to the symbolic order of art;
d   of the role of the creative arts in human development;
e   of theories of the human psyche, its ills and range of remedial regimes;
f   of the cultural roots of the individual;
g   of *poiesis* and *techne* in artistic symbolic creativity;
h   of the repertoire of therapeutic skills appropriate to an arts therapy treatment;
i   of professionalism within the treatment community;
j   of the dynamics of the therapist–client relationship.

Summary

The arts therapist's work is to service the client's Identity Project through expression in the arts. The basic role model is the good-enough mother. The principal method will be play; the medium, art. The aim of treatment will be to help the client produce satisfying artistic work that represents the authentic world of feeling, allowing the expression of their deepest commitments and desires and a sharing of themselves with others. The therapist will use arts activities to identify problems in the functioning of the client's expressive system, including their capacity to play. She/he will work to remove blocks, restore balance, strengthen weaknesses and facilitate creative harmony and flow to the expressive system as a whole, understood as the making and handling of presentational symbols. To be capable of dispensing appropriate and effective treatment, the arts therapist will require a thorough grounding in psychology and therapeutic techniques, and foundation skills and understandings in their chosen medium or art form. The therapist will be a knowledgeable and enthusiastic art lover and a deeply compassionate person. They will understand what playing for one's client means. Her/his work will be informed by, based upon and accountable in terms of a coherent conceptual framework (e.g. the Syncretic Model).

This book presents one among many competing frameworks for developing an arts-based therapeutic practice – a model with strong, traditional connections to healing. The Syncretic Model could be the basis of co-created, formative and summative appraisal, allowing the systematic evaluation of the art work as a therapeutic experience. It could also provide a framework for professional appraisal and for evidence-based research.

In their work, the therapist is, inevitably, pursuing not only the client's recovery but also their own Identity Project – both as an individual and a professional. Their professional identity will have authenticity at its centre, and will amount to the professional expression of empathy. At each stage of their work in supporting and tending the client's creative play as an artist, the therapist will be engaging and dealing with their own cycle of emotions and creative responses, i.e. expressing themselves as a reflective practitioner.

Composing this chapter, I have been very aware of writing as an outsider. However, given the emphasis throughout this book on the experience of change, I was heartened to read the following lines by Jocelyne Samuels in her recent article for the *British Journal of Psychotherapy Integration*:

> Supporting people in managing the change process works for me as a simple aim for psychotherapy in general. The pace of change is rapid today and therefore adaptation has to be fast moving in order for people to cope. Individuals, families and organisations have to be very dynamic to survive. Change brings with it the transference of all our personal histories with their abandonments, bereavements and betrayals, as well as the anxiety attached to uncertainty in our anticipation of the future. Not surprisingly it can be very scary.
>
> (2006: 42)

As someone working with the remarkable Kids Company in London, Jo should know.

Footnote: patient or client?

My use of the word 'client' in this chapter will have caused, perhaps, most readers no problems. It is the conventional usage these days, in the UK and the USA particularly, when speaking of persons seeking and receiving therapy. However, I know that, for some readers, the close connection the word has with the notion of the commercial consumer will strike the wrong note for a human, interpersonal relationship that seems to have more of the 'gift economy' about it than the marketplace. I have actually looked for a possible alternative – one that might also, at the same time, cover the teacher–student relationship. The use of the older term 'patient' now seems generally on the decline in therapeutic circles (though, as we have seen, still happily adopted by Stern and his colleagues in America), not least because of the stigma attaching to the idea that the person seeking help from a therapist must always or necessarily be 'sick'. In some countries this unfortunate and inaccurate description has been dropped in favour of the word 'participant', with its suggestions of a more equal and interactive relationship and a less traumatic practice. However, I am unconvinced by the word, not least because it tends to blur what, to my mind, is central to the relationship, namely the principle of professional 'distance'.

I take for my authority in persisting with the term 'client' the account given in the *SOED*. In particular, I refer to the dictionary's account of the word *clientele*, which speaks of 'the professional connections' of practitioners such as lawyers and physicians with those they serve. It seems to me that the notion of the client properly suggests that those receiving (and usually paying for) the services of a professional are the one's taking the initiative in the relationship and in keeping it going. The professional is invited into their lives on the basis of some kind of mutually agreed arrangement. They are expected to draw on a particularly high level of expertise appropriate to the difficulty the client presents, underwritten by their profession's own rules of practice and conventions of excellence. The client is always free to terminate the relationship.

But the relationship does not hinge upon the fee. It pivots on the principle of professionalism, central to which is the idea of what I shall call 'disinterested interest'. I mean by this that in seeking the services of a professional, we assume that our best interests will always be decisive in all their decisions – irrespective of every other consideration. Where this principle is deemed to have been broken, then every profession worthy of the name has its own mechanisms for calling the membership to account. At root, the relationship of client to professional is one of trust, whether the professional benefits financially or not, and if it is, whether such remuneration comes directly or indirectly from the client.

For arts therapists interested in taking some of these ideas further and exploring in greater depth what Five Elements theory has to say about the emotional and physical problems associated with weakness or malfunction of individual elements in the cycle, I would strongly recommend the sensible book by Rothfeld and Levert (2001) cited earlier.

So, to conclude: whilst acknowledging that 'client' might not always sit comfortably with certain 'professional connections', I feel that it is probably the only serviceable term that I have available in discussing and describing the relationship of therapist to therapee. Now there's an idea. Despite Collingwood's warning, I hope not to have made too much of a fool of myself, treading where even angels hesitate.

11 Valediction

In this chapter, we reiterate the message that cultivating the arts in our lives demands the reinstatement of 'contemplative action' at the heart of education and therapy. This means not only the rejection of the hegemony of the 'technical, promotional, media, digital operation', but also the adoption of ways of teaching and healing based on a co-created, expressive conversation in the arts. The discussion covers a range of topics: the confrontation between the arts and the contemporary 'ceremonies of marketing'; the role of the arts in a world at war; the safeguarding of the sacred in art; the re-balancing of the creative cycle of culture.

> **The adventure of modern art is over. Contemporary art is contemporary only with itself. It no longer knows any transcendence either towards past or future; its only reality is that of its operation in real time and its confusion with that reality. Nothing now distinguishes it from the technical, promotional, media, digital operation. There is no transcendence: . . . merely a specular play with the contemporary world as it takes place. It is in this that contemporary art is worthless: between it and the world, there is a zero sum equation.**
>
> **Jean Baudrillard, *The Intelligence of Evil, or the Lucidity Pact* (2005: 105)**

After Auschwitz

Theodor Adorno, the German-born philosopher and musicologist, famously said that after Auschwitz there could be no more poetry. Al Alvarez (*The Savage God*) logged the sad catalogue of broken lives among artists who gave up and killed themselves. If art is good for you, what good was it to Sylvia Plath or Virginia Woolf? And then there was George Steiner's demolition, in *To Civilize our Gentlemen*, of the Victorian cultural act of faith that literature could have a civilizing, an ennobling, influence through education. Steiner took as his case in point the Nazi officers appointed to run the death camps – many of whom were keen music lovers, some organizing their Jewish prisoners into camp orchestras.

178

Janine di Giovanni has reported many wars. In the early part of 2010 she returned to Sarajevo, to the scenes of the Bosnian conflict that she had lived through as a journalist. Her account of the experience, carried in *Granta* magazine, Issue 111 (2010), is both searing and awesome. During the conflict she had met and fallen in love with a young soldier, and, with the war over, she arranges to meet him again. He has changed – adapted to the new Sarajevo. Their meeting is fraught: the gulf between them somehow unbridgeable.

> 'Every war drowns out another', he tells me. 'Rwanda drowned out Bosnia. Somalia drowned out Rwanda. Sierra Leone drowned out Somalia. Iraq drowned out Israel. Afghanistan drowned out Iraq…and so on and so on until no one remembers anything.'
>
> Later I ask him what happened to this city. Why did the people rip each other to pieces? Everyone calls it an ethnic war, or a religious war, but it was neither. It was about politics, greed, land-grabbing, and how it can eat you up, turn you crazy, make you turn on your neighbour. It was about politicians and power.
>
> 'You should let it go', he says, finally.
>
> He looks distant, remote. He says nothing. He gets up to take his long, black coat. I want to cry, but I don't.

These are all terrible stories and they drain us. We fall to our knees. They are somehow beyond speech, certainly beyond answers. And yet none of them can be allowed to be decisive. That individual creative lives might be unsettling in themselves and, for all the brilliant fruit they yield, finally prove unsustainable to the artists themselves, has to be accepted as a fact of life – and death. But it is the exception rather than the rule. As for the Nazi officers, whatever else was going on with them, they managed to split their habit of art from their habit of life. The seemingly endless tally of modern wars plays to the basest and most degraded estimate of human being. It may seem irrelevant, even improper, to talk about the arts in the same breath – and yet we must. Our claim here is that the arts – belonging as they do to the contemplative realm – are an undisputed civic good and play a central part in our idea of a civilized world, no matter that world so often seems to fail us. They should also, where they can, be deployed to alleviate suffering and sickness. For all the sadness and disillusionment of her writing, Janine di Giovanni's bearing witness is somehow itself a heroic message of hope. Wherever a society acknowledges that there is more to life than getting and spending, than politics and power, an investment in the arts is also just such an investment in hope, in our old idea of the soul.

Wise teachers and therapists are able to find a middle way between thought and intuition, between accountability and risk-taking, between nourishing and challenging, between finding answers and asking questions. It is perfectly right that society should demand evidence in support of the claims we make for the efficacy of our work. But, by the same token, that evidence must be appropriate to the claim: so this is likely to be in terms of the eye-witness rather than the speed camera. Some activities we have to judge not for the quality of what comes out of them but for the quality of what goes into them, for the opportunity and occasion of investment. For we are inveterate investors in life – gamblers I suppose – as well as tallymen. Life is at least as much to do with the quality of what we have attempted and the integrity of our commitment, as with success in terms of coffers filled and gongs lifted. We often have fonder memories of training sessions and rehearsals than of the actual performances themselves, win or lose.

'Respond to the dance'

Kazuo Ohno, the co-founder of modern Japanese Butoh dance, died on 1 June 2010. I saw his slow-motion troupe dance at Dartington some years ago and one performance was sufficient to make an enduring mark upon my work. In an obituary by Martin Childs in the *Independent* (7 July 2010), Ohno is quoted as follows:

> The best thing someone can say to me is that while watching my performance they began to cry. It is not important to understand what I am doing; perhaps it is better that they don't understand, but just respond to the dance.

If we can cry at a dance it is precisely because we understand – but not as the world commonly understands. Not *Logos* but *Eros*. We understand in feeling rather than with our heads. Ohno seems to be saying that we don't need to supply the dance with a narrative or a reference system: the symbol system of the dance is non-referential, it is, as we have discussed elsewhere, 'presentational'. And the presentational symbol works directly through the intelligence of feeling, which is to say immediately upon the right brain (soma), rather than via left-brain discursive thought. The intelligence of feeling is 'intelligent' in as much as it actively probes and processes questions. It is interrogative and formative. Where we open ourselves to artistic experience we are deliberately exposing ourselves to the principle of 'rogation', which is searching, testing, probing or questioning. We may think that it is we who are asking the questions, but we go to art to be tested, searched, explored and interrogated by other minds, so as to have the horizons of our own enlarged; to be laid open, revealed, disclosed and understood – at the deepest level available to consciousness.

Such laying open and deep probing of the self is the way of art – it is also more generally the way the intelligence of feeling or sensibility works in our lives. It is our most intimate form of cognition; it is also the oldest. When we weep spontaneously at a dance or at a piece of music (we are on the surest ground the more 'abstract' or purely formal the stimulus, for this will help to fend off the superficial appeals of 'content' to cliché and sentiment), our deepest emotions are being stirred by intelligent feeling. Feeling is not emotion, it is sensibility and speaks to the soma, to our bodily perception of orientation, stability, motion, direction, ambience and atmosphere. Intelligent feeling tells us directly how the sensate being feels at any given moment, whereas it is the function of the emotions to transmit information about our relationship to the world, to what in the environment we need to give our attention. Emotion, as Nussbaum argued, provides the signal to act in the world. Consciousness is 'punctured' by emotion to trigger instant reaction to changes in our circumstances for good or ill. Feelings are intelligent in the sense that they identify and search problems of being *reflexively*, in parallel with left-brain thinking – contemplatively. Feelings are free to attend to qualitative information, to monitor and adjust our being so we come closer to our heart's desire, whereas emotions are burdened or charged with reactive potential, and rational thought is about computing our best advantage. Aristotle's basic distinction between contemplation and calculation applies here.

In her little book *Absence of Mind*, the American novelist Marilynne Robinson takes issue with the hegemony of modern science in its brutal denial of the intelligence of feeling. Robinson doesn't actually put it like that, but that is what she means. She argues that modern science, or, as she terms it, 'parascience', has built 'an unshakeable bulwark' (quoting Freud's words) against the spirit, wonder, intuition, the arts, wisdom, folklore, myth, mysticism, religious sensibility and the actual felt experience of the living subject. It has instituted a 'threshold' mentality – a kind of fortress science – which brooks no half-measures in the pursuit of reason. If you conform to its positivistic strictures you may abide within its walls; otherwise, quite simply, you've got it wrong. Parascience is the new Puritanism; a culture in retreat from the body and the spirit. Robinson, who believes 'it is only prudent to make a very high estimate of human nature', attacks what she calls 'parascientific literature' for its pseudo-certainties. She explains:

> By this phrase I mean a robust, and surprisingly conventional, genre of social or political theory or anthropology that makes its case by proceeding, using the science of its moment, from a genesis of human nature in primordial life to a set of general conclusions about what our nature is and must be, together with the ethical, political, economic and/or philosophic implications to be drawn from these conclusions.
>
> (2010: 32)

She goes on to track the way this kind of reductive thinking – in such writers as Auguste Comte and, more recently, Daniel Dennett, E. O. Wilson (The Ant Man), Richard Dawkins and Steven Pinker – marks so much of our contemporary modernist, 'debunking' culture. She argues that in thinking so, we wilfully abandon not only so much of our cultural inheritance – including the transcendent roots of science 'proper' in awe, wonder, imagination and creative speculation – but also condemn ourselves to a kind of obdurate single-mindedness that shuts down half the human brain and leaves us bereft of our deepest resources of personal and collective wellbeing and happiness. She comes very close to echoing Darwin's lament that he had forfeited his happiness in order to become a computer. I say, for modern science read also modern business, where the dangers of positivistic mono-vision are perhaps even more dangerous because they are more ruthlessly pervasive in their influence on all of us. Robinson (who wrote *Gilead*) has no problem rendering unto Caesar what rightly belongs to him, but not at the expense of ignoring the spirit and denigrating the old-fashioned idea of the recognizably human in man.

For me, the argument is to be made in terms of *Logos* and *Eros*. In making a plea for the reinstatement of the intelligence of feeling in our lives and, more specifically, the authenticity of the subject, we are echoing Gablik's demand for the 're-enchantment' of art. I am also suggesting that this is to pay due tribute to the importance of the erotic principle, which I understand to lie at the root of free creativity, free play and, of course, the free arts. Creativity, play and art cannot be other than free – and freedom is the drive that *Eros* supplies. 'Freedom' is the cry of *Eros* – and is the principle incorporated in the Syncretic Model. The subject must be free to seek her own good within the bounds of authenticity and empathy, knowing herself to be vulnerable and dependent, understanding that to be free means knowing how to be with, how to create and play with others. The sign of healthy being is playfulness; all that works against free playing, such as the threshold mentality of the 'pseudo' scientist and the competitive, cost-effective mantras of corporate business, works against the inherent freedom of the old idea of the soul and serves to erode the deepest source of intelligence available to us – the intelligence of feeling.

Staying with the theme of the dance, here is Coomaraswamy answering the question, 'Why does Shiva dance?'

> He dances to maintain the life of the cosmos and to give release to those who seek Him. Moreover, if we understand even the dance of human dancers rightly, we shall see that they too lead to freedom. But it is nearer the truth to answer that the reason of his dance lies in his own nature, all his gestures are own-nature-born, spontaneous, and purposeless – for his being is beyond the realm of purpose.
>
> (2009: 92)

The soul hunters

In writing this book I have explored Chinese Five Elements theory as a metaphor for deepening understanding of the creative process in the arts, particularly in the contexts of arts education and therapy. These two fields of practice, in common with acupuncture itself, my initial point of departure, work to the betterment of the human condition and are thereby conceived as pro-life, as constructive interventions. To the extent that my emphasis in interpreting Five Elements theory has been uniformly positive, I am guilty of a distortion. The Five Phases of Change is a holistic model of the circumstances in which human life is realized, and as such, presents both the negative as well as the positive sides of change. To provide the complete picture, to do full justice to the model, would entail my offering a more strictly balanced account of the woe to which change exposes us as well as the weal. Human progress is matched by human decline; good fortune must be weighed against ill; we are both blessed and cursed in our lot. Life offers us joy in one hand and horror in the other. Either way, we have to learn to adapt, to be flexible, to be philosophical, drawing equally upon the collective wisdom and our own personal experience to survive and prosper as best we may. 'If all goes well' we shall find meaning and happiness to reward our perseverance. Arts education and arts therapy are practices conceived in the hope of making as good a life for ourselves as fortune allows, of maintaining the balance between happiness and computing.

It is almost time to go, but before I do, here's the promised story of the soul hunters. Once again we have a repeating cycle of events, and one strangely echoing the model we have been exploring.

The Yukaghir are a small community living under extreme conditions in remote eastern Siberia. Their story is told by the young Danish anthropologist Rane Willerslev (*Soul Hunters: Hunting, Animism, and Personhood among the Siberian Yukaghirs*). Willerslev found himself in trouble with the Russian police, so he says, and had no choice but to join a Yukaghir hunting party and head for the deep forest. There he observed and participated in their rituals – and, as a scientist, attempted to theorize what he saw. His book makes fascinating reading. I abstract from it the bare bones of the hunting cycle, as another beautiful metaphor for the creative process, and as another illustration of the pervasiveness of the cyclical, four- five- six-part-model in our thinking about the world. Fundamental to the Yukaghir hunt is their animism – their belief that not only humans but also animals, trees and plants – all living things in fact – have souls. 'Soul' here means the life-force itself. Insofar as the material world contains animate creatures, they are understood to be ensouled. There is a sense in which our Syncretic Model tracks the journey of the soul as it follows the life-force in its cycle. Nicole C. Karafyllis (2008) points out that 'Looking across cultures, in ontologies of nature the activity of soul, and thus life, starts with plants, that is, what Aristotle regarded as (Latin) *anima vegetative* (or Greek: *psyche threptiké*)' (Karafyllis and Ulshöfer, 2008: 242).

Life, for the Yukaghir, is to be understood on at least two levels running in parallel and regularly crossing over and interacting. The one level is that of physical nature, the other of the soul or spirit world. Hunting the body of the elk meant also hunting the animal's soul. Such a matter of life and death could not but be a sacred transaction. For the Yukaghir hunter it meant wooing the soul of the elk, seducing it to fall in love with him and yield up her life to him. The danger for the hunter was to be seduced by the power of his animal suitor – and go native. The hunt itself has six distinct phases:

1   The village. The hunting party leaves the village full of hope, makes camp in the forest and, drawing upon traditional wisdom, ritually prepares for the hunt.
2   The camp. The hunters take care of the practicalities: preparing the weapons, securing supplies and so forth. There were rituals to be followed as part of the spiritual process of 'opening up' to the hunt.
3   The hunt. The hunters tended to work alone. They would track their quarry through the forest and, when the moment seemed right, would lure the animal from its hide by performing a dance. This involved the hunter's donning an elk skin and 'dancing' in a suitable clearing – also cupping his hands and making a particular call. The animal would be seduced into moving from the security of the trees into the clearing, to take a closer look at this display, by a creature that was not an elk, but not *not* an elk. (Doing tai chi in my garden or in the woods or beside a river, I am often approached by the wild. Once, in Langdale in Cumbria, an otter came out of the river and sat so close to watch me I could see the beads of water on its whiskers.) With the elk surrendered to his charms, the hunter dispatches it and his work is done. The soul of the slaughtered animal then migrates to another elk.
4   Back at the camp, the hunters relax and celebrate their kill. The drink flows and each man tells his story, sings his own songs. Sharing and festivity, storytelling and merry-making. The hunter prepares to return to the village.
5   At the centre, in line with the Syncretic Model, is the hunter's prowess – his fitness, his integrity, his honour, his authenticity as a hunter. At every stage of the cycle, it is this central principle that secures the truth, the authority, the integrity of the work, that ensures its essential sanctity or holiness.
6   The (hopefully) successful return to the village, where the families are waiting anxiously for the safe return of their menfolk and the whole village for the meat that will see them through the coming winter. Each man's story is retold and reputations puffed and polished. Meanwhile the elders appraise the hunt's success and the prowess of individual members of the team.

Deploying the Chinese principles of *Sheng* and *Ke* to this particular instance of creativity is, once again, to grasp the dynamics at play holding the whole system together; a system governed by the complementary principles of nurturing and controlling. Similarly, Harré's key words correspond neatly to this practice:

Village: conventionalization/Metal
Opening up: appropriation/Water
The hunt: transformation/Wood
Celebration: publication/Fire
The hunter: authenticity/Earth
Village: the gift

My practical workshops follow the same pattern. Insofar as I take the role of the hunter, what I seek in the end is a transaction of souls.

Here is Simone Weil:

> Extreme attention is what constitutes the creative faculty in man and only extreme attention is religious…The poet produces the beautiful by fixing his attention on something real. It is the same with the act of love…The authentic and pure values – truth, beauty and goodness – in the activity of a human being are the result of one and the same act, a certain application of the full attention to the object…Teaching should have no aim but to prepare, by training the attention, for the possibility of such an act. All the other advantages of instruction are without interest.
>
> (2005: 234)

Arts educators and therapists are in the same business of 'extreme attention' as the Yukaghir hunters.

The pool of time

There is a pivotal moment In Virginia Woolf's novel *To the Lighthouse* (1927) when all seems to be on the point of being lost. It is the decisive moment of the book's own pivotal centre, the section called 'Time passes'. Woolf has been describing the passing of the years when the house used by the Ramsay family for their seaside summer holidays in Scotland had stood empty. (Woolf is drawing on memories of her childhood holidays in Cornwall.) The First World War had come, holidays were out of the question: there was news of Mrs Ramsay's death, of the death of her daughter Prue in childbirth, of Andrew her son killed in France. No-one came, no one wrote. Mrs McNabb, the housekeeper, herself old and crippled, made desultory attempts to dust and tidy up, but it had all become too much for her. And yet she carried on, and she remembered. But nature threatened to overwhelm the empty house, with its fecundity, its 'insensibility', its 'equanimity' – Woolf's words.

> For now had come that moment, that hesitation when dawn trembles and night pauses, when if a feather alight in the scale it will be weighed down. One feather, and the house, sinking, falling, would have turned and pitched downwards to the depths of darkness.
>
> (1960: 160)

We are invited to imagine the house, which by this time in the novel we have come to love, not least for the people into whose intense playings and realities Woolf has tenderly drawn us, finally abandoned to picnickers, lovers, the occasional shepherd or tramp. The roof will fall, briars and hemlock will blot out the paths, the carnation mate with the cabbage, swallows build in the drawing room, thistles push through the floor tiles in the kitchen. (Woolf revisited Talland House in St Ives, Cornwall, some 20 years after the family left it.)

The feather does not fall. If it had, the house would have 'plunged to the depths to lie upon the sands of oblivion'. The cultural (contemplative) impulse is not quite extinguished: it stirs to reassert itself and restore the balance with nature – which otherwise would simply have annihilated it. The long-awaited 'word' arrives: the family is coming back, and the boy James's long-postponed dream mission to the lighthouse will be resumed, many years after bad weather had thwarted his dreams. There is something gently comic in the moment of redemption, as Woolf describes it:

> But there was a force working; something not highly conscious; something that leered, something that lurched; something not inspired to go about its work with dignified chanting or solemn ritual. Mrs McNabb groaned; Mrs Bast creaked. They were old; they were stiff; their legs ached. They came with their brooms and pails at last; they got to work…Slowly and painfully, with broom and pail, mopping, scouring, Mrs McNabb, Mrs Bast stayed the corruption and the rot; rescued from the pool of Time that was fast closing over them now a basin, now a cupboard; fetched up from oblivion all the Waverley novels and a tea set one morning; in the afternoon restored to sun and air a brass fender and a set of steel fire-irons.
>
> (ibid.: 161)

I would gladly settle for some such account of the habit of art: this 'staying of the corruption and the rot', this rescuing 'from the pool of Time'. There is an unsettling foreshadowing in these lines of Virginia's own 'pitching downward to the depths of darkness'.

All the while I have been writing this book, Virginia Woolf's novel has haunted it, at the edge of vision, somehow insisting, questioning, looking for a way in. Rather like the 'airs' Woolf describes, nosing and nibbling and fanning around the deserted house above the beach. She sees them 'questioning and wondering, toying with the flap of hanging wallpaper, asking, would it hang much longer, when would it fall?' I began to play with the idea that the whole novel might be structured around the model. In a way it had to be, since I have always felt it to be the purest poetry, the most beautiful of stories. In my speculations I placed the section we are now examining ('Time passes') at the centre (Earth), seeing it somehow as the novel's fulcrum. Woolf found it the most challenging section to write – saw it as incredibly risky. And I managed to find a more or less plausible way of disposing of the remaining phases of the novel around that centre, as it moved from the opening scenes of Mr Ramsay's brutal deflation of his son's hopes (Metal) to its final moments, as father and son step out of the boat onto the rocks where the lighthouse stands (Metal again).

It was a pleasant surprise, therefore, to discover, looking at what Hermione Lee (1996) has to say about the novel, that Woolf made her own little drawing of the shape she had in mind for it – and you don't have to push quite beyond the bounds of plausibility to see the quincunx lurking within it! Woolf mentions Sir Thomas Browne's *The Garden of Cyrus* and his writing about the quincunx in Chapter V of her novel *Night and Day* (1919). At all events, she places 'Time passing', as I do, firmly in the middle. She describes the diagram as 'two blocks joined by a corridor'.

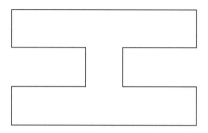

Figure 11.1 Virginia Woolf's model for *To the Lighthouse*

This middle section seems important to me now, which is why, at the very last, I have been able to respond to the novel's importunate nudges and winks. It speaks of the turning point, the tipping point, of the cycle of time, the transitional moment. It speaks not so much of the potential 'space' – although in many ways the haunted house at the centre of the book is just such a space – but of the potential 'time'. Potential spaces and potential times wait just out of sight, just beyond our reach, like these naturally occurring places and times when the world turns, when the scale tips, when the feather drops – or fails to drop. These are the moments of transition between conscious and unconscious, sleep and waking, night and day. They occur at the turning of the tide, at the turning of a corner, at a turn of the weather: transitional or liminal moments marking change, the crossing from one space, one time, into another. T. S. Eliot writes of such times, such places, in his poem 'Four Quartets'. We have, following Winnicott, spoken of these 'potent' spaces and moments in connection with the opportunity to cross from reality into play. Set in the context of a holiday, interrupted by brutal reality and then resumed again, the narrative of *To the Lighthouse* is concerned with the transitional and the playful, with disclosure, creativity and, yes, epiphany. The book's final sentence testifies to the artist Lily Briscoe's having 'had her vision'.

These moments of transition are pivotal points in life: dusk, dawn and twilight. My favourite French word is *le crépuscule*. The 'twi-' in twilight means 'two': two things at the same time: both light and dark, both day and night. Which? Neither? Both? These are the magical times, the moments when we drowse, doze, are dazed, fazed – the sharp focus of reality gives way to mists and haze (and de-differentiation). Not to true dreaming, night dreaming, but to day dreaming. At such moments of ambiguity, we partake of both sides of ourselves, the open and the secret, the manifest and the hidden, the dextrous and the sinister, the bright and the dark. In a sense, here and only here we may appear whole to ourselves; dropping off in the haunted house at dusk, or coming to at break of day. Art arises when we invest in such moments, of our own making and by our own entreaty, or when we are surprised by their sudden appearance and we recognize them for what they are. There are dangers, of course. At such times and in such places we are blithe in our vulnerability. We are in neutral with the brakes off; in free fall, as Golding would have it; exposed, open, receptive, off our guard, suspended, available, potent, potential, waiting, ready, unachieved, available. And we choose to go there, choose to spend that kind of time or tide, in order to restore and rebuild our capacity to stop the corruption and the rot, to deny the pool of time, to insist upon the relevance of the good, the true, the beautiful – the old idea of the soul.

Woolf insists upon these things, as we have done consistently throughout this book of ours.

> Then indeed peace came. Messages of peace breathed from the sea to the shore. Never to break its sleep any more, to lull it rather more deeply to rest and whatever the dreamers dreamt holily, dreamt wisely, to confirm – what else was it murmuring – as Lily Briscoe laid her head on the pillow in the clean still room and heard the sea. Through the open window the voice of the beauty of the world came murmuring, too softly to hear exactly what is said – but what mattered if the meaning were plain? – entreating the sleepers (the house was full again; Mrs Beckwith was staying there, also Mr Carmichael), if they would not actually come down to the beach itself at least to lift the blind and look out. They would see the night flowing down in purple; his head crowned; his sceptre jewelled; and how in his eyes a child might look. And if they still faltered (Lily was tired out with travelling and slept almost at once; but Mr Carmichael read a book by candle-light), if they still said no, that it was vapour this splendour of his, and the dew had more power than he, and they preferred sleeping; gently then, without complaint, or argument, the voice would sing its song. Gently the waves would break (Lily heard them in her sleep); tenderly the light fell (it seemed to come through her eyelids). And it all looked, Mr Carmichael thought, shutting his book, falling asleep, much as it used to look years ago.
>
> (ibid.: 165)

Woolf's impulse here is the same as Collingwood's plea for resisting what he called 'the corruption of consciousness', in insisting upon the distinction between 'art proper' and 'pseudo art' or art 'so-called'. It is the same as Frank Oppenheimer's impulse to put the muse back into museum, designing his Exploratorium in San Francisco as an 'undesigned' space for play and exploration, so that no child should be afraid of knowing or feeling, or be tricked into believing that understanding was beyond them; in the arts as well as the sciences. The resistance of art (Adam Phillips calls it the 'rage' of art) is to be found in the spirit of John Donne's love poetry; in Wordsworth's celebration of childhood; in Gerard Manley Hopkins's passion for nature; in the courage of love in W. H. Auden; in the reclamation of the religious spirit in the poetry of George Herbert; more recently, in the personal refusal of poet Jo Shapcott. Winnicott wrote against the corruption of play and to stop the rot of mothering; Shakespeare wrote against the corruption of power, wherever and by whomever. Kathleen Jamie writes of the bird flying out of the waterfall, of the blue boat sailing north in the twilight, with its lantern 'like our old idea of the soul'. And what is all of this? What does it amount to, all this turning away from 'getting and spending'? What is it if not a ministering to, an invocation of, the soul? There is no other word for what we are speaking of here. I want still to be able to use it, with the confidence of the Yukaghir, of Woolf and Heaney and Jamie. This, finally, is the habit of art.

How many miles to Babylon?
   Three score and ten.
Shall I get there by candlelight?
   Yes, and back again.

Paula Rego has made a strong picture of this old verse, full of lighted candles and wild girls dancing back home again in the night sky, saying 'yes'.

The end of *To the Lighthouse* brings night and day together: the visions of the artist (Lily the painter and Mr Carmichael the poet) and the troubled longings of the bereaved practical man (Mr Ramsey), stepping out of the boat with his parcel in his arms, onto the lighthouse rocks. As Lee says, this is a book about endings. It is also a book about the strain on the artist of leaving the safe haven of the past and venturing into the unknown, a topic we have already looked at. There are two houses in the book: the house of light and the house of dark. The house of light is a kind of illusion that beckons, not only the book's characters but also the reader, to imagine something (a love?) radiant beyond mere 'understanding'. The dark house is the house of potent space, and it is boundless; it is also the house of timeless depth. It is the house of the soul. Depth is our experience of potent time, and time is the measure of life. Were the Syncretic Model sometime in the future to acquire a third dimension, as Donna once built it in an inspired moment, time (*Kairos*) will probably be it.

I noticed a quite unexpected echo in Woolf's lines with which she closes this interlude, of the elegiac passage that closes James Joyce's story 'Death' in his collection *The Dubliners*, published some 13 years earlier and made into the perfect film adaptation by John Houston and his daughter Angelica.

Woolf: The sigh of the sea breaking in measure round the isles soothed them; the night wrapped them; nothing broke their sleep, until, the birds beginning and the dawn weaving their thin voices in to its whiteness, a cart grinding, a dog somewhere barking, the sun lifted the curtains, broke the veil of their eyes, and Lily Briscoe stirring in her sleep clutched at her blankets as a faller clutches at the turf on the edge of a cliff. Her eyes opened wide. Here she was again, she thought, sitting bolt upright in bed. Awake.

(ibid.: 166)

Joyce: Yes, the newspapers were right: snow was general all over Ireland. It was falling on every part of the central plain, on the treeless hills, falling softly upon the Bog of Allen and, further westward, softly falling into the dark mutinous Shannon waves. It was falling, too, upon every part of the lonely churchyard on the hill where Michael Fury lay buried. It lay thickly drifted on the crooked crosses and headstones, on the spears of the little gate, on the barren thorns. His soul swooned slowly as he heard the snow falling faintly through the universe and faintly falling, like the descent of their last end, upon all the living and the dead.

(1993: 288)

I have traced both these pieces, with their characteristic 'dying fall', to a passage in George Eliot's *The Mill on the Floss* (Book 2, Chapter 2) – another novel whose theme is death. Eliot is also describing a fall of snow.

Eliot: Snow lay on the croft and river-bank in undulations softer than the limbs of infancy; it lay with the neatliest finished border on every sloping roof, making the dark-red gables stand out with a new depth of colour; it weighed heavily on the laurels and fir-trees till it fell from them with a shuddering sound; it clothed the rough turnip-field with whiteness and made the sheep look like dark blotches...

(2003: 161)

Death does indeed, as Lee suggests, wander the margins of Woolf's book, very much as *To the Lighthouse* has wandered the margins of mine: there is a time for everything, and death shall be no exception. But death has no final dominion in either her book or Joyce's – or indeed George Eliot's – for they speak of a potential place and a potential time, and though the habit of art as resistance must partake of decline and death at the end, in striking a bargain with death, art belongs firmly with the journey to Babylon, from which all travellers may hope to return. 'In their death they were not divided.' As Lee points out at the end of her piece:

The ending of the novel is poised between arriving and returning, getting somewhere ('he must have reached it') and being finished. This dark book of loss and grief begins and ends with sentences starting 'Yes'.

(1996: 483)

She points to the book's deep cyclical structure. But this is no 'dark' book; it has a dappled beauty, a 'pied beauty' – as in Hopkins's poem. It is a book of sunshine and shadow, of tears and laughter, of sunset and sunrise, of decay and renewal, of setting out and time passing and coming home.

Seasoning

I was walking out one morning before breakfast in the grounds of the Gliffaes Hotel beside the River Usk in South Wales – a holy place for me since so much of this book has been conceived, drafted and worked out there – when I passed a pile of sawn timber planks stacked in a field, all of prodigious thickness and width. I had noticed the huge oak felled beside its vast stump over a number of years, and now someone had sawn its massive trunk into a set of boards. They stood piled one on top of the other, out in the weather. I have no notion how long they will be left there to 'season' – perhaps the process takes many years. And the thought came to me that our English verb 'to season', meaning to expose wood to the vagaries of the passing seasons as a process of hardening or making durable, carries another connotation: the notion of making a dish more appetizing by adding spices to it. This seemed a handy way of encapsulating the central claims of this book. The habit of art is indeed such a seasoning process: as we repeat the seasonal cycle (and the arts have their own 'seasons' of course), so our souls become more durable and more richly fragrant and delightful. I am reminded of George Herbert's poem 'Vertue' – the title of which signifies, in its original sense, not only the moral quality but spiritual power or energy too. The final verse reads:

> Onely a true and vertuous soul,
> Like season'd timber never gives;
> But though the whole world turn to coal,
> > Then chiefly lives.

Behind and beyond the woodpile hovers the ghostly past life of a fallen giant: flourishing for hundreds of years. It is much the same with the story of the Yukaghir: there is just so much more to it than I have been able either to grasp or to tell. It is so, too, with the Chinese theory of the Five Elements and my application of it. I fear I may be guilty of a reductive handling, cutting its complex mysteries down to size for my own convenience – mysteries of enormous power and potential for human good. I must hope that the reader will not imagine that what I have offered in this book is all that there is to be said. Whether considered as underpinning the Syncretic Model or, more profoundly, on its own ancestral terms, there is far, far more to discover about Five Elements theory than has come within my compass. The woodpile tells me but a fraction of the story of the 'great rooted blossomer' (Yeats). Metal marks the end of the quest for inspiration and meaning, and it marks the beginning. I like to think that those who have followed me thus far will find themselves at the beginning rather than at the end of a story.

> Here and there one sees a face on a checkout clerk, or a boy pushing a broom which seems so fresh and well intentioned that one knows the human race will outlive the ceremonies of marketing.
>
> John Cheever, *The Journals* (2010: 360)

Epilogue

Ah, not to be cut off,
not through the slightest partition
shut out from the law of the stars.
The inner – what is it?
if not intensified sky,
hurled through with birds and deep
with the winds of homecoming.

Ahead of All Parting, Selected Poetry and Prose of Rainer Maria Rilke

In his little book on Thomas Hardy's boundless (and bountiful) *The Mayor of Casterbridge*, my old Cambridge tutor Douglas Brown observes that in his art Hardy does not seek to provide 'closure' but rather 'to hold the balance'. To do otherwise, to have come down either on the side of the doomed world of the corn-factor Michael Henchard or the emergent world of the young merchant Donald Farfrae, would have been to betray the role of the artist, which, says Brown, is that of a *mediating consciousness*. It would have been to surrender art to the polemical impulse; to close it within the bounded; which makes me think that the symbol in art is about the power to release impacted (potential) energy into the kinetic world of action – to convert unknowing into knowing. This is the very business of 'holding the balance'. In terms of our model, it means unblocking and releasing the creative flow of energy; it means enabling the student, the client, to rejoin the cycle of change with more of their experience available to transformation and celebration. Art, Brown seems to be suggesting, is not about finding answers or consolation but about rejoining the action, with more of our experience active within us. The symbol in art is critical in 'mediating' the processes of converting potential to active emotional energy, to converting unknowing into knowing (in education), dis-ease into ease (in therapy). The symbol in art offers the brain (intelligence of feeling) an imaginative structure for the processing of trauma, for negotiating the cloud of unknowing and, from time to time, finding illumination. My thesis is that impacted (potential) emotional energy remains inert and troubling when it cannot be processed, cannot be converted into mental/emotional activity: symbol-making and symbols are the catalysts of affective transformation. Arts education and arts therapy pivot on the art symbol. Our Syncretic Model shows that we dock with such symbols at Metal, where they exist for us in the cultural repertoire, and launch them at Wood, where we create them for ourselves.

Brown's argument in his treatment of Hardy's novel is about accepting that our destiny is to live with change, to negotiate personal meaning in the face of uncertainty, to remain active in a world that is for ever urging us on, always threatening to unsettle us. In such a world, to lose or lack available energy is to risk marginalization and eventual irrelevance – to invite annihilation. We use the art of a writer like Hardy, Brown suggests, to establish or re-establish ourselves as 'mediators of consciousness', as fit for action. I have been arguing that the means to that end are supplied by the arts – through the disciplined activity of contemplation, through the habit of art. A 'mediating consciousness' is a consciousness alive to possibility, adapted to change, charged with creativity – for its own good and for the collective good. That is the 'goodness' we have described as 'sovereign' – it is the core condition of the good life. Here is Brown himself, drawing his unfolding of Hardy's book towards full disclosure:

> I come back, finally, to the kind of saga-story that embodies the imaginative valediction, and exploration of change, in defeated provinces. It is grand and formal in outline. Its adhesions, its proliferations of plot and character, take such force as they have from the vigour of the sustaining saga. The elements of its fiction are like flotsam on subtle tideways; they exhibit the essential pulls and currents and movements of the deeper waters. They take the eye at the surface, but not to satisfy it: to trouble and to reveal.
>
> (1962: 48)

You have followed this book thus far; you can have no doubt why I find this passage, stumbled upon so late in the writing, providential. Brown's final sentence tells us what to expect of art, and why we cannot do without it. It points to the interplay of subject matter and meaning: where the subject matter commands our attention, the symbol works at a deeper level, at the level of meaning, of 'signification'. It is signification and meaning that are threatened by the loss of the symbolic life – by the failure to resolve the cloud of unknowing, by submitting to what Collingwood called, 'the corruption of consciousness'. The symbol in art is the embodiment of 'mediated consciousness'. A little later on in his piece, Brown adds these telling words, 'Like the art of *The Mayor* itself at its best, it is absorbed in the incidents themselves, in what happened; the signification can speak for itself.' Signification always does and can only 'speak for itself': a theme we have touched upon many times in this book.

When Shakespeare's Prospero, in his late play *The Tempest*, finally forswears his magic and observes that 'we are such stuff as dreams are made on', he is speaking of art as signification. The drama is a dream, just as the novel, the painting, the opera, the concerto, are all dreams. Other cultures speak of and revere 'the dream time': we have been calling it *Kairos*. Unless we somehow can access that special ('enchanted') time 'in between', that potential ('enchanted') space that Winnicott says awaits us half awake, there is no hope of art – art 'properly so called' that is. And if you ask what these dreams of art are about, the answer is clear: our grief, our fear, our rage, our joy, our love, our fellow-feeling. Therapy addresses not so much our dreams as our dreaming. The Propero speech continues: 'Our little life is rounded in a sleep.' If we were to read 'rounded' as 'surrounded', then the whole passage suggests that to dream the dream of art we must hover in the time and space between sleeping and waking. I dare say many, if not most, of the problems to do with our expressive life occur as forms of insomnia – as an inability to let go, to shift from left to right brain, from *Logos* to *Eros*, from reality to playing, from *Chronos* to *Kairos*, from reason to feeling, from the referential to the presentational symbol, from potential to kinetic energy.

The art is not the life. The art is 'the little life' – like the *petit mal*, a kind of trance we fall into, a spell we fall under. But the little life of art is essential to the bigger life because it nourishes and questions feeling, keeps feeling intelligence alive. The little life of art simulates rather than replicates real dreaming, which, of course, is unconscious. Art-making and reception are activities of the conscious (semi-conscious) mind and that is necessary if the dreams of art are not to go the same way as the dreams of night. Art captures our dreaming in symbols that remain potent and resonant in experience and thus continually accessible as means to the refreshment of cognitive feeling.

I am so glad to have been able to invoke the lost voice of Douglas Brown. I have no idea why I should suddenly think of him as I drew this writing to a close. Douglas died aged only 43, in 1965. I had known him but a few years and remember being shocked and distressed at the news of his sudden death. His lectures in the 1960s at the Madingley Hall Winter and Summer Schools, his readings of Hardy, Donne and George Herbert, were unforgettable – he opened up literature for me in a way no other don had come even remotely close to doing whilst I was an undergraduate. And not just literature but music too: for instance, the settings by Benjamin Britten of Donne's *Holy Sonnets* (sung by Peter Pears) made a huge and lasting impact when Douglas first played them to us on his 78 recording.

At a meeting with my editors shortly after drafting this Epilogue I was handed a copy of Robin Alexander's *Essays on Pedagogy* (2008) – as an example of the kind of layout I might want to choose for myself. I opened the book at random and there was Douglas! I could scarcely believe my eyes. I was immediately offered the book as a gift, and on the journey home read Alexander's splendid chapter on the man, Alexander having himself been Brown's student at the Perse School in Cambridge.

Deep blow the winds of homecoming.

Appendix 1: Good habits

Perhaps my richest resource in this writing has been the *Shorter Oxford English Dictionary*. Its two volumes sit beside me within arms reach as I write – and I reach for one or the other every day. The edition is dated 1973 – it was bought with research money for the Arts and the Adolescent project and each volume bears the impress of the project's old rubber stamp. It is my desert island book, not least for words such as waly, wamara, wamble, wame, wampee and wampumpaeg. When I opened Volume I to check the spelling of habitué (two es or one?), I realized that I had never thought to look up the word 'habit' in all this time. The thing about the *SOED* is that it can spring delightful surprises. For example, I recently checked the word 'contingent', having found Winnicott writing of the mother's progression from continuity with the child, to her contingency, her being close by the child. And there I discovered contingency's connection to the verb 'to touch' (L. *tangere*). Motoring into Exeter the same day I saw a man and a child standing together by the roadside. The little girl turned to her father and wrapped her arms around him as I passed. Perhaps the traffic scared her. I remembered 'contingency' and understood how touching, embracing, is the child's way of being separate *with* rather than separate *from* the other. And I thought how we never lose the power and meaning of the need for contingency.

There are so many dictionary entries for 'habit' and its derivatives, and most of them speak to the project of this book. Habitat, for instance, and habitation, habitual, habituate, habitude, inhabit – not forgetting habitué of course. 'Habit' has four particular meanings or uses as a noun in English:

1   Dress. Bodily apparel or attire; clothes, garment
2   Bearing, deportment, behaviour, posture; bodily condition, or constitution; the bodily system; *Zool.* and *Bot.* the characteristic mode of growth and appearance of an animal or plant
3   Mental constitution, disposition, character; a settled disposition or tendency to act in a certain way, *esp.* one acquired by frequent repetition of the same act; a settled practice, custom, usage; a customary manner of acting; familiarity
4   *Logic*. The eighth of the categories or predicaments of Aristotle: Having or possession. L. *habitus*

I shall spend a moment taking each of these usages in turn, for each is useful to us.

1   *Apparel, garment, dress.* A respected colleague once advised me strongly against continuing to use the word 'arts' in the context of education. He said that it was a turn-off among politicians and policy-makers and should be avoided. We should now be talking instead of culture and creativity, he said — this was in the mid-1990s. Especially creativity. 'But they're not the same thing,' I protested. 'Nonetheless,' he continued, 'the arts as a serious topic in education are anathema to the powers-that-be and you'll get nowhere trying to talk about them.' He was right. Some weeks later I was explaining the idea of the reflective conversation as a way of assessing achievement in the arts to a visiting senior government adviser and he could barely contain his impatience. More recently, at a meeting convened by the Parliamentary Select Committee on Education to discuss revisions to the national curriculum, my argument for restoring the arts to a central role was brusquely dismissed by the Minister for Schools with a tetchy, 'Oh, for heaven's sake! We're not going back to the 70s, thank you very much'. Not mentioning the arts has simply been a form of collusion in their disappearance from the education debate.

2   *Bearing, mode of growth in nature, bodily system.* Now this one was the surprise. It's an unexpected reference to the Syncretic Model. For what is the Syncretic Model if not 'the bodily system' or the 'characteristic mode of growth' in nature? So my choice of 'habit' for the theme of the book was more apposite than I had imagined. We can use the notion of habit to cover the Five Phases of Change and the system of the Five Elements as they promote the growth of individual identity and the development of the intelligence of feeling. In other words, the Syncretic Model fittingly presents the cultivation of the habit of art as a defining feature of human being. The 'system' is fully articulated, funded and self-renewing, on a similar model to the cycle of the seasons. In Winnicott's scheme of the good-enough mother, the Syncretic Model becomes the repeated sequence:

Metal: holding
Water: handling (the beginnings of play)
Wood: presentation of objects (the beginnings of creativity)
Fire: reflecting back (the mother as mirror)
Earth: maternal empathy and authenticity.

To the centre of Winnicott's scheme, where ours has Earth, I add a mother's authentic love — her complete and enduring adaptation to the child's neediness and insufficiency.

3   *A settled practice, custom, usage...acquired by frequent repetition. A customary manner of acting. Familiarity.* I have been arguing in this book that it is the job of the arts

teacher and arts therapist to cultivate the habit of art to enrich the lives of young people growing up, to repair the stricken lives of people who have lost, failed to discover or been prevented from discovering the power and confidence to act expressively in furthering their own identity project. 'Frequent repetition' is built in to the idea of the cycle of creativity or change that is the Syncretic Model. It is also the very stuff of an arts education and therapy. The identity project is never finished. 'My self must I remake,' wrote Yeats. The self is remade through successive acts of subject-reflexivity; i.e. in essence, through the symbol-making (*poiesis*) that is the creative arts. We are talking about a therapy or a teaching that is not about the endless pursuit of novelty or confessional opportunities but the deep acquisition of the habit of transformation that repays repeated application and perseverance. It is about the quality as well as the frequency of artistic experience: that is to say, experience that is undertaken in the 'contemplative' spirit of a long-term commitment to averted vision, to an indirect, allusive and illusory, slow-dawning immersion in the symbolic order. It is not about explanation and interpretation – Winnicott himself felt that interpretation was not essential to psychotherapy, and he says so repeatedly. Others in this book endorse that view. Stern and his colleagues, as we have seen, echo this point; which is not the same as saying that he doesn't believe in what Winnicott called 'reflecting back'. Again, Stern sheds more light on this idea with his theory of attunement.

The arts are a lifetime and daily investment – they help to constitute the tone of personal being, moment to moment. I am William Blake, Virginia Woolf, Benjamin Britten, Thomas Hardy, Kieslowsky. These are the people, the events and the images that furnish my mind and beat in my heart; that hold, constrain, sustain and reflect back to me my deepest sense of personal being. The habit of art is a commitment to a participatory practice marked by what the philosopher Bergson called 'indwelling'. The habit of art must be worked at devotedly, must be perfected as a way of life, worn as a familiar garment, easily and with confidence. When the College of Arts was evicted from its home at Dartington after 50 years, the students blacked out the word 'art' embedded in the word D**art**ington on all the local road signs. They understood the significance of the sign. Rather wonderfully, the clumsy attempts by the local Highways Authority to make their protest disappear has only served to reinforce the message.

4   *Having or possession.* Aristotle again – just where one least expected to find him. A bit of research was called for since I knew nothing of his *Categories or Predicaments.* The eighth category, I learn, describes the state of 'having' or 'possession'. For St Augustine, who wrote a commentary on the *Categories,* man's first possession, citing the story of Adam and Eve, was the fig leaf! With nakedness and guilt, the first 'habit' (or dress) covering guilty nakedness also marked the beginning of the sense individuation, and prefigured all our cultural activity to come. The Fall was a falling into separation and all the rigours and

trials of individuation. It was also a falling into nakedness and the beginnings of culture. I think this is a nice idea – and a happy discovery. These are crucial themes for Winnicott who argues that in play we find the third area of being. His potential space bridges the inner world of the subject and the outer world of the object, maintaining the possibility of the experience of subject-reflexivity which was the hallmark of the good-enough mother–infant relationship. Individuation need not mean isolation but rather co-presence within a touching (contingent) conversation – it is the same with the teacher–student, therapist–client relationship.

Our expressive project is a sign of our humanity. Culture emerges in human history as the habitual redress of congenital neediness and insufficiency. It is in our very expressivity that we both admit our neediness and insufficiency and take steps to handle the situation. To have is to hold and we have already had a good deal to say about holding and handling in the context of human relationships and human expression. Holding is the first intuition of the mother and the first experience of life for the baby: holding and being fed, within the womb and after birth. Being possessed and possessing constitute the beginnings of the Identity Project.

I am not qualified to pronounce on whether or not our sense of self is an admission of guilt – except to say that it might seem natural to suppose that if we are born both needy and insufficient to our own wellbeing, we might be tempted to think (and feel) we were being punished. Where did we go wrong?, we might ask. Might the roots of empathy lie in a shared sense of collective guilt? Our natural inclination to humility (humus = earth) becomes us. The habit of art is the way back to union, to reconnection with the source of the good. That it is illusory seems not to matter at all. It is the bridgework that guarantees what Winnicott calls 'the avoidance of separation'. This is for sure a redemptive or, to use Seamus Heaney's term, 'redressive' act. The truth we seek in art is embodied in the artist's empathic (intuitive) mastery of the skills of symbol-making, of opening magic casements for us and putting us in touch with our deepest longings. The 'elected' habit of art guarantees its authenticity.

Appendix 2: Dangerous play

In returning to Winnicott at the end of this writing I have yielded to a homing instinct. He of all my mentors since my partnership with Witkin, save perhaps Louis Arnaud Reid, has been the bedrock of my work and my understanding of it. Where Louis's notion of 'cognitive feeling' deepened my grasp of 'the intelligence of feeling', Winnicott's insistence on the therapeutic relationship being grounded in play opened my eyes to the possibilities of working 'from within the pupil's expressive act'. The impulse to return arose as a particular concern, however. I had been thinking about his theory of play and about what seemed to me significant misunderstandings prevalent among teachers and therapists whose work I had been looking at. I have in the course of this writing begun to feel increasingly certain that play is no infantile thing, a sort of never-never land for stressed adults and children to regress to – but rather, that play is dangerous, and in its danger lies its usefulness. In the Syncretic Model, I associated play particularly with the Water phase and I had begun to feel that it was no accident that it should be associated with fear. So I wanted to discover, never having noticed it before, whether Winnicott had said anything on this score – anything about the play space, about play time, being dangerous.

In fact, as people who know their Winnicott better than I will already be aware, he actually uses the phrase 'danger area' (1971: 107) in connection with play, and speaks of the threat of disaster attending poor management of the client's play by the therapist. And he repeatedly has a good deal to say about the dangerous side of play as such. The play space/time is inherently dangerous because of its confusing, liminal character: it exists at the boundary between the vulnerable subjective self and the dangerous real world of intractable objects and consequential actions. In play, nothing is what it seems. Play is at the tipping point between psychological balance and unbalance: in some ways it amounts to the deliberate sacrifice of balance and security for the delights of unbalance, and of recovering it, recognizing it as something new. All our rule-bound contact sports are about physically putting our balanced bodies at risk. None of the joys and rewards of sport can happen without the transition from balance, through unbalance, on to balance again.

Play is potentially dangerous because in play (at play) we suspend the routines of vigilance, of self-protection, that are habitual in our day-to-day transactions. We suspend them – as we 'suspend our disbelief' – for the freedom that intimacy requires. Freedom, openness, truthfulness. As we have seen, speaking of the play of the infant, Winnicott proposes a crucial role for the mother. In early play the mother plays with the child and induces him/her into playing through immersion, through a shared encounter, the mother managing both playfulness and her child's protection. In this mode, the mother plays not so much *with* the child as *for* the child. This shared play in time gives way to solitary play, in which the child plays alone, learns how to be *at play*. (Later on comes full social play with others: play-mating.) The mother's role has now shifted from participation to watching over – Winnicott speaks of her as emotionally 'covering' the child's playing. I take him to mean that the mother makes the child feel guarded or safe, when absorbed and so 'off guard' themselves. Absorption, together with openness, freedom, truthfulness, become the essential conditions of playing, as they are of all potentially dangerous forms of intimacy.

Playing in a clinical setting, where intimacy may also include the sharing of confessional or threatening material, necessarily leaves the client exposed, off guard, at risk. What is threatened by such confidence sharing is the client's continuing sense of their own integrity and self-worth. Unable to defend themselves properly they are vulnerable to any attack upon that inner core of being, whether intended or accidental. The first duty of the therapist teacher in situations of intimacy is to protect the client from harm, harm by others (including the therapist teacher) and self-harm, intended or accidental. (Protection from harm doesn't, of course, guarantee protection from pain.) Making the client/student feel safe not only facilitates the sharing, making it good or good-enough to matter, but is also a basic condition of its proving effective. The professional's vigilance and understanding will help them provide the emotional cover necessary to compensate for the client's suspending their own defensiveness; their disinterested love will keep the client safe from harm.

Professionals inclined to follow Winnicott in *playing for* their client (as a way of inducing playfulness where otherwise it would be lacking) will be careful either to avoid or secure full-on *playing with* the client, since this, by definition, would leave both parties to the play defenceless, if there were no-one to cover for each of them. Where free play or any other form of intimacy requires the professional to join the client on *equal* terms, it follows that a second professional should not only be present but should also be managing the encounter, for the time being. Partnered free play is always dangerous where no disinterested third party is available as referee or umpire. It is usual, to return to Winnicott's mother–infant relationship, to find a group of mothers keeping an eye on children playing together – as it is to have the school playground patrolled by one or more teachers. Play that is truly, as it must be, 'free', even within an understood set of rules, always hovers at the boundary with the dangerous and the illegitimate. It is in the nature of play to breach that boundary under the pressure of play itself, driven as it is by the pleasure impulse, by an imperious desire. Therapists and teachers often make much of their formal 'contracts' with their charges, but it is frankly disingenuous to suppose that what is an essentially left-brain regime could be maintained by anyone, or any pair, surrendered to and absorbed in a right-brain activity. The security guaranteed by these 'contracts' is illusory in my view. They are potentially another source of danger.

Where professionals offer artistic experiences as forms of play, they also function as forms of intimacy. Art may be openly confessional and threatening or it may not. It is, when authentic, always unguarded and representative of the artist's core sense of being. The anxiety of the artist over self-exposure is a commonplace of creativity, matched only by the felt imperative to publish – and be damned, if necessary. Where they are forced by the free play of their minds and imaginations to lower their guard and put their souls at risk, they not infrequently turn to friends, lovers, their muse, their agent, their publisher, their fellow artists, the play's director, the orchestra's conductor or their patron for the emotional 'cover' they need. The much-derided so-called 'luvvie' culture of the theatre is simply another manifestation of this same need for mutual succour. The free play of the creative mind is only possible as an act of total surrender and complete absorption, inviting 'cover' by some third party or parties. I prefer Gadamer's account of play as 'the play of light' to Winnicott's here. Winnicott's pairing of playing with reality tends to make playing a kind of infantilism, although I sense they are both ultimately describing the same thing: a frame of mind. Free play is the mind freed of intentionality, receptive, passive in following its own inclinations, associations and correspondences, monitored not by forms of reflection but intuitively, by a knowing in one's bones. It is the mind 'abandoned' but intensely active, as Adam Phillips describes it in one of his essays on creativity. Such abandonment induces a kind of trance-like, mesmerized, surrendered state in which the possible takes precedence over the probable, the indeterminate over the determined. It is pure play as a semi-autonomous activity.

The notion of aesthetic 'distance' or disinterestedness' is simply another way of describing this abandonment or surrender of the intending self, the self undefended. Intentionality in art is a kind of intentional inattention, as it is purposely purposeless. It is the intention of feeling, more an awaiting and an awakening than a construction or execution of a premeditated design. Where Schön refers to reflection in action, the philosopher John Searle writes of 'intentions in action' (1991: 67). The dramatic actor's action of impersonation is also, in an important sense, 'impersonal'. The personal, the defended subject, is left out of the artistic/aesthetic equation so that mind, emotions and the expressive project of symbolic forming may have completely free play. The arts therapist committed to engaging with intimate materials ('issues', to use the common parlance), and choosing to do so though the arts, is thereby doubly obliged or committed to distance themselves from the client's absorption and guard their unguardedness.

The client's predicament, their vulnerability, albeit elected and necessary to the playing, is potentially dangerous, and the professional's first consideration must be to assume the role of guardian of their client's soul. Some might argue that the professional need not go much beyond that, since playing, properly understood, is itself a way of knowing. Free play of the mind, including artistic play, elicits and evokes the autonomous 'seeking' for meaning in information randomly generated that is the habitual mode of intelligence at work. Such play is fundamentally cognitive in its orientation. What makes it special is its quality of intentional unintentionality. Being a good-enough guardian requires specialist knowledge, professional understanding and the kind of expertise in partnering that it has been the business of this book to promote. There seems every likelihood that if the client's artistic playing (alone or partnered) is good enough, then playing itself (creating a satisfying art work or responding deeply to the art work of others) will deliver the hoped for outcome.

The impersonal care of the disinterested therapist, teacher, priest, doctor, nurse, friend is a special love: in Greek it is called *agape*. Mother love is of the self-same kind, and as with a mother's love, so with a teacher's and therapist's. The love is the medium through which the healing and the learning are delivered: the love is the animating force, the life of the practice, the ultimate source of meaning. As successful teachers and therapists everywhere will vouch, the secret of good teaching and good therapy lies in the quality of the living relationship between the cared for and the other who cares – between the one made sacred by their need, by their vulnerability and dependency, and the other who cares enough to minister to them.

Simone Weil says: 'To love purely is to consent to distance, it is to adore the distance between ourselves and that which we love' (2005: 293).

Bibliography and further reading

* All translations from the Polish are by Jolanta Gisman-Stoch.

Alexander, R. (2008) *Essays on Pedagogy*. Oxford: Routledge.
Aristotle (1980) *The Nicomachean Ethics*, trans. David Ross. Oxford: Oxford University Press.
Armstrong, R. P. (1975) *Wellspring: On the Myth and Source of Culture*. London: University of California Press Ltd.
Barrantes-Vidal, N. (2004) 'Creativity and Madness Revisited from Current Psychological Perspectives', *Journal of Consciousness Studies*, 11: 58–78.
Barrs, B. J. (1999) 'Art Must Move: Emotion and the Biology of Beauty', *Journal of Consciousness Studies*, 6: 59–61.
Baudrillard, J. (2005) *The Intelligence of Evil or the Lucidity Pact*. Oxford: Berg.
Benjamin, W. (1992) (trans. Harry Zohn) *Illuminations*. London: Fontana Press.
Bennett, A. (2009) *The Habit of Art*. London: Faber and Faber.
Bohm, D. (1980) *Wholeness and the Implicate Order*. London: Routledge and Kegan Paul.
Bohm, D. (1996) *On Creativity*. London and New York: Routledge.
Bohm, D. (1996) *On Dialogue*. London and New York: Routledge.
Boston Change Process Study Group (2010) *Change in Psychotherapy: A Unifying Paradigm*. New York, NY: W. W. Norton & Co.
Brown, D. (1962) *Hardy: The Mayor of Casterbridge*. London: Edward Arnold.
Brown, J. (1999) 'On Aesthetic Perception', *Journal of Consciousness Studies*, 6: 144–60.
Brown, L. (2009) *Aristotle: The Nicomachean Ethics*. Oxford: Oxford University Press.
Brown, Sir T. (1658) *The Garden of Cyrus*, R. H. A. Robbins (ed.) (1972) Oxford: Clarendon Press.
Buber, M. (1970) *I and Thou*. Edinburgh: T. & T. Clark.
Cabanac, M. (1999) 'Emotion and Phylogeny', *Journal of Consciousness Studies*, 6: 176–90.
Cary, J. (2005) *What Good Are the Arts?* London: Faber and Faber.
Cheever, J. (2010) *The Journals*. London: Vintage.
Clarkson, P. (1989) *Gestalt Counselling in Action*. London: Sage.
Collingwood, R. G. (1938) *The Principles of Art*. Oxford: Clarendon Press.
Collingwood, R. G. (1960) *The Idea of Nature*. Oxford: Oxford University Press.
Coomaraswamy, A. K. (2009) *The Dance of Shiva*. New Delhi: Munshiram Manoharlal Publishers Ltd.
Craft, A., Gardner, H. and Claxton, G. (2008) *Creativity, Wisdom, and Trusteeship: Exploring the Role of Education*. Thousand Oaks, CA: Corwin Press.
Csikszentmihalyi, M. (1996) *Creativity: Flow and the Psychology of Discovery and Invention*. New York, NY: HarperCollins Publishers.
Csikszentmihalyi, M. (1999) 'Implications of a Systems Perspective for the Study of Creativity',

in Sternberg, R. (ed.) *Handbook for Creativity*. Cambridge: Cambridge University Press.

Dillard, A. (1998) *Pilgrim at Tinker Creek*. New York, NY: HarperCollins Publishers.

Dillard, A. (2008) *The Maytrees*. London: Hesperus Press Ltd.

Dissanayake, E. (1988) *What Is Art For?* Seattle and London: University of Washington Press.

Doctorow, E. L. (2009) *Homer and Langley*. London: Little, Brown.

Ehrenzweig, A. (1967) *The Hidden Order of Art: A Study in the Psychology of Artistic Imagination*. Berkeley, CA: University of California Press.

Eliot, G. (2003) *The Mill on the Floss*. London: Penguin Books.

Ellis, R. D. (1999) 'The Dance Form of the Eyes: What Cognitive Science Can Learn from Art', *Journal of Consciousness Studies*, 6: 161–72.

Feist, K. J. (1999) 'The Influence of Personality on Artistic and Scientific Creativity', in Sternberg, R. (ed.) *Handbook of Creativity*. Cambridge: Cambridge University Press.

Fraleigh, S. and Nakamura, T. (2006) *Hijikate Taysumi and Ohno Kazuo*. New York, NY: Routledge.

Gablik, S. (1991) *The Reenchantment of Art*. London: Thames and Hudson Ltd.

Gadamer, H-G. (1986) *The Relevance of the Beautiful and other Essays*. Cambridge: Cambridge University Press.

Gardner, H. (1973) *The Arts and Human Development: A Psychological Study of the Artistic Process*. New York and London: John Wiley and Sons.

Gilroy, A. (2006) *Art Therapy, Research and Evidence-based Practice*. London: Sage Publications.

Goguan, J. A. (2000) 'What Is Art?' *Journal of Consciousness Studies*, 7: 7–15.

Golding, W. (1959) *Free Fall*. London: Faber.

Gombrich, E. H. (1960) *Art and Illusion*. London: Phaidon Press.

*Gombrowicz, W. (1989a) *Dziennik 1953–1956*. Krakow: Wydawnictwo Literackie.

*Gombrowicz, W. (1989b) *Dziennik 1957–1961*. Krakow: Wydawnictwo Literackie.

*Gombrowicz, W. (1989c) *Dziennik 1961–1966*. Krakow: Wydawnictwo Literackie.

Harré, R. (1983) *Personal Being: A Theory for Individual Psychology*. Oxford: Basil Blackwell Ltd.

Harth, E. (1999) 'The Emergence of Art and Language in the Human Brain', *Journal of Consciousness Studies*, 6: 97–115.

Heath, M. (1996) (trans.) *Aristotle: Poetics*. Harmondsworth: Penguin Books.

Heidegger, M. (1929) *Was ist Metaphysik?* Bonn: Cohen.

Holmes, R. (2005) *Footsteps: Adventures of a Romantic Biographer*. London: Harper Perennial.

Hyde, L. (1983) *The Gift: How the Creative Spirit Transforms the World*. Edinburgh: Canongate Books Ltd.

Jacobsen, T. (1976) *The Treasures of Darkness: A History of Mesopotamian Religion*. London: Yale University Press.

Joyce, J. (1993) *The Dubliners*. Ware: Wordsworth Editions Ltd.

Karafyllis, N. C. and Ulshöfer, G. (2008) *Sexualized Brains: Scientific Modelling of Emotional Intelligence from a Cultural Perspective*. Cambridge, MA: MIT Press.

*Korczak, J. (1978) *Pisma Wybrane*. Warszawa: Nasza Ksiegarnia.

Langer, S. K. (1967) *Philosophy in a New Key*. Cambridge, MA: Harvard University Press.

Lanier, J. (1999) 'What Information Is Given by a Veil?' *Journal of Consciousness Studies*, 6: 65–8.

Lee, H. (1996) *Virginia Woolf*. London: Chatto and Windus.

Lévinas, E (1993) *Totalité et Infini: Essai sur l'exteriorité*. Boston, MA and London: Kluwer Academic Publishers B.V..

Lubart, T. I. (1999) 'Creativity across Cultures', in Sternberg, R. J. (ed.) *Handbook of Creativity*. Cambridge: Cambridge University Press, pp. 339–50.

Macfarlane, R. (2007) *The Wild Places*. London: Granta Books.

McGilchrist, I. (1982) *Against Criticism*. London: Faber and Faber.

McGilchrist, I. (2010) *The Master and His Emissary*. New Haven, CT and London: Yale University Press.

McNiff, S. (2004) *Art Heals: How Creativity Cures the Soul*. Boston, MA and London: Shambhala Publications, Inc.

Maslow, A. H. (1968) *Toward a Psychology of Being*. New York: Van Nostrand Reinhold.

Mitchell, S. (2004) *Gilgamesh*. London: Profile Books.

Morrow, G. R. (1962) *Plato's Epistles*. New York: The Bobbs-Merrill Company Inc.

Murdoch, I. (1991) *The Sovereignty of the Good*. London: Routledge and Kegan Paul.

Nussbaum, M. C. (1990) *Love's Knowledge: Essays on Philosophy and Literature*. New York and London: Oxford University Press.

Nussbaum, M. C. (2001) *Upheavals of Thought: The Intelligence of Emotions*. Cambridge: Cambridge University Press.

Paglia, C. (1990) *Sexual Personae: Art and Decadence from Nefertiti to Emily Dickinson*. Newhaven, CT: Yale University Press.

Panksepp, J. (1998) *Affective Neuroscience*. Oxford: Oxford University Press.

Phillips, A. (1988) *Winnicott*. London: Fontana Press.

Phillips, A. (1998) *The Beast in the Nursery*. London: Faber and Faber.

Phillips, A. (2010) *On Balance*. London: Hamish Hamilton.

Read, H. (1943) *Education through Art*, London: Faber and Faber.

Reid, L. A. (1986) *Ways of Understanding and Education*. London: Heinemann Educational Books.

Rifkin, J. (2009) *The Empathic Civilization: The Race to Global Consciousness in a World in Crisis*. Cambridge: Polity Press.

Robinson, M. (2010) *Absence of Mind: The Dispelling of Inwardness from the Modern Myth of the Self*. New Haven, CT and London: Yale University Press.

Ross, E. D. (1997) 'Right Hemisphere Syndromes and the Neurology of Emotion', in Schachter, S. C. and Devinsky, O. (eds) *Behavioral Neurology and the Legacy of Norman Geschwind*. Philadelphia, PA: Lippincott-Raven, pp. 183–91.

Ross, M. (1975) *Arts and the Adolescent*. London: Evans Brothers.

Ross, M. (1978) *The Creative Arts*. London: Heinemann Educational Books.

Ross, M. (1984) *The Aesthetic Impulse*. Oxford: Pergamon Press.

Ross, M., Radnor, H., Mitchell, S. and Bierton, C. (1993) *Assessing Achievement in the Arts*. Buckingham: Open University Press.

Rothfeld, G. S. and Levert, S. (2002) *The Acupuncture Response*, New York: Contemporary Books.

Samuels, J. (2006) 'Reflections on the Transpersonal Dimension in Integrative Psychotherapy: Art, Imagination and the Creative Process', *British Journal of Psychotherapy Integration*, 3(2): 40.

Sawyer, R. K. (2006) *Explaining Creativity: The Science of Human Innovation*. New York: Oxford University Press.

Scarry, E. (2,000) *On Beauty and Being Just*. London: Gearlad Duckworth and Co..

Schön, D. (1983) *The Reflective Practitioner: How Professionals Think in Action*. Avebury: The Academic Publishing Group.

Searle, J. (1991) *Minds, Brains and Science*. London: Penguin Books.

Sennett, R. (2008) *The Craftsman*. London: Penguin Books.

Solso, R. L. (2000) 'The Cognitive Neuroscience of Art', *Journal of Consciousness Studies*, 7: 75–85.

Stern, D. N. (1985) *The Interpersonal World of the Infant: A View from Psychoanalysis and Developmental Psychology*. New York, NY: Basic Books.

206

Stern, D. N. (2004) *The Present Moment in Psychotherapy and Everyday Life*. New York, NY: W.W. Norton.

Stern, D. N. (2010) *Forms of Vitality*. New York, NY: Oxford University Press.

Sternberg, R. (ed.) (1999) *Handbook of Creativity*. Cambridge: Cambridge University Press.

*Tarkowski, A. (1991) *Czas Utrwalony*. Warszawa: Pelikan.

Tillyard, E. M. W. (1942) *The Elizabethan World Picture*. London: Macmillan.

*Tischner, J. (1992) *Świat Ludzkiej Nadziei*. Krakow: Znak.

Trimble, M. R. (1988) *Biological Psychiatry*. Chichester: John Wiley and Sons.

Trimble, M. R. (2007) *The Soul in the Brain: The Cerebral Basis of Language, Art and Belief*. Baltimore, MD: Johns Hopkins University Press.

Tusa, J. (2003) *On Creativity: Interviews Exploring the Process*. London: Methuen Publishing.

Unschuld, P. U. (1985) *Medicine in China: A History of Ideas*. London: University of California Press.

Warnock, M. (1976) *Imagination*. London: Faber and Faber.

Watt, D. F. (1999) 'Consciousness and Emotion (Review of Panksepp)', *Journal of Consciousness Studies*, 6: 191–200.

Weil, S. (2005) *Simone Weil: An Anthology*, S. Miles (ed.). London: Penguin Books Ltd.

Willerslev, R. (2007) *Soul Hunters: Hunting, Animism, and Personhood among the Siberian Yukaghirs*. London: University of California Press.

Willis, B. (2000) *The Tao of Art: The Inner Meaning of Chinese Art and Philosophy*. London: Random House UK Ltd.

Winnicott, D. W. (1971) *Playing and Reality*. London: Tavistock Publications.

Witkin, R. W. (1974) *The Intelligence of Feeling*. London: Heinemann Educational Books Limited.

Woolf, V. (1960) *To the Lighthouse*. London: J. M. Dent & Sons Limited.

Young, J. Z. (1978) *Programs of the Brain*. Oxford: Oxford University Press.

Zeki, S. (1999) *Inner Vision: an Exploration of Art and the Brain*. Oxford: Oxford University Press.

Zeki, S. (2009) *Splendors and Miseries of the Brain: Love, Creativity, and the Quest for Human Happiness*. Chichester: Wiley-Blackwell.

Acknowledgements

My students have been my partners in the making of this book. It is in their company over many years that I have built my experience and learned my trade. In lots of ways this is their book and I offer it to them in gratitude and happy remembrance of their bright shining.

My friends and family have faithfully backed this writing from the start and I thank them all. Sincere thanks go particularly to Dennis Carter, Jodie Davies, Sally Mitchell, Sarah Scoble and Ronnie Wood.

I am deeply grateful to Kathleen Jamie for her personal permission to quote the two poems I have used to root this book, and to John Tusa for allowing my 'quarrying' – for analysis in Chapter 6 – of the interviews in his book *On Creativity*.

Three individuals must have special mention.

Without the help and inspiration of Donna Ashton, my acupuncturist and friend, I should never have conceived of this book. It was Donna who set me thinking about creativity and the Five Elements in the first place and worked with me to devise and present the Syncretic Model for the first time. Her commitment and care have been a continuing source of creative energy and courage to me.

Jola Gisman-Stoch has provided me with a second academic home in Poland for almost 20 years. I am so grateful to her, her husband Jarek, Anīa her daughter and Jollie the Scot, and to her students at the University of Silesia in Cieszyn for the warmth of their friendship and their infectious commitment to our work together. They have, all of them, in their own ways, remade my life.

My soul's companion all the crooked way towards the completion of this book has been my wife Kicoula. Not only has every idea come under her scrutiny, but most of them have also been transformed by it. She has stayed the course as first reader, been an infallible soothsayer and an incisive soul-searcher. When I needed slack she gave it me; when I was tempted to walk the coals, she stayed me. For her constancy and patience I am immeasurably in her debt.

Finally, I wish to thank my editor, Bruce Roberts, his assistant James Hobbs, their colleagues at Routledge and Mark Livermore at FiSH Books for their sustained and sustaining care of my work and me. That my friend and former Dillington student, John Dean, should agree to design the book's cover has been a delightful bonus.

Index

acupuncture 4, 26, 36, 38, 48–9, 70, 108, 181
Adorno, Theodor 177
aesthetic experiences 71, 121, 169
'affective cues' 55–6, 167, 169
agape 151, 202
Alexaki, Hari 134
Alexander, Robin 194
Alvarez, Al 177
'ambivalence crisis' (Nussbaum) 163
Apollo 78–9
appraisal 64, 66, 156, 175
appropriation 14–15, 21, 59, 65, 91
Arendt, Hannah 49
Aristotle 2, 49, 84, 87, 89, 94, 96, 106, 134, 137–8, 180, 182, 197
Arnold, Matthew 89
art, role and function of 62, 74–7, 81–3, 102
art appreciation 155–6
art criticism 67
artistic responses 73
arts teaching 56, 84, 110–20, 135–7, 141–56, 158, 169, 182, 192–3, 197; repertoire of skills for 153; vocation for 119–20
arts therapy 9, 56, 84, 123, 157–61, 165–75, 182, 192–4, 197; overarching theory of 174
Ashton, Donna 4–5, 38, 40, 70, 151–2, 188

assessment in the arts 13, 65
'attunement' concept 19, 53–8, 66, 101, 164, 197
Auden, W. H. 1–2, 188
Auerbach, Frank 86, 88–95, 98–101, 104
Augustine, St 197
authenticity 15, 40, 43–7, 58, 62, 66, 67, 87, 89, 97, 100, 102, 104, 106–7, 138–9, 164, 175
autumn 42–7
axis mundi model 39

Barrantes-Vidal, N. 79–80
Barrs, Bernard J. 81
Baudrillard, Jean 177
beauty, experience of 122, 139
Beethoven, Ludwig van 148
Benjamin, Walter 49–50, 57
Bennett, Alan 1–2
Bergson, H. 197
bestowal, concept of 130
Bierton, Kathy 13
bird flocking 51
Birtwistle, Harrison 86, 90, 94–101
Blake, William 197
Boston Change Process Study Group (BCPG) 20, 53, 55, 57
brain structure and function 2, 50–1, 72–83, 163, 167, 170–1, 201
Britten, Benjamin 9, 148, 194, 197
Brown, Douglas 192–4

Brown, Jason 82
Browne, Sir Thomas 39, 186
Buber, Martin 113

Campbell, Peter 67–9
Caro, Anthony 9–10, 88–91, 94–5,
    98–101, 145
Carter, Elliott 88–92, 96, 98
ch'i, flows of 26, 27, 36
challenging of clients 64
Cheever, John 135, 191
Cheevers, Tony 85
children, treatment of 120, 122; see also
    arts teaching; education; mother-child
    relationship
Childs, Martin 179
Chinese philosophy and medical theory
    26–9, 35–8, 47–50, 77, 79, 132; see
    also Five Elements theory
Clarkson, P. 18
Claxton, Guy 3–4, 128–9
'client', use of term 175–6
Collingwood, R. G. 11, 129, 131, 149,
    157, 176, 187, 193
compass points 39–40
Comte, Auguste 180
Conrad, Joseph 9, 129
consciousness studies 72, 78, 81, 83
conventionalization 14–15, 20, 47, 65, 87,
    147
Coomaraswamy, Ananda K. 37, 181
correspondences, principle of 23–5
cosmological models 38–9
Craft, Anna 3–4, 124, 127–9, 168
creativity 40, 43–4, 48–51, 74, 83,
    124–32; definition of 125; evolution of
    80; and madness 79–81; myths of
    125–6; processes of 10, 102; social
    aspect of 98; sociocultural model of
    124–6; use of term 86; see also
    Syncretic Model of creativity

Csikzentmihayli, M. 124, 126, 128
cultural animation 111
cultural heritage 120
cyclical patterns in nature 24, 29, 131, 137

dancing 48, 49–50, 79, 121, 187
Dartnell, Lewis 37, 50
Darwin, Charles 181
Dawkins, Richard 180
de Bono, Edward 125
Dennett, Daniel 180
dialectic 63, 69, 135–7
di Giovanni, Janine 178
Dillard, Annie 43, 143–4, 148
Dionysus 78–81, 94, 148
directionality 56–7, 60
'disinterested interest' 176
Doctorow, E. L. 149
Donne, John 77, 132, 188, 194
Doré, Gustav 103–4
dyadic nature of the therapeutic process
    57

Earth as an element 30–2, 35, 38, 44–8,
    58, 62, 66–7, 93, 100–1, 151–3
education: totalitarianism in 118; trends
    in 3–4; and upbringing 115–16; see
    also arts teaching
Eggleston, William 67–9
Ehrenzweig, A. 18
Eliade, Mircea 121
Eliot, George 189
Eliot, T. S. 43, 83, 94, 186
Ellis, Ralph D. 82–3
emotional cycle 33, 155
emotional health 159
emotions 74–8, 81, 165–9, 180; and the
    Syncretic Model 153–5
empathy 47, 49, 78, 93, 98, 101–2, 106,
    151, 154, 161, 164, 167–70, 175, 198
eudaimonia 157, 161–2, 168–9

evaluative judgements 169–70
expressive dimension of life 107, 158–9, 165–6

feeling 10, 179–80
Feldman, Morton 66, 68
Fire as an element 30–2, 35, 47, 57–8, 61, 66, 87, 92, 97–9, 145, 148–51
'fittedness' 56–7
Five Elements theory 2, 4–5, 23–40, 48–50, 70, 137, 139, 176, 181–2, 190–1, 196
Fonteyn, Margot 148
formative judgement 65, 93, 175
'forms of vitality' 56; see also 'affective cues'
Frost, Robert 165

Gablik, Suzi 89, 133, 181
Gadamer, Hans-Georg 17–18, 61, 66, 93–4, 130, 201
Gardner, Howard 3–4, 127–8
'genius' school of thought on creativity 96
Gestalt cycle 18
Gilgamesh epic 20–1, 43, 46, 110, 123
Giotto 100
Gisman-Stoch, Jolanta 20–2, 46, 110–11, 123
Goguan, Joseph A. 72, 126
Golding, William 53, 187
Gombrowicz, Witold 118, 120
Gonne, Maud 148
good-enough caring 161–2, 174, 196, 198, 202
Grace 121
grief 11, 33, 42, 59, 78, 87–8, 101, 103, 138–9, 154–5, 160

habit, different meanings of 195–8
Hallam, Arthur 148

Hals, Franz 90
Hardy, Thomas 192–4
Harré, Rom 8, 11–21, 37–40, 47–8, 51, 64–5, 80, 148, 151, 165, 167, 183
Harrison, Tony 88, 91, 95–102, 147, 172
Harth, E. 81–2
Heaney, Seamus 39, 75, 103, 188, 198
Heidegger, Martin 34, 124
hemispheres of the brain 2, 51, 72–80, 167, 179, 201
Herbert, George 60–1, 188, 190, 194
He Tu 38
'hidden curriculum' 115
'holding form' 93–6, 145–6
hope, experience of 83, 113–14, 163–4
Hopkins, Gerard Manley 34, 98, 188, 190
hormonal systems 32
Houston, John and Angelica 188
Hughes, Ted 94, 147–8
Hyde, Lewis 98, 124, 126, 129–33

'identity project' matrix (Harré) 13–14, 19–20, 37–40, 47, 51, 64–5, 80, 151, 158, 165, 167, 172, 175, 197–8
'immersion' principle 14
Incy-Wincy Spider syndrome 32
indoctrination in art education 118–20
innovation 125–7
intelligence of the emotions 169
intelligence of feeling 169, 179–81
'inter-subjective consciousness' (Stern) 55
inter-subjectivity 58, 60, 63–4, 76, 174

Jacobsen, Thorkild 20
Jamie, Kathleen 143, 188
Jesus Christ 120, 139
Joyce, James 188–9
Jung, Carl 23

Kailish (mountain) 39
Karafyllis, Nicole C. 182

Ke cycle 28–32, 43–4, 50, 58, 63–4, 68, 78, 126, 132, 145, 147, 152, 183
Kids Company 175
Klee, Paul 147
Korczak, Janusz 111, 117, 120–3

language 74, 76, 82
Lanier, Jaron 81
Lao Tzu 48
Lawrence, D. H. 102, 168
Leach, Edmund 121
Lee, Hermione 186, 189–90
Levert, S. 26, 32, 139, 141, 176
Lévinas, E. 46, 112–13
loving relationships in therapy and teaching 170
Luo Shu 38

Macfarlane, Robert 3, 39, 144–5
McGilchrist, Iain 2, 76–8
McNiff, Shaun 157
Magritte, René 39
Marcuse, Herbert 113
market forces 127–8
Maslow, Abraham 11–12, 148, 162
'meridians' in the human body 26
Messiaen, Olivier 90
Metal as an element 30–4, 38, 42–7, 59, 65, 87, 90, 93, 97, 138–43, 147
Mitchell, Sally 13, 16
models and model-making 37–8, 50
Moore, Henry 9–10, 88
Morrow, Glenn R. 134–7
mother–child relationship 19, 51, 55, 58, 101, 159–65, 198, 200, 202
Murdoch, Iris 139
muses 130, 148–9

Neil, A. S. 128–9
neuroscience 72–4, 81–3, 89, 92, 126, 141, 163

Nietzsche, Friedrich 75, 77–8, 102
nourishing process 63–4
Nureyev, Rudolph 148
Nussbaum, Martha 157–71, 180

Ohno, Kazuo 179
one-person psychology 55
Oppenheimer, Frank 187–8
opportunity in the arts 9–10

Paglia, Camille 78–9
Panksepp, Jaak 72, 83
participatory practice in the arts 8–10, 54, 64
'patient', use of term 176
Pears, Peter 9, 148, 194
pedagogy in the arts 16
Pericles 169
Philip IV of Spain 101
Phillips, Adam 75, 79, 188, 201
Pinker, Steven 180
Plath, Sylvia 148, 177
Plato 63, 132, 134–9, 147, 171
play 12, 18, 51, 75, 79, 122, 142, 162–3, 174, 181, 199–202; dangerous aspects of 199–200
poetry 75, 91, 168, 171–2
poiesis 2, 56, 74, 130–3, 138, 174, 197
Portuguese language 104
profiling of clients 69–70
progress, assessment and recording of 64–5
protolanguage 74, 76
Proust, Marcel 159
'pseudo' art 11, 149, 187

quincunx figure 39–40, 186

Radnor, Hilary 13
Raleigh, Sir Walter 23, 25
reactive feelings 10–11

Read, Herbert 10
reception theory 65, 107
reflecting-on-action and reflecting-in-action 54–5, 63, 93, 201
reflective conversation 13, 64
reflective practitioners 53, 116, 175
reflexive feelings 10–11
Rego, Paula 9–10, 84, 86, 94, 97–8, 102–6, 149, 188
Reid, Louis Arnaud 199
religious experience 75–6, 140
responsibility, excess of 118
Rilke, Rainer Maria 192
Robinson, Marilynne 180–1
rogation 63, 179
Ross, E. D. 74
Roth, Gabrielle 50
Rothfeld, G. S. 26, 32, 139, 141, 176

Samuels, Jocelyne 175
Sarajevo 178
Sawyer, Keith 124–9
Schön, Donald 13, 53–4, 63, 201
Searle, John 201
seasonal cycle 29, 131, 137–8, 190
seasoning processes 190
self-actualization 162
Sen, Amartya 9, 130–3, 138
Sendak, Maurice 145
Sennett, Richard 62
Shakespeare, William 40, 131, 155, 157, 171, 188, 193–4
Shapcott, Jo 188
Sheng cycle 28, 30–2, 35, 43–4, 50, 58, 63, 78, 80, 83, 126, 132, 145, 147, 150, 152, 183
Shorter Oxford English Dictionary 195
Socrates 137
soul hunters 147, 182–3
Spark, Muriel 89, 91, 96–102
spring 44–7

standards in the arts 87
Steiner, George 89, 177
Stern, Daniel 19, 53–60, 63, 74, 101, 161, 166–7, 174, 176, 197
Sternberg, R. 127
Stravinsky, Igor 88, 92
'subject-knowing' theory (Witkin) 11–12
subject-reflexive action 10
summative appraisal 175
summative judgement 93, 175
summer 45–7
Sunderland, Margot 18
symbolism in art 193
sympathetic nervous system 32
Syncretic Model of creativity 2, 4–5, 8–9, 18, 23, 37–41, 47, 51–3, 57–8, 62–71, 74, 77–89, 93, 97, 100, 102, 107, 110, 125, 129, 132–8, 157–61, 164–9, 172, 175, 181–3, 188, 193, 196–7, 199; and the emotions 153–5; original and revised versions of 41
Szymborska, W. 160

Tao Te Ching 48
Taoism 48–50
Tarkowski, Andrej 116–18
Tennyson, Alfred 148
tessera hospitalis 18, 94, 130
therapeutic assessment 172–3
therapeutic relationship 12, 55–8, 161, 176, 199
Tillyard, E.M.W. 24–5
Tischner, Józef 111–17, 121–3
Tolstoy, Leo 8
tragedy 77–8
transformation of language 14–15, 21
Trimble, Michael 73–82
trusteeship 128–9
Tsou 27
Tusa, John 84–7, 91–2, 95, 97, 100–2, 106–7, 125, 132, 145, 169, 172

two-person psychology 55
Unschuld, Paul U. 24–30, 40, 50

Van Gogh, Theo 9, 148
Van Gogh, Vincent 68, 148
Velazques, Diego 93, 101
Warnock, M. 169
Water as an element 30–4, 43–7,
    57–60, 65–6, 70, 90, 92, 96, 141–7,
    150–1
Watt, D.F. 83
Weil, Simone 184, 202
Wheel of Fortune 39
Wheeler, Charles 90
Willerslev, Rane 182
Willing, Victor 9–10, 103
Willis, Ben 49–50
Wilson, E. O. 180
Winnicott, D. W. 12–13, 55, 57, 64, 79,
    95, 98, 142, 160–3, 170, 186, 188,
    194–201

winter 43–7, 142–3
Witkin, Robert 8–13, 26, 69, 75, 93, 105,
    145–6, 169, 199
Wood as an element 30–5, 44–7, 60–1,
    66, 87, 92–8, 144–9, 152–3
Woolf, Leonard 70–1, 148
Woolf, Virginia 1, 70–1, 146–8, 177,
    184–9, 197
Wordsworth, Dorothy 148
Wordsworth, William 148, 188

Yeats, W. B. 19, 106, 148, 191, 197
yin and yang 25, 32–3, 38, 58, 79, 138
Yukaghir community 147, 182, 188, 190

Zeki, Semir 157, 170–2